FEMINISM, DIGITAL CULTURE AND THE POLITICS OF TRANSMISSION

FEMINISM, DIGITAL CULTURE AND THE POLITICS OF TRANSMISSION
Theory, Practice and Cultural Heritage

Deborah Withers

ROWMAN & LITTLEFIELD
INTERNATIONAL

London • New York

Published by Rowman & Littlefield International Ltd.
Unit A, Whitacre Mews, 26-34 Stannary Street, London SE11 4AB
www.rowmaninternational.com

Rowman & Littlefield International Ltd. is an affiliate of Rowman & Littlefield
4501 Forbes Boulevard, Suite 200, Lanham, Maryland 20706, USA
With additional offices in Boulder, New York, Toronto (Canada), and Plymouth (UK)
www.rowman.com

British Library Cataloguing in Publication Information Available
A catalogue record for this book is available from the British Library

ISBN: HB 978-1-78348-350-1
       PB 978-1-78348-351-8

Library of Congress Cataloging-in-Publication Data

Withers, Deborah M.
  Feminism, digital culture and the politics of transmission : theory, practice and cultural
heritage / Deborah Withers.
      pages cm
  Includes bibliographical references and index.
  ISBN 978-1-78348-350-1 (cloth : alk. paper) — ISBN 978-1-78348-351-8 (pbk. : alk.
paper) — ISBN 978-1-78348-352-5 (electronic) 1. Feminism. 2. Feminism and mass
media. 3. Digital media. 4. Feminist theory. I. Title.
  HQ1155.W58 2015
  305.42—dc23   2015022616

∞™ The paper used in this publication meets the minimum requirements of
American National Standard for Information Sciences—Permanence of Paper
for Printed Library Materials, ANSI/NISO Z39.48-1992.

Printed in the United States of America

Contents

Acknowledgements

THIS BOOK WAS RESEARCHED AND written as I laboured precariously on short-term teaching contracts and time-limited Heritage Lottery Fund (HLF) grants. These peculiarly stressful and hyperflexible circumstances have shaped the observations in the book. What follows is informed by a mixture of theory, practice and personal experience, punctuated by long periods of uncertain waiting, which, although profoundly stressful, afforded plenty of time for reading, writing and thinking.

As someone operating outside conventional academic environments, I have had to grasp collegiality and intellectual companionship in nonstandard settings. I am supremely grateful to people who have supported my work, either through sharing ideas, conversations, resources and practices or by commenting on sections of the book and being excited by what they read. It is not easy being a scholar working under these conditions. It requires determination, self-belief and a fair amount of cunning. I would therefore like to dedicate this work to anyone pursuing scholarly activity outside or alongside academic institutions. Your research matters, as do your ideas—have courage in your convictions and all power to your struggle.

I am particularly grateful to Adrian Finn from Great Bear Analogue and Digital Media in Bristol, who gave me an opportunity to research, write and learn about the issues relating to the care and preservation of magnetic tape collections and digital artifacts. All of this (ongoing) work is documented on the Great Bear tape blog, http://www.thegreatbear.net/blog/.

Massive thanks must also be extended to Hannah Lowery, my fellow Feminist Archive South trustee and archivist at Special Collections at the

University of Bristol, who has always been supportive of my desires to rummage and reconfigure the archive's contents, as well as immeasurably kind and insightful about archival matters.

For intellectual companionship, thank you to Victoria Browne, whose thinking has greatly informed this work, and Michelle Bastian, whose facilitation of the Temporal Belongings meetings and network is nothing short of awe-inspiring. Thanks also to Alex Wardrop for your love of words, thinking and learning, which has been a great form of sustenance and inspiration.

Thanks likewise go to my mum and dad, Alexandra Kokoli, Margaretta Jolly, Ellen Malos, Patrick Crogan, Charlotte Cooper, Frankie Green, all at the Glasgow Women's Library, Rachael House, Jo David and all at Space Station Sixty-Five, Maud Perrier, Emma Thatcher, Eva Megias, Jan Martin, Alison Rook, Rosie Lewis and all at Imprint, Rachel Cohen, Gail Chester, Anna Feigenbaum, Andrea Hajek, Susan Croft, Niamh Moore, Sian Norris, Sue Tate, Laura Sterry, Tom Perchard, Annie Gardiner, Josie McLellan, Trishima M. Khan, Hannah Little, Julia Downes, Kate Eichorn, Finn Mackay, Michael O'Rourke, members of the Fabulous Dirt Sisters, the York Street Band and Siren Theatre Company and participants in the Sistershow Revisited project.

Thanks also to Sarah Maguire for sharing Gertrude Stein's '30 minutes a day' writing practice, which has been an invaluable disciplinary technique, Sanjay for being a wonderful companion specie and Maggie Nicols for inviting me to live with her at Melin Dolwion as I completed this book. Thanks must also go to Chris Weedon and Glenn Jordan for their work establishing and sustaining the Butetown History & Arts Centre in Cardiff, and all the incredible people who have worked there over the years, and for Chris in particular, who passed this manuscript on to Martina O'Sullivan at Rowman & Littlefield International. Thank you also, Martina, for taking this project on.

This book is dedicated to the loving memory of Mike, Joan and John Withers and Zouïna Benhalla. *I still miss you.*

Finally, gargantuan gratitude goes to Natalie J. Brown for always being such a super-trouper.

Introduction

IT IS THE AFTERNOON OF Saturday, October 12, 2013, and I am sitting in a café near King's Cross St. Pancras Station in London with Jalna Hanmer, a retired professor of women's studies. Jalna was an activist in the Women's Liberation Movement (WLM) and was instrumental in setting up Women's Aid Services in the UK.[1] We are taking a moment to relax after attending the annual meeting of the Feminist Archive, of which we are both trustees.[2] A few hundred yards up the road is the British Library, where a unique event of staged conversations between feminists from different generations is taking place. It is poor timing that our meeting is held on the same day, because we would both liked to have witnessed such collaborative acts of live, public memory-making. It is gratifying, however, that the event, which sold out within hours of its announcement and then moved to a larger venue, is happening. It is testimony to the swelling interest in activist legacies of the UK WLM, which place transgenerational exchanges at the centre of renewed explorations.[3]

In the café Jalna and I talk about her move to Britain from Oregon, USA, and the stultifying boredom of the 1950s. Then, seemingly out of the blue, she begins to recount a story about her activism in the WLM, meditating upon one incident in particular. In the bustle of the café it is hard to hear her talk; the background music merges with the deep tone of Jalna's voice. As the story is elaborated, I tune in to it directly because it is one I have never heard before, despite being a keen listener to oral histories from the women's movement, from Brian Harrison's suffrage interviews[4] to my own work interviewing WLM activists.[5] Jalna tells me about an extraordinary meeting held in 1977 that was to decide the fate of Fawcett Library's collection, which at that time was the largest repository of women's history in the UK. The location of the library, 27 Wilfred Street, SW1, had been put up for sale, and quick action was needed if all the items in the collection were to be kept together. Historian Jill Liddington remembers that the library

> seemed from the outside an unremarkable house . . . in an ordinary London street, my abiding impression was of neglect and despondency. I felt I was trespassing into an older parallel universe, tiptoeing trepidatiously into a forgotten world on its uppers, hanging by a perilously thin thread. Were there really too few working light bulbs to cast enough light into the gloomy rooms? It seemed a 'library' at its last gasp, run by a dwindling band of increasingly frail volunteers.[6]

Finding a stable home for the Fawcett Library's collection (later the Women's Library) has always been an issue, as Angela John recounts:

> The Library dates back to the 1920s when it was housed in Marsham Street, Westminster. The Women's Service Library was linked to the London Society for Women's Service (formerly the London National Society for Women's Suffrage). It was a valuable resource for newly enfranchised women and gained support from figures such as Vera Brittain and Eleanor Rathbone. In the early 1930s it took over the Cavendish Bentinck Library which had supplied, as Viscountess Rhondda explained in her autobiography *This Was My World*, 'all the young women in the suffrage movement with *the books they could not procure in the ordinary way*.'[7]

In the café in 2013, Jalna told me about the moment in 1977, when institutions were invited to make proposals to become custodians of the collection.[8] There wasn't massive interest and two institutions emerged as front-runners: the London School of Economics (where the collection moved in 2013) and City Polytechnic (now called London Metropolitan University). Jalna remembered that the two offers were very different: LSE wanted to break up the collection, keeping those parts they deemed important and could enter into the Dewey decimal system and discarding the rest. City Polytechnic proposed to keep the collection together in its entirety and develop it through further acquisitions. Fawcett member Baroness Seale had done extensive negotiations with the LSE, and it looked likely that a move there would be favoured despite the very grave consequences for maintaining the integrity of the collection.

The final fate of the Women's Library was to be decided by a vote at a meeting of the Fawcett Society, who were at that time custodians of the collection. Only members of the Fawcett Society could cast a vote, but the organisation policy stipulated that women could join and vote immediately on proposed actions. In the days leading up to the extraordinary meeting, a rush to join

Fawcett ensued, as concerned women's liberationists and other women activists aimed to wield their voting power in order to protect the collection. It should be noted that the aims of the WLM and the Fawcett Society were not politically congruent, as Jalna qualified in an email:

> At that time the Fawcett Society members were not impressed with the WLM. Fawcett saw the WLM as concerned with sexual liberation, not an issue historically or currently relevant to the Fawcett Society. One of the staff told me that she did not approve, as no doubt did others, and the Fawcett Society was not collecting WLM material. This was in the 70s when the WLM first began. Because there was a gulf between the views of the Fawcett and WLM interests and activities, joining the Fawcett only occurred because of the danger to the continuation of the collection. This was the most extensive collection of women's history internationally at that time. I think many of the women who joined to attend this meeting understood that people without a history are truly oppressed. These books, pamphlets, journals and newspapers, and other items, such as banners and badges, had to be protected.[9]

Jalna recounted how she turned up at the meeting and could not enter the room; so many women attended they were spilling out of the hall. The women on the Fawcett committee could not believe what they were witnessing. From her place in the corridor Jalna could just about hear the unfolding of proceedings, occasionally stealing a glimpse inside the room. There was Dame Margery Corbett Ashby, a veteran suffragist campaigner now in her mid-nineties, sitting on the stage, steadied by her cane, which was adorned with a smart ornamental cap. Corbett Ashby was so important within the Fawcett Society that the chair of the meeting read out her address, which delivered a damning indictment of plans to break up the Fawcett Library's collection. Another woman in the audience, whom Jalna believed to be in her eighties, echoed this outrage, proclaiming that her mother would be appalled if the collection was split up. As votes were counted it became clear that there was overwhelming support for the move to City Polytechnic. Jalna's eyes gleamed with excitement as she told me this story, and emphatically declared it to be 'one of the great meetings of my life'—quite a statement for someone who has spent a lifetime in political activism. The texture and vivacity of Jalna's memory was so forceful that I felt I was there in 1977, lurking, just outside the room, with Dame Corbett Ashby and all the other mobilised women.

I didn't know about the continual threats to the Women's Library collections when I first went there in 2007 to learn about the history of feminist activism. The library had been just a few years in its custom-built home in Aldgate East, paid for by a £4.2-million grant from the Heritage Lottery Fund. At that time the library was well staffed; several receptionists greeted me as I walked through the door and there were always plenty of librarians on hand to offer help with enquiries. Staff numbers dwindled drastically as the 2000s unfolded, and, of course, the library had to move in 2013 because London Metropolitan could not afford to run it anymore. As I browsed the collections in 2007 I didn't know that the material I was consulting could have been very different, or even not been there at all, had a significant intervention not been made by activists in 1977. Until Jalna told me about the extraordinary meeting, I had no idea it had ever taken place. As she stopped speaking, I asked if she had recounted it before—perhaps to the recent *Sisterhood and After* project for which she was interviewed? But she wasn't sure, so I took these notes and wrote it down a week later to ensure that it was recorded.

Accessing Legacies

Feminism, Digital Culture and the Politics of Transmission examines the processes through which feminist ideas, knowledge and cultural practices are transmitted across generations. A central claim in the book is that feminism is defined by generation *as such*, and because of this it is necessary to attend to how generational formations are composed through transmission. To be clear from the start: My aim is not to *oppose* 'generation' and 'transmission,' but to demonstrate how transmission processes *compose* feminist generations. That is, we cannot go *beyond* feminist generations but only *within their composition.* To do this we need to grapple with the many challenges that occur when we think through and elaborate a feminist politics of transmission. When we encounter feminist generational claims we are only accessing the tip of the transmission iceberg, even if they are evidence that transmission is at play—evidence that is signposted throughout feminist thought. Generational claims are integral to the formation of feminist identities and modes of belonging, and are often used to designate particular aesthetics, vocabularies, political ideologies and strategic approaches to feminism in different times and places. Generational claims, fashioned most clearly through the metaphor of the wave, operate within feminism as meta-narratives that structure and account for the back-and-forth[10] quality that underpins feminism's long and continuous struggle for social revolution. Generational narratives are vital for the coherency of feminism as a conceptual system rooted in their connection with other feminist traditions across historical time; they are, Victoria Browne argues, part of 'feminism's "great hegemonic model."'[11] Yet often these anchors that structure feminist thought, and thereby hold *the idea* of feminism together, cover up the *material and technical processes* through which generation is composed. It has become normative to 'tell stories' *about* feminist generations in order to implicitly justify certain knowledge claims.[12] Such actions occur, however, without having to do the difficult work of taking seriously feminism's generational composition and therefore think through the compelling issues that are engendered through considering transmission processes.

In this book, then, I outline ways we can understand the material and technical processes that compose feminist generational knowledge, a cavernous information-entity I will call *feminism's already-there*. My exploration of the transmission of feminism's already-there refers to two related things: first, the practical organisation of memory resources and their dissemination through popular culture, libraries, archives, museums and the internet, as well as in educational institutions such as universities where feminist ideas acquire epistemic and cultural value; secondly, how individuals and groups *adopt* feminist ideas and form circuits through which feminism's already-there is transmitted. The formation of a transmissive circuit can be a very modest encounter, occurring between one person and a feminist book, film or song, or it can aim to involve significant numbers of people through an exhibition or digital archive. In either case, the transmission of feminism's already-there does not just happen out of thin air—it is always a *technical process* that requires a lot of hard, often unpaid or low-paid labour, so that such information can be *organised* and *operationalised* through acts of transmission.

This book elaborates a politics of transmission within the context of feminist political, activist and epistemic communities, examining how feminism's already-there is organised and distributed. I want to affirm again that this argument does not *oppose* generational thinking with a politics of transmission. Rather, it demonstrates how a politics of transmission arises *from within* the idea of feminist generations itself; it affirms the necessity that they must be thought together. Feminist generations are not simply narrative tropes that can be treated as neutral or inevitable historical facts; they are the consequence of the complex composition of transmission processes, and such processes must be scrutinised and understood—there can be no generation without transmission. Furthermore, if those invested in feminism are not well equipped to interpret, understand and *take care of* the processes of transmission peculiar to diverse feminist communities, there is a risk that both the potential of and threats to feminism's already-there will be misrecognised or overlooked.

Heritage Practices

The book is largely informed by my personal practice as a curator and custodian of feminist archives. I became professionally involved in the cultural heritage sector by accident. In 2007 I had the good fortune to volunteer, and later work, at the Butetown History & Arts Centre (BHAC), a people's history museum based in Cardiff.[13] Working at BHAC introduced me to the basics of attractive exhibition design delivered within fairly low budgets. It also demonstrated to me how exhibitions are powerful educational tools, which can enable public encounters with ideas, images, ephemera, film, sound and objects. The skills, or should I say *techniques*, that I acquired from working at BHAC infused my approach when I began to (re)search (for) the cultural heritage of the WLM. At around the same time I started working at BHAC I began to root around feminist archives, particularly the Feminist Archive South (FAS) based in Bristol, propelled by a desire to understand the dissonance between the flat, monodimensional stories about feminism's recent history I had inherited from popular culture and academia, and the other life of feminism I intuited to have existed.[14] As Clare Hemmings's work has shown, the academic feminist picture of the '1970s,' the filter through which this dogmatic 'image of thought'[15] was transmitted, had been tainted by claims of 'essentialism' and a lack of critical sophistication. This effectively made the resources created by women in the WLM and within that decade— an important part of feminism's already-there—'off-limits.'

Yet for me the limits were easily breached. In my first visits to the FAS I quickly found compelling examples to counter the static and often dismissive stories about the '1970s' (read: WLM or 'second-wave feminism') I had inherited from academic feminism. One example stood out in particular. Flicking through a written summary document of an oral history with poet, activist and artist Pat VT West collected by the FAS in 2000/2001, I read about the existence of Bristol-based agit-prop feminist theatre troupe Sistershow, whose members engaged in gender-bending antics that aimed to politicise what it meant to be a 'woman.'[16] Sistershow was clear evidence of a vibrant cultural activism that challenged sweeping generational stereotypes about the 'second-wave' and 'third-wave.'[17] Even so, the activities of Sistershow, and many other forms of WLM activism, seemed to have no influence whatsoever on the static representations of 'the 1970s' or 'second-wave feminism' that circulated authoritatively as 'feminist knowledge.' I witnessed how Sistershow's existence had been organised and documented in Pat's oral history, yet as a *resource composing feminism's already-there* the materials remained largely inoperable.[18] As Pat wrote to me in a letter shortly before she died in 2008, 'One does such tapes, *wondering if anyone will ever hear them*, let alone understand or be inspired.'[19] Early on in my engagement with feminist archives, I learnt a key lesson: that the existence and organisation of materials is only one (but of course a crucial) part of the political struggle. If the vastness of feminism's already-there is to be accessed and mobilised, they have to be actively and deliberately transmitted.

In a very general sense, the technological changes fashioned by digitisation have normatively transformed societal attitudes towards transmission. 'I transmit, therefore I am' could be a rewired maxim for early twenty-first-century life. Digital technologies have made it easier than ever before to organise, transmit and connect people with marginalised feminist histories too. Crucially, they have enabled people with no archival skills or training to reconfigure the meaning of 'the archive' and the practice of archiving as it mutates within the digital environment. Chapters 6 and 7 of this book explore the problems and possibilities of an archival world gone digital, and how this changes access to feminism's already-there, reflecting on my work co-founding the Women's Liberation Music Archive (WLMA).[20]

Working in a heritage context that lends itself to thinking about responsibility, custodianship, curation and *caring for* historical materials also oriented my thinking *within* feminism's already-there differently. Heritage practices and theories, which are not usually applied to the heritage of radical political movements such as feminism, provided me with frameworks to understand how communities utilise resources such as texts, monuments, music, dance, images and so forth to construct identities and senses of cultural belonging. Throughout the extensive generational framing of feminism's self-identity as a political, intellectual and social movement, such a heritage value was often implicitly appealed to, yet rarely *explicitly practiced*. Indeed, given the spectre of generational conflict that continues to hang close to many debates about second-, third- and even fourth-wave feminism, such valuations—which would encourage orientation within feminist 'roots'—are positively discouraged.[21] What are the theoretical and practical consequences, then, if I understood feminism's archive as a *heritage resource* that could be used to transmit the values, knowledges, techniques, practices and cultural forms feminists have created across historical time? How would such an orientation to the material transform my relationship and responsibilities to it? If the material encountered in the archive is not simply *historical evidence*, but a patchwork of ideas, energies, possibilities and world-making tools through which I orient my sense of being in the world, *my cultural heritage*, what different intellectual and affective claims does such material elicit? How does thinking of feminism, which I experience as a revolutionary social movement with leftist (indeed anti-capitalist) leanings *as* cultural heritage, challenge how heritage in general is thought of as social phenomena?

A Wider Conversation

Like most books, what follows is a contribution to wider conversations. The discussions informing this work have been gaining momentum across academic and activist feminist communities since the turn of the twenty-first century. The question of feminism's recent history, and feminist generational knowledge, has been a topic of rich debate within academic circles and informs ideas addressed in this book. If the mournful, postfeminist 'we-are-all-empowered-now-feminism-is-dead-or-redundant' refrains gained a lot of credence within academic circles and popular culture throughout the 1990s, the early twenty-first century offered something different. Grassroots feminist activists began to interface their concerns with internet technologies,[22] North American subcultural travelling concepts,[23] queer politics and revived WLM traditions.[24] Chapters 1 and 2 will nevertheless respond to the enduring quality of postfeminist and stereotypical imagery through my discussion of the *immediately-there*.

Within academia there was also a marked desire to understand feminist generations. This was often expressed in a revisionary mode, such as trying to grapple with 'the feminist seventies,' or through an attempt to understand the unique characteristics of this particular 'third-wave' generational moment.[25] Emerging from such debates was an increased interest in epistemology and feminist knowledge, often examining how historical ideas and ideas *about* feminist history are entangled. Theorists such as Clare Hemmings, Victoria Hesford and Lisa Diedrich have demonstrated that to revisit how feminists are oriented to/within recent feminist history is to also reconsider the question of what feminist knowledge is. It is to examine the *historical grounds* on which feminist knowledge claims are (re)produced and secured.[26] This issue is examined in chapter 2 of this book, 'Feminist Knowledge Formation and the Already-There.' Such work was complemented by a renewed interest in strategy, evident in Iris van der Tuin's desire to use theory creatively in order to escape rigid epistemological claims lodged within negative appeals to a feminist generation.[27] Other strategists, such as Sophie and Kath Woodward, have engaged in empirically rich transgenerational writing experiments to reembody the maligned figure of generational conflict: the mother-daughter relationship.[28]

Feminist generational debates have stimulated thinking about temporality, often inflected by queer theorisations. Questions of untimeliness, anachronism, futurity, lagging, dragging and nonlinearity have all factored in these discussions in the twenty-first century.[29] In this book I offer further tools to think about feminist generations and temporality differently. This will be practiced through an operationalisation of feminism's already-there that aims to establish a non-futural feminist political imaginary. This will orient the possibility of collective attention within feminist ideas *whose time has come*, rather than a futural logic that is always deferred, *to come*. Within feminist theory there has also been interest in archives, both as historiographical tools and as repositories of feelings.[30] These debates have further converged with conversations in cultural memory studies that have explored the enduring images, phrases and references that compose feminist generational memory across mainstream and grassroots media.[31] This book aims to think with and across these rich theoretical resources in order to develop frameworks to understand the politics of transmission within the context of feminist generations.

What follows is, of course, not informed by theory alone; it is deeply influenced by *practices* of heritage and memory-making that I have either been directly involved in or witnessed as a community participant. As such, this book responds to and is enriched by wider efforts 'outside' of academia (although not exclusively, because there are always people who occupy multiple and contradictory positions in, out of and alongside academia). These actions have facilitated the curation, organisation, interpretation, archiving and transmission of feminist cultural heritage within the twenty-first century.[32] Such initiatives have often emerged from within communities of interest, community-led organisations, grassroots activist groups and individuals, or driven by the efforts of 'independent' curators and scholars. They have covered diverse issues such as the history of alternative feminist theatre, transnational feminist zines, the WLM as a national and local phenomenon, inspirational European women, feminist youth work, black feminism and the British Black Panthers, feminist film collectives, music and theatre in the suffrage movement, WLM posters, the East London Federation of Suffragettes and South Asian Striking Women. Their modes of creation and dissemination are digital or physical archives, theatre or performance, collaborative zines, film screenings, oral histories, comic books, films, podcasts, witness seminars, workshops, exhibitions, curated websites, networks, performances, protests and discussions.[33] While this book does not and cannot examine in detail all of these different examples of how feminism's already-there has been transmitted in the 2000s and beyond, they are all testimony to the central role feminist traditions perform in relation to contemporary feminist politics, a politics that is always located within the dynamics of transmission.

Accessing Feminism's Already-There

Within this book I argue that it is vital to understand the integral role *technical processes* perform in transmission and, therefore, the formation of feminist generations, identities, politics and acts of world-making. Central to my argument is the concept of *feminism's already-there*, a modification of a concept—the already-there—developed by French philosopher of technology Bernard

Stiegler already the

Stiegler. Stiegler's wide-ranging philosophical, and increasingly political, project places the question of generational transmission and its technical organisation at the centre. For this reason it is surprising that his ideas have not yet been widely adopted within heritage or memory studies.[34] His work has certainly not been considered in relation to feminist thinking or practice; yet what follows is not an attempt to *apply* Stiegler's ideas to feminism, or claim his work for the feminist political project. Instead my concern is to articulate a politics of tradition, inheritance and transmission informed and enabled by Stiegler's thinking and theoretical techniques. This will, in particular, reside within an elaboration of *feminism's already-there.*

Stiegler's already-there fuses Martin Heidegger's notion of *dasein*, 'the already-there that is its past, always having preceded it and from out of which it "is" this particular "who,"'[35] and Gilbert Simondon's notion of 'the pre-individual.' Together they compose the field of inheritance comprising books, monuments, photographs, film, sound and digital technologies—what Stiegler describes as hypomnemata[36]—'techniques of memory and communication'[37] from which critical faculties, techniques and social bonds are forged. For Stiegler, what is encountered already-there, what we inherit, defines the contours of the world we inhabit *as we move through, into and within*, so that we may adopt techniques, behaviours, orientations, information and knowledge.[38] In this sense the already-there could be perceived as mundane, the *there-being* of what is readily available, akin to the most basic of social functions. Yet what is already-there cannot be underestimated—it *forms* and *de-forms* individuals, communities and wider society; from the already-there's *forms* 'we' and 'I's' *are* fashioned. In this respect, the already-there is necessarily a site of struggle, contention and invention.

Another way to understand this suggestion is that our milieu conditions how we *can* think, act, relate, learn, know and so forth. A crucial point to grasp is that, for Stiegler, any milieu is conditioned by its 'techno-logical constitution.'[39] The already-there cannot be thought of apart from its inscription in technics, a term that encompasses both technologies *and* techniques. In this double sense, technics such as writing and reading, playing a musical instrument or listening to a vinyl record, knitting a jumper or sowing seeds to grow vegetables are all activities exterior to life, but nonetheless come to compose life through *a process* of 'taking within,' or interiorisation. Stiegler explains:

> They are of experiences I have not myself lived but that I have nevertheless *adopted*: this is the case for everything of which I have been told, of that into which I have been initiated, or of that which I have been taught . . . they have been conceived, selected, projected and lived by others, and have constituted their own pasts, from of their own presents . . . *collective, common, inherited*

by everyone as the past of everyone . . . constituting *horizons of expectation common to a group.*[40]

It is the constitutive importance of inheritance and memory inscribed in technical forms addressed in Stiegler's work that I want to develop in relation to feminist generations. I want to suggest that feminism, *as a field of inheritance*, is composed of its own transmission trajectories and circuitry whose specificity is not accounted for in Stiegler's thinking, which pursues a *general* approach to these problems. This book aims to outline, therefore, the contours of feminism's already-there. Accessing feminism's already-there is not as simple or immediate as, say, turning on the radio to listen to the 'feminist news,' or going to the public library to consult certain key feminist texts. Very prosaic factors get in the way: radio stations run by commercial ventures or the state may not wish to promote feminist culture, and the library does not stock the book you want to read. Even in an age of apparent information abundance, there remains the problem of accessing '*the books they could not procure in the ordinary way*' for marginal knowledges such as feminism. As much as feminism is defined by generation, it is also defined by a problem of accessing inheritance from within generation. The circuitry of feminism's already-there always requires work; its transmissive trajectories have to be constructed, elaborated and continually (re)affirmed. Feminist traditions, and the resources they offer, *are already-there*, but their arrangement is often fragmented and dispersed—'scattered,' van der Tuin suggests, 'ruled out by a logic of One which develops into a norm and marks all the rest as deviant (Other).'[41]

This book is an outline of how access routes to feminism's already-there become fragmented, blocked, obfuscated and directed in particular ways due to the technical transmissive systems they are embedded within (the mainstream media, academic articles, websites, archives, digitised artifacts and performance, to name a few). It is also an enactment of how it is possible to be oriented within such transmission processes differently by paying attention to how 'transmission is determined by the explicitly technological forms recording forms of knowledge, by the conditions of *access* they provide.'[42] As Stiegler makes clear, when the dominant technical apparatus changes—for example, with the movement from analogue to digital—so do the technical capacities of the already-there as conditioning context for societal becoming. Building political lexicons that mobilise *what is already-there* aims to encourage scholars, thinkers and activists to explore the resources that compose an emergent feminist tradition. Examining the role technical processes perform in defining conditions of access to feminist knowledge may also enable diverse feminist communities to take better care of those complex inheritances *in the long term*. My fashioning of the already-there is neither normatively *modifiability of already there.*

positive nor negative, in the sense that what is encountered within conscious searches for tradition, as well as within everyday lived experience, can make one feel uncomfortable, unhappy, distressed, embarrassed, disgusted and even traumatised. Yet the compositional power of the already-there must, however, be accounted for because it cannot, ultimately, be escaped; it operates as technical anchor conditioning the coemergence of the world through processes of transmission.

This may be misrecognised as an argument for technological determinism, that I am arguing we can do nothing to change history or memory, and are condemned to inheritance or tradition. Yet this is far from the case. Even though 'the default of origin cannot be corrected'[43]—that is, the compositional co-evolution of human and technical culture cannot be reversed—it can be confronted and 'worked through.' The already-there cannot, therefore, be escaped, but *it can be modified*. It can be confronted, selected and elaborated through practices of operationalisation. Indeed, understanding the processes of transmission, and acquiring appropriate techniques and practices of selection, can mitigate the extent to which what is already-there is passively reproductive of normative and even destructive social and technical arrangements. A politics of the already-there, a politics of transmission, is to understand how, why and where these technical processes occur so that transmissive practices attentive to questions of selection and circuitry can be elaborated and established. A politics of the already-there will also seek to understand how different communities of knowledge and practice are wired up differently, as it were, with specific forms of organisation, tradition and transmission that cannot be understood within a general conception of the already-there.

Structurally, this book is organised into seven chapters that seek to enact, as well as explore, the problem of accessing feminism's already-there. Chapters 1 and 2 outline the feminism that is most immediately-there, within the realms of both popular culture and academia. These sites are significant because they condition how feminism's already-there is accessed, often through transmitting congealed signals that can smother curiosity and encourage narrow interpretations, even if they act as 'entry points,' as signs that the transmitted sign-al of feminism's already-there exists. Chapters 3 and 4 examine the techniques of generational transmission, focusing on the articulation of the ancestral within black and women of colour feminism. These chapters also discuss how transmission practices have been theorised within heritage studies and international heritage policies, demonstrating how feminism's transmission processes both diverge and intersect with established frameworks. Chapters 5–7 explore how digital technologies have reconfigured access to feminism's already-there, through my (re)search for the music-makers of the WLM. Less restraint is practiced within these chapters, as previously suppressed layers of the already-there emerge within the text. The text thus unravels, critically, not in the quest for truth as such, but as a means to enact a different kind of access within feminism's already-there, enabled by digital conditions. With such a trajectory outlined, we can ask of feminist tradition: What is already-there?

Notes

1. A biography of Jalna is available on the *Sisterhood and After* website: 'Sisterhood and After,' accessed 27 October 2013, http://www.bl.uk/learning/histcitizen/sisterhood/bioview.html#id=144025&v=true&id=144025.

2. See 'Feminist Archive South,' accessed 27 October 2013, http://feministarchive .org.uk.

3. For more information on the conference, please go to 'History of Feminism,' accessed 27 October 2013, https://historyfeminism.wordpress.com/conference-2013/. Personal responses from attendees commented that there was a tendency at the event for 'younger activists' to blame 'older activists' for their political 'failures,' such as not developing a trans-positive politics in the WLM, and that they found this 'frustrating.'

4. Brian Harrison's 'Oral Evidence of the Suffrage Movement,' deposited in the Women's Library, accessed 27 October 2013, http://twl-calm.library.lse.ac.uk/Calm View/Record.aspx?src=CalmView.Catalog&id=8SUF.

5. For projects such as 'Sistershow Revisited' (2011), accessed 27 October 2013, http://sistershowrevisited.wordpress.com; 'Music & Liberation' (2012), accessed 27 October 2013, http://music-and-liberation.tumblr.com.

6. Jill Liddington, 'Fawcett Saga: Remembering the Fawcett Library Across Four Decades,' *History Workshop Journal* (2013): 268, accessed 27 October 2013, DOI: 10.1093/hwj/dbt026.

7. Angela V. John, 'To Make That Future Now: The Women's Library and the TUC Library,' *History Workshop Journal Online*, 20 April 2012, accessed 24 October 2013, http://www.historyworkshop.org.uk/to-make-that-future-now-the-womens -library-the-tuc-library/.

8. This, of course, prefigured similar activity in 2012, which led to the collection being rehoused yet again.

9. Jalna Hanmer, email message to the author, 20 October 2013.

10. Victoria Browne, 'Backlash, Repetition, Untimeliness: The Temporal Dynamics of Feminist Politics,' *Hypatia* (2012), accessed 27 October 2013, DOI: 10.1111/ hypa.12006.6.

11. Victoria Browne, *Feminism, Time and Non-Linear History* (Basingstoke: Palgrave, 2014), 15.

12. Clare Hemmings, *Why Stories Matter: The Political Grammar of Feminist Storytelling* (Durham, NC: Duke University Press, 2011).

13. To learn about Butetown History & Arts Centre's work, please visit 'About Butetown History & Arts Centre,' accessed 13 February 2015, http://bhac.org.c31 .sitepreviewer.com/.

14. See also Niamh Moore, *The Changing Nature of ECO/Feminism: Telling Stories from Clayoquot Sound* (Vancouver: University of British Columbia Press, 2013).

15. Gilles Deleuze, *Difference and Repetition*, Paul Patton, trans. (London: Athlone Press, 1994), 129–168.

16. See 'Feminist Archive South,' 'Personal Histories of Second Wave Feminism,' accessed 12 November 2014, http://feministarchivesouth.org.uk/collections/personal-histories-of-second-wave-feminism-oral-history-project-2000-2001/.

17. See Deborah Withers and Red Chidgey, 'Complicated Inheritance: Sistershow and the Queering of Feminism,' *Women: A Cultural Review* 12:3 (2010): 309–323.

18. The oral histories collected by the FAS were, in fact, recorded on mini-discs, which by 2007 was a format approaching obsolescence. I migrated the recordings on mini-disc to WAV files in 2013.

19. Pat VT West in Deborah Withers, *Sistershow Revisited: Feminism in Bristol, 1973-1975* (Bristol: HammerOn Press, 2011), 7.

20. 'Women's Liberation Music Archive,' accessed 13 February 2015, http://womensliberationmusicarchive.co.uk.

21. Astrid Henry, *Not My Mother's Sister: Generational Conflict and Third Wave Feminism* (Bloomington: Indiana University Press, 2004).

22. The UK-based website 'The F-Word,' which aimed to create a voice for contemporary UK feminism, was established in 2001. 'The F-Word,' accessed 15 November 2014, http://www.thefword.org.uk/. Consider also the rise of 'the feminist blogosphere.'

23. For example, Ladyfest, first held in Olympia, Washington, 2000. Ladyfests remain a popular, transcultural phenomenon, as communities around the world use the model to create platforms for women and queers to perform music, display art, share skills and so forth. According to one person who attended the original Ladyfest in Olympia, the invitation to organise similar events in other cities was not merely a call to arms to spread the feminist revolution, it was so that people would not move to Olympia—a small town in the Pacific Northwest—and take all the jobs (Nicola Elliott, personal communication with author, 2013).

24. Reclaim the Night was restarted in 2004 in London, and many other cities have held similar marches; Radical Feminism remains controversial and popular. 'Reclaim the Night,' accessed 27 October 2013, http://www.reclaimthenight.co.uk.

25. Ann Kaloski, ed., *The Feminist Seventies* (York: Raw Nerve, 2003). The collection was published following a conference of the same name, now archived at 'The Feminist Seventies,' accessed 13 February 2015, http://www.feministseventies.net/; Stacy Gillis, Gillian Howie and Rebecca Munford, eds., *Third Wave Feminism: A Critical Introduction* (Basingstoke: Palgrave Macmillan, 2007).

26. See Hemmings, *Why Stories Matter*; Lynne Segal, 'Generations of Feminism,' *Radical Philosophy* 83 (1997): 6–16; Lisa Diedrich and Victoria Hesford, 'Experience, Echo, Event: Theorising Feminist Histories, Historicising Feminist Theory,' *Feminist Theory* 15 (2014): 103–117.

27. See, for example, Iris van der Tuin, 'Jumping Generations: On Second- and Third-Wave Epistemology,' *Australian Feminist Studies* 24:59 (2009): 17–31.

28. Sophie Woodward and Kath Woodward, *Why Feminism Matters: Feminism Lost and Found* (Basingstoke: Palgrave Macmillan, 2011).

29. Elizabeth Freeman, *Time Binds: Queer Temporalities, Queer Histories* (Durham, NC: Duke University Press, 2010); Victoria Browne, *Feminism, Time and Non-Linear History*; Sam McBean, *Feminism's Queer Temporalities* (London: Routledge, 2015); for queer theorisations of temporality, see José Esteban Muñoz, *Cruising Utopia: The Then and There of Queer Futurity* (New York: New York University Press, 2009); Lee Edelman, *No Future: Queer Theory and the Death Drive* (Durham, NC: Duke University Press, 2004).

30. Ann Cvetkovich, *Archives of Feelings: Trauma, Sexuality, and Lesbian Public Cultures* (Durham, NC: Duke University Press, 2003); Kate Eichorn, *The Archival Turn in Feminism: Outrage in Order* (Philadelphia: Temple University Press, 2013).

31. Victoria Hesford, *Feeling Women's Liberation* (Durham, NC: Duke University Press, 2013); Red Chidgey, '"A Modest Reminder": Performing Suffragette Memory in a British Feminist Webzine,' in Anna Reading and Tamar Katriel, eds., *Powerful Times: Cultural Memories of Nonviolent Struggles* (Basingstoke: Palgrave Macmillan, 2015). My personal relationship with Red Chidgey was formative in regard to feminist generations, and shaped much of my early thinking and activism in this area. Between 2006 and 2009 we shared similar passions and political grievances about how our inheritance had been transmitted and the ways in which the question of generation was being framed within academic feminism. I want to thank her here for both profound inspiration and early companionship in thinking through these issues.

32. The *Sisterhood and After* oral history project is a good example of an academic project that aims to communicate its content to a wide range of diverse audiences from schoolteachers, community members, academic researchers, the media and so forth. 'Sisterhood and After,' accessed 24 January 2015, http://www.bl.uk/learning/histcitizen/sisterhood/.

33. See, for example, 'Feminist Archives and Libraries Network,' accessed 24 January 2015, http://feministlibrariesandarchives.wordpress.com/; 'Translation/Transmission Women's Film Season,' accessed 24 January 2015, http://translation transmission.wordpress.com; 'Unfinished Histories: Histories of Alternative Theatre, 1968–1988,' accessed 24 January 2015, http://www.unfinishedhistories.com; 'Bolton Women's Liberation Oral History' Project, accessed 24 January 2015, http://www.bolton-womens-liberation.org/; 'Striking Women,' accessed 24 January 2015, http://www.striking-women.org/main-module-page/striking-out; 'Shape and Situate: Posters of Inspirational European Women,' accessed 24 January 2015, http://www.spacestationsixtyfive.com/exhibitions_and_projects.php?project_id=140; Petra Bauer's exhibition, 'Me, You, Us and Them,' which focused on 1970s film collectives, accessed 24 January 2015, http://www.focalpoint.org.uk/archive/exhibitions/18/, and subsequent publication, Petra Bauer and Dan Kidner, eds., *Working Together: Notes on British Film Collectives in the 1970s* (Southend: Focal Point Gallery, 2013); 'East London Suffragette Festival,' accessed 24 January 2015, http://eastlondonsuffragettes.tumblr.com/; 'Remember Olive Morris,' accessed 24 January 2015, https://rememberolivemorris.wordpress.com/; 'Grassroots Feminism,'

accessed 24 January 2015, www.grassrootsfeminism.net; Nic Green's 'Make Your Own Herstory' project, accessed 24 January 2015, http://nicgreen.wix.com/make yourownherstory; 'See Red Women's Workshop,' accessed 24 January 2015, https://seeredwomensworkshop.wordpress.com/.

34. According to Grant David Bolmer, memory studies have tended to privilege accounts of psychic and individual memory, rather than paying attention to the role material technologies play in shaping individual and psychic memory. See Grant David Bolmer, 'Virtuality in Systems of Memory: Toward an Ontology of Collective Memory, Ritual, and the Technological,' *Memory Studies* 4:4 (2011): 450–464.

35. Bernard Stiegler, *Technics and Time, 1: The Fault of Epimetheus*, Richard Beardsworth and George Collins, trans. (Stanford: Stanford University Press, 1998), 207.

36. Bernard Stiegler, *The Decadence of Industrial Democracies*, Daniel Ross, trans. (Cambridge: Polity, 2011), 76.

37. Bernard Stiegler, *The Re-Enchantment of the World: The Value of Spirit Against Industrial Populism*, Trevor Arthur, trans. (London: Bloomsbury, 2014), 6.

38. Increasingly, Stiegler's work is intent on demonstrating how such a process is short-circuited, compromised or impossible due to the technical conditions in hyper-industrial society.

39. Stiegler, *Technics and Time, 1*, 205.

40. Stiegler, *The Decadence of Industrial Democracies*, 112–113. Italics in original.

41. Iris van der Tuin, *Generational Feminism: New Materialist Introduction to a Generative Approach* (New York: Lexington, 2014).

42. Stiegler, *Technics and Time, 1*, 210.

43. Bernard Stiegler, *Technics and Time, 2: Disorientation*, Stephen Barker, trans. (Stanford: Stanford University Press, 2009), 95.

1

Feminism's Already-There?

T his book is concerned with feminism's already-there and explores how these resources can be accessed, preserved and cared for through practices of selection, organisation and transmission. As stated in the introduction, the already-there is our key concept that will orient thinking actions as we move through the book. The already-there enables us to think through and account for the role exteriorised, technical memory resources perform in the formation of knowledge, identities and culture. Considering feminism's already-there enables us to respond to feminism as an epistemic, cultural and political field defined by generations yet simultaneously inattentive to the *technical processes* through which memory resources are transmitted across generations. It is these processes that must be thought through, and attendant practices developed, as we elaborate a feminist politics of transmission.

How then are we to recognise the already-there? The already-there operates as a *technical compost*, an arena of composition and decomposition from which ideas, practices, knowledges and techniques emerge and diverge through dynamic processes of transformation, becoming, disintegration and solidification. The already-there is a stratified constellation of technical memory matter, composed of resources that shape political and cultural imaginaries. This stratification should not be thought of merely as *across*, but also in terms of depth, height, scale, extensiveness and duration. Entities within the already-there are capable of moving in different directions, and can sometimes move through materials such as concrete, bodies and metal. Sometimes what is already-there makes material vibrate or change consistency or temperature corresponding to the terms of its operability. Its forms may change and content migrate, accruing or shedding textures in the process. To access what is already-there is to operationalise it, to put it into use and action. Such activations cannot be valued as inherently positive or negative—all kinds of ideas and actions can be mobilised from within the already-there. The already-there includes material artifacts such as books, monuments, pamphlets, paintings, photographs, film and music. The already-there can also be embodied and gestural, comprising *techniques* that are kept alive deliberately or by chance—contingency, accidents *and* planning shape its existence, and relational access to it.

The already-there is spatial, temporal, fibrous, liquid, resonant, electronic, mechanical, inscribed, geophysical,[1] deep, aquatic,[2] shallow, mineral, metal, wooden, computational, inauthentic, modifying and plastic. In varied forms it transmits, forgets and disintegrates, betraying resilience and vulnerability. There are cultural, economic and governmental strategies that aim to control what is already-there and monitor the effects of encounters that emerge from within it. There are always contingencies at play in its operation, and therefore the possibility of transformation *as well as* reaction to its contents. The mnemonic technical organs that compose the already-there are collected and sometimes catalogued for ease of reference and coherency, but they can equally be dispersed, hidden or displaced and not form part of any recognisable story or collection. Such 'unofficial' annals of the already-there are not necessarily lost forever—they can be reclaimed by individuals, communities, institutions and governments who may care enough to reinvigorate access to them at a historical time amenable to their articulation.[3] Furthermore, such dynamics of disappearance and reappearance cannot always be anticipated in advance, or always appear as the result of *intentional* reclamation.

Even as we acknowledge the pliable contingency of the already-there, what we find already-there can be rigid, established and organised in deliberate ways. It is not an amorphous mass that is indeterminable; it *is* technical although it may seem intangible. The already-there composes the ground through which actions, social lives, relationships and identities emerge across different historical contexts; it is the locus from which transgenerational responsibility is supported and practiced. What is already-there acts as the very condition for thinking itself: exteriorised technical inscriptions that *support* and compose the *movement* of thought, resources from which ideas, lives, politics, desire and culture are woven. Yet what is already-there is not straightforwardly cumulative. It does not *automatically* become richer as traditions are created, recorded or documented; it belies progression and is oriented in the everywhere. Such a deep archive may exist in the already-there in terms of material *volume*, as years pass and collections swell—but it may not always be accessible, either in content *or* in form. What emerges through

[handwritten marginalia: "transmission", "accumulation", "lean + just in time production —", "see Marx 33", ""]*

the already-there in one historical moment may disappear in another. This may be for a variety of reasons including active suppression, accident, technological obsolescence or neglect. The already-there functions across varied layers of access conditioned by technical systems that filter what *can be* already-there; by the cultural, economic and political context in which what is already-there is valued, dismissed, represented, interpreted, modified or policed; and finally by people struggling to compose themselves within the already-there's cavernous infinitude. Residing within the already-there's *compositional* role, shaping social worlds and imaginations, is to elaborate a politics of tradition and heritage, and 'the theme of "heritage" . . . cannot be thought apart from an already-there.'[4]

Elaborating a Politics of Tradition and Heritage in Digital Culture

There has been widespread debate as to whether 'the digital' marks a significant historical rupture or substantial reorganisation of technical and symbolic life.[5] For Stiegler, the appearance of the internet, and subsequent widespread, 'connective'[6] digitisation, amounts to an undeniable 'mutation . . . unified by the TCP-IP[7] protocol [that] has manifestly changed the organizational set up of the program industries. And there is no doubt that this transformation of industrial technology, via the digital, renders new perspectives conceivable.'[8] Furthermore, there are significant political stakes in these transformations. He writes:

> With the advent of very advanced control technologies emerging from digitalization, and converging in a *computational* system of globally integrated production and consumption, new cultural, editing and programming industries appeared. What is new is that they are technologically linked by universal digital equivalence (the binary system) to telecommunications systems and to computers. [This] . . . constitutes the hyper-industrial epoch strictly speaking, dominated by the categorization of hyper-segmented 'targets' ('surgically' precise marketing organizing consumption) and by functioning in real time (production) through lean production and *just in time* (logistics). . . . The upheavals induced by digitalization [are] often compared to a 'third industrial revolution' (also called the 'information society' or, more recently, the 'knowledge society'—the digital system permitting, on the side of industrial conception, the systematic mobilization of all knowledge in the service of innovation).[9]

For Stiegler, the *hyper-industrial* synchronisation of diverse memory communities into precise, targeted constituents of consumption is symptomatic of a very serious and extensive crisis.[10] At an everyday level it produces banal homogeneity, 'the de-composition of the *I* and the *we* (or the collapse of the

I and the *we*),'[11] which in turn results in widespread pseudo-individualism[12] and 'herdish' behaviour. For Stiegler, we are currently embroiled in nothing less than a 'war without rules,' resulting in the 'alienation of desire and of affects, where the weaponry is organized by marketing.'[13] The hyper-industrial digital, manipulated by the programming industries, has reorganised 'epigenetic memory of individual experience, which becomes transmissible through technical objects,' the tertiary retentions (i.e., exteriorised mnemo-technical resources such as books, films and websites) that 'condition [the] bond between *I* and the *we*.'[14] In the context of this book, we could say that such transformations have qualitatively altered the access to the already-there, and its operating capacities, rendering them anticipatory and synchronised.

The hyper-industrial digital is also marked by a profound *dis-adjustment* in the compositional grafting of human and technics, amplifying the 'fragility . . . of those who are born to prostheticity.'[15] As technologies acquire increasing computational sophistication, they require less technical skill and knowledge on behalf of the human operator to make them work. Increased automatism deprives humanity of technical and social knowledge, as the exteriorised alterity within the human—digital technics, if you like—*operate* human life in the service of capitalist accumulation. The human, as composed technical being, is pulled out of place and time, continually *adapting* to accelerating technological innovations that render them perpetually de-skilled and disoriented. If all this sounds rather bleak and deterministic, it is important to remember that Stiegler's diagnosis of the contemporary technical condition is a means to elaborate a pharmacological politics[16]— that is, a political programme attentive to the deeply poisonous aspects of digital technics *and* their curative potential.[17]

Long-Circuits and Short-Circuits

Transmission and generational exchange are central themes in Stiegler's diagnosis of the problems created by the '*extensive, more intensive and more complex*'[18] forms of calculation that define the hyper-industrial digital environment. In *Taking Care of Youth and the Generations* (2010) Stiegler argues that 'psychotechnological' devices such as mobile phones, video games and the internet, as well as older media forms such as television, have 'ravaged the mental and physical health of the entire population,'[19] shortening capacities for attention. For Stiegler, a robust and healthy population is one capable of paying sustained attention to an object or practice (the ability to 'take care' of knowledge), thus keeping techniques and knowledge (heritage and tradition) *alive* through practices of exchange. Such practices are demonstrative of generational responsibility, a process of caring for *the action of* transmission. Psychotechnologies, on the other hand, are compromising collective and individual capacities for care by short-circuiting networks of inheritance across generations, eroding basic critical faculties and social knowledge. Deprivation of such skills, Stiegler writes, evacuates 'the responsibility that defines human existence, [and] also short-circuits the psychic links between the generations. . . . Psychopower destroys the transmission and education of *philia*, the intimate connection among the generations.'[20]

The question of heritage and transmission as 'the *intimate* connection among the generations,' then, becomes extremely political within a digital environment where powers of circuitry are radically truncated. Here is a world where short-term satisfaction not only is the norm but also operates as the technical infrastructure *composing* reality. To challenge this viewpoint we might agree with Peter Gratton, who argues that neither 'the culture industry nor its consumers are as homogeneous as Stiegler suggests.'[21] Gratton also contends that Stiegler, ironically, excludes the voices of younger generations in *Taking Care* and speaks in their place, therefore undermining his arguments about generational exchange and responsibility. Additionally, and this will be key as we seek to elaborate a politics of transmission that *can respond* to the challenge of generational exchange and responsibility *within feminism*, there is the problem that Stiegler offers us a *general* critique. He does not do enough to differentiate how knowledge is transmitted among different social groups and communities *before* he writes of their erosion by the 'psychotechnical apparatus that controls attention.'[22] Stiegler offers a very persuasive *general* theory of how a politics of generational transmission can be a serious political question, but he does not pay enough attention to how heritage and knowledge are always already differentiated across communities and identities (be they spatial, temporal, gendered, ethnic, of interest, age or class). It is important to emphasise that not everyone accesses the already-there in the same way. Furthermore, everyone's already-there is different, even if the threat posed by hyper-industrial synchronisation—the synchronisation of the already-there—is palpable.

There are brief moments when Stiegler acknowledges the limitations of his general approach. In *Acting Out* he writes, 'These memories I share with others—*more or less*. . . . There are conflicts over sharing, over heritage. There are localizations in the capacities for appropriating the preindividual potential that open common scenes of individuation forming precisely the *we*.'[23] Yet such a claim is rare within Stiegler's oeuvre, which remains largely localised within scenes common to the particular demographic he inhabits. This is reflected when he writes about the loss of ethnic particularities connected to the rapid evolution of the technical system, discussed at length in *Technics*

and Time, 2,[24] in which he is arguably talking about the loss of a particular
heritage, and a particular kind of world—the ethnic communities, knowledge
and heritage of the white, majoritarian Western man.[25] Moreover, Sophie
Fuggle points out that the kinds of generational transmission Stiegler favours
in *Taking Care of the Youth and Generations* are those distributed within the
hierarchical structures of the (presumably heterosexual) family.[26] It is then
familial structures, governed by an authoritative, deferential patriarchal logic,
that Stiegler describes as breaking down in the face of emergent psychotechnological attention capture.

These are predictable feminist critiques to make of a writer who makes no
attempt whatsoever to engage in feminist political thought across his significant corpus of writing. Yet they are important criticisms because Stiegler as-
sociates tradition, or the loss of it, within a limited compass. The challenge he
opens up, but arguably does not fully realise, is to think tradition and generational transmission without necessary recourse to, or recuperation by, *a single
idea of tradition* situated within the *general* project. We cannot assume that
the traditions meant for us are always those we *immediately* inherit. There are
always *Other* traditions, as feminist, black, queer and anti-colonial struggles
indicate, and these traditions help us to think differently, know differently
and act differently in the world—they open up other spatial and temporal
orientations, and harbour potential to communicate alternative forms of historical experience. Such traditions often emerge après-coup (after the fact), as
'untimely,'[27] reinserted materials of the already-there, because there is usually
not enough technical infrastructure to secure their consistent transmission
across time, spaces and communities of practice wherein traditions co-evolve
with and through technics.

It is also possible to read an assumption within Stielger's thought that the
transmission of knowledge across generations was once whole but is now
dangerously fragmented. Yet such a claim does not apply easily to alternative
traditions such as feminism. Within feminist worlds there has never been a
continual transmission of knowledge across generations. There have always
been breakdowns in the circuits, dispersal, disappearance, destruction and
loss due to the peripheral nature of these traditions, and the lack of technical
support for the transmission of feminist cultural heritages. Significantly, at
historical moments when continuity and security is sought after within feminism, it is often articulated in generational terms. Furthermore, establishing
repositories and circuits where feminism's already-there can be transmitted,
such as libraries, archives and websites, is central to the elaboration of feminist worlds. I use the term 'feminist worlds' here to gesture towards the power
of feminism to enact different political imaginaries through the use of creative
strategies that articulate claims, actions and ways of living that *can* place

women's lives, and political concerns, at the centre; it is to engender further 'respect for *feminism as a maker of community.*'[28] Feminist worlds cannot be wholly assimilated to any dominant tradition, even though normative aspects do, of course, appear within feminism, often in the form of the discourse of constitutional reform, the fight for equality or incorporated rhetorics of 'choice' and 'empowerment' that Rosalind Gill names as the 'postfeminist sensibility.'[29] I want to assert throughout this work that feminist worlds establish their own trajectories, forms of belonging, identity, relationality and desire, as well as specific modes of transmission, that are for the most part unrecognisable by the terms laid out by any *general* idea of tradition. The aim of this book is to elaborate tools so that recognitions of feminist traditions can become possible, and emergent forms of knowledge reclaimed, through carving out orientations *within* feminism's already-there.

Feminist worlds are also plural *across* historical time and space and cannot be reduced to *each other*. I am not interested here in *recuperating* feminist worlds in order to perpetuate what Joan Scott calls the 'fantasy' of feminist history, whereby 'successive generations of women (activists and historians) . . . write themselves into these similarly structured scenarios.'[30] Outlining the technical composition of tradition and its transmission is not the same as salvation, retrieval or correction. On the contrary, the elaboration of feminist tradition is drawn from concrete and sometimes disjunctive contexts. It has to be capable of considering—indeed, caring for—the differences between, across and within historical situations. It is therefore a complex conception of tradition that remains open for interpretation and understands the dipping in and out of touch, sight, sound and body that is peculiar to feminist tradition, yet not exclusive of it. Feminism's already-there is composed of tangible and intangible remains, preserved in material culture, oral traditions and the dispersed ephemera so often produced by marginal cultures. We find it sometimes by accident, while echoes and suggestions sometimes confront us in the *immediately-there* of popular culture—the commonsense layer of the already-there that we shall turn to now.

Common Sense and the Immediately-There

In most cases we often do not go far enough with what is already-there. If the already-there were a very large house with several staircases and many rooms, for example, we would just stop and rest in the first room we come to, and settle in its ease, comfort and sensory plenitude. We do not feel impelled to investigate further because the risk of feeling small in its awesome presence is a terrifying proposition. Or it simply feels like too much effort because we may not know the way around, and how can a route be established without the appropriate tools (techniques)? Another way to conceptualise the already-there is in terms of depth. And it is here that we may encounter the commonsense *immediately-there*, which stops movement through the presentation of shallow encounters, 'a compendium of well-tried knowledge, customary beliefs, wise sayings, popular nostrums and prejudices' that appear as 'a product of Nature rather than of history.'[31] The immediately-there can appear like a never-ending cycle of amnesiac-inducing newness, embodied by shiny, yet dull, objects, captivating in their *lack* of intensity. The commonsense immediately-there seals over contours and depths—other realities struggle to escape its cellophane suffocation. Or, as Stiegler describes, through the immediately-there's apparent 'simultaneity and universality, temporal industrial objects tend to suspend all contextuality. Memory's industrialisation achieves a general decontextualisation.'[32]

With the already-there, however, you should always go further, and never trust what is immediately encountered. What has risen to the surface—what appears closest and without *active selection*—is a distillation of the already-there filtered through the contours of capitalism, racism, sexism and classism; cultural forces that are likely to evaporate deeper access to memory resources that may provide radically different viewpoints and critical tools that are likely to destroy what appears *immediately-there*. The digital immediately-there is often conceptualised as enabling access with greater *immediate* force, 'a new temporality . . . variously described as *instantaneous time, timeless time, time-space compression, time-space distanciation, chronoscopic time, pointillist time, or network time.*'[33] The digital immediately-there is therefore furnished within the immediate, sensory environment, undoubtedly wielding enormous power to shape subjectivities that can be hard to escape from, at times facilitating the formation of *decompositional* circuits located in novel forms of bodily and psychic control.[34] Within such a context it is imperative to remember that there are imaginaries, political ideas, societies and ways of living different from what is *immediately presented as all there is*. The profound problem with the immediately-there is that it can short-circuit access to the deeper resources of the already-there, where seeds of other worlds, and ways of being, are latent and ripe for awakening. As we have already seen with our discussion of Stiegler's outlining of psychotechnological capture, technics operating within the nexus of the digital immediately-there are incredibly sophisticated in the manner through which they control attention and, therefore, consciousness. Such sophistication is not omnipotent, and hardly experienced in a homogenous, unilateral manner by everyone, but it must be taken seriously when elaborating a politics of transmission within digital culture.

The Feminism That Appears Immediately-There

As far as we are aware, there is not a black British feminist herstory and/or archive association, and this is urgently needed.[35]

Feminism is all around us. . . . It is impossible to pinpoint where feminism has
started, where it is at and where it is supposed to lead us.[36]

If second wave feminism engaged in an enormous feat of remembering, in
which women's histories, achievements and the wrongs perpetrated against
them were recovered to collective memory and recorded for posterity, then
postfeminism might often seem to partake in the countervailing work of dis-
membering and forgetting.[37]

These three quotes offer different perspectives on 'where' feminism appears
immediately-there. The first outlines the *problem of access* to black British
feminist history that conditions the circuit trajectories of such knowledge,
and, as a consequence, influences which kinds of feminist voices dominate
debates within feminism's immediately-there. Without a specific organisation dedicated to collecting and transmitting black British feminist 'herstory,'
there is limited capacity for these much-needed voices and perspectives to
become part of the immediately-there because the materials are dispersed
and disorganised. *Despite being already-there*, the transmitted signal is not
concentrated and therefore lacks consistency.[38] Such a point is evidenced
by Terese Jonnson's work, as she outlines how the legacy of black British
feminism has had little impact on the framing of contemporary grassroots
feminist activism within mainstream left-leaning liberal media. The result
of this is that whiteness continues to define the political agendas of contemporary feminism's immediately-there.[39] Of course, there is no inevitable
correlation between the organisation of black British feminist history and the
shaping of news stories within papers such as *The Guardian*. Nevertheless,
the perspectives, feelings, images, agendas, voices and orientations of black
British feminist history have to be transmitted, and transmitted with velocity,
organisation, deliberation, emphasis and security, so that they can be known,
and *known widely*. That is why, as Burin and Ahaiwe Sowinski stress, the fact
that these histories do not have a specific home or organisational structure is
a pressing *political* problem, a problem that concurrently shapes which information circulates and becomes part of feminism's immediately-there.

The second quote invokes feminism as a general environmental presence
within contemporary culture, a presence that nevertheless remains 'impossible to pinpoint.' This suggests there is a reinvigoration of feminist political
viewpoints within the immediately-there, an indication of revival, ubiquity

and perceived relevance. The final quote outlines the complex processes of forgetting that characterise what the authors call the 'post-feminist mystique,'[40] which incorporate and distort the tenor of feminist political claims as anachronistic and irrelevant. Read together, these three observations help us understand the curious constellations of a feminism that appears immediately-there in the twenty-first century. It is a feminism still dominated by white feminist political claims and frames, underscored by the limited organisation and transmission of black British feminist perspectives; it is a revitalised feminism that could be said to appear everywhere; it also therefore remains a potentially decontextualised feminism, vulnerable to postfeminism's procedures of mnemonic mystification.

Feminism's immediately-there circulating in the twenty-first-century media cultures has recovered, it seems, from the death of feminism that was widely and fashionably proclaimed in media and academic discourses in the 1990s.[41] The 'post-feminist masquerade'[42] celebrated by popular 1990s TV programmes such as *Ally McBeal* and *Sex and the City*, and further championed in books such as *Bridget Jones's Diary*, has lost credence in the face of economic depression and austerity cuts.[43] It is hardly the case in 2015, as I write, that 'no one uses the word sexism anymore.'[44] In the past five years, several popular books have been published with the intention of 'reclaiming'[45] feminism and shattering the 'illusion'[46] that gender equality has been achieved, while a visible 'new swell' of grassroots activism is regularly reported. All these factors indicate that contemporary feminist activism has become newsworthy again in certain sections of the media, as much as it demonstrates an increase in the number of people engaged in feminist activism.[47] Yet feminism remains a contradictory and contentious ideological field, as evidenced by *The Guardian*'s decision in 2013 to give a platform to a feminist writer spouting transphobic hate speech, the Islamophobic feminist activism of FEMEN and the sexualised protests of Slutwalk, to name but a few areas.[48] There are, however, increased points of access to feminism's already-there in contemporary popular culture; there is not the outright dismissal, erasure, ridicule, backlash and silence that characterised preceding decades.

The changing landscape of what is immediately-there in contemporary media culture is not just the result of a (re)growing amenability to feminist ideas. Digital technologies have played a key role. Of course, saying that digital technologies have transformed the way we consume, or 'prosume,' media is as obvious in 2015 as it is banal. Yet it is an important point to emphasise when discussing the changing conditions of access to feminism's technically composed immediately-there. A crucial difference in the media cultures of the twenty-first century is that official media gatekeepers have not previously approved the majority of media objects that *visibly* and *widely* circulate.

The digital milieu creates conditions, Mark Hansen optimistically suggests, of 'possibility for self-expression, and hence for self-exteriorization, today's digital hypomnemata restore a positive dimension to our coevolution with technics.'[49] In a practical sense we have seen such claims in action with the proliferation of feminist blogs. Furthermore, the opinions of independent bloggers and Twitter users can at times be taken as seriously as the professional journalist or academic or established expert, particularly among communities of interest. Another crucial aspect of digital media, and one that will be explored in depth in the second half of this book, is that contemporary media objects are not only *news* objects that reflect historical incidents currently happening but also digitised or born-digital *archival* objects that emerge from a vast array of different historical times. These archival objects circulate and 'break,' and can be consumed alongside the latest news items in the same promiscuous manner (in bed, walking down the street, at a desk, on the train).[50] They operate inside the 'endless rhythm of things appearing and disappearing . . . the continuing-across of Things . . . [and] existential interweave'[51] of digitised temporal historicity.

The digital has then enabled greater *immediate* access to feminism's already-there via digitisation, as well as emergent proximities to archival materialities existing under the digital skin-screen. Encountering feminism in the digital immediately-there is to *potentially* find a diversity of feminist voices and positions that emerge from grassroots political activism of different historical eras.[52] Much has been made of the simultaneity and coexistence of historical times in the so-called decontextualised time-space compression of the digital immediately-there. Yet there has been little, if any, serious appraisal of the demands this places upon contemporary historical actors participating within widened articulations of generation. This book attempts to offer a response to this situation by arguing that it is necessary to find our way within the digital composition of the already-there: 'Just as territory only exists when it is crossed, memory exists only when it is recalled. *One must find one's orientation in and to the already-there of memory* just as one must find it in and to territory.'[53] Of course, it would be a mistake to herald the digital moment as a uniquely liberated one. This would be not only very naïve theoretically but also politically dangerous within networked 'societies of control,' where media encompasses 'everything from social media and data-mining to passive sensing and environmental microsensors . . . [a] shift from [a] past-directed recording platform to a data-driven anticipation of the future.'[54] Yet it remains a seemingly innocuous, but nonetheless significant, fact that technical recordings of marginal voices are widely available in the immediately-there, enabling more extensive access that would not have been possible prior to digitisation.[55] One need only think of the difference in numbers between the readers of a paper zine and a digital, networked blog, for example, to appreciate the differences *in scale* here. Yet again it is important to appreciate that *quantity* of transmitted signal is not the same as *quality* of signal. That is, the potential of widespread connectivity should not be confused with the actualisation of such connections, and the formation of transmissive circuits from which knowledge emerges. For example, a single blog visited by ten viewers, consumed amid a sea of other digital information, may not have the same impact as a self-published zine read by ten people, each of whom go on to make their own publications or organise events in their communities.[56] The affective impact of different media forms such as blogs and zines, although an immensely important subject to investigate, is, however, beyond the scope of this book. My concern is to further outline the contours of the immediately-there, and this will be done with a discussion of feminist waves.

The Waves

This book aims to understand *how* to access feminism's *already-there*, as well as what is politically and epistemically at stake in transmission processes. Generational narratives define feminism as a political philosophy, a social movement and a popular cultural form. Within these narratives, particular modes of thinking and action are performatively reproduced as specific to feminist generations, signposted through the metaphoric-mythography of 'feminist waves,' as well as temporal markers such as the '1970s' or '1980s.' Often cultural or political practices (such as campaigning to get the vote, consciousness-raising groups or zine making) become attached to particular generational cohorts, as a means to differentiate politicised articulations of feminism across time. As Clare Hemmings's[57] work has demonstrated, such typologies and hearsay become far more influential than close scrutiny of the incredibly diverse political texts and actions continuous with feminist activisms across historical time, space and generations.

Generational *narratives*, although cursory evidence of transmission *at play in the world*, risk containment and undermine expansive approaches; they prevent nuanced engagements with what is already-there. When feminist generations are performatively announced in an action that brings those categories into being, the chaos of life, action and historicity is rendered flat and unknowable. There is nothing of interest; 'we know' already what is already-there within the generational imaginary, what feminist generations 'are.' In this manner generational narratives *conceal* access to feminism's already-there: Their apparent conclusiveness prevents complex engagements with the materials, controversies and resources that compose feminist generations. Yet such narratives also *reveal* the generational composition of feminism's mnemo-technical reserves; as a transmissive circuit hardened through recitation, they offer a means to *access* feminism's already-there. It is a form of access that is, however, insufficient for the purposes of this book, which attempts to carve out conditions where feminism's already-there can be 'ceaselessly reactivated in order to be relayed with new givens and new unknowns.'[58] To do this we must resist the temptation to claim to move *beyond* feminist generations. Instead the imperative is to move *within* them.

How then do we access feminism's already-there? What tools are needed to understand how certain techniques act as gatekeepers, monitoring circuits of transmission and positioning the time-space map of feminist knowledge? How is it possible to avoid being 'boxed along spatiotemporally fixed generational lines'?[59] To consider this problem in more detail, let us consider briefly how the wave metaphor operates as the main conduit for the transmission of generational knowledge within feminism, and how it can wash over historical specificities and geographical particularities. Indeed, feminist waves are such a central part of feminism's immediately-there whose origins can be traced, significantly, from publications such as the *New York Times* and *Ms.*,[60] 'mass media' implicated in the 'delivery of memory . . . organized in mediated systems . . . that favour the broad over the narrow, the simple over the complex, the uniform over the differentiated, form over content . . . playing to mnemonic certainty.'[61] Such framings effectively come to organise collective relationships to history, time, generation and identity. To offer a generic example of the wave metaphor in action, let us briefly consider a 2013 news article reflecting on the resurgence of contemporary feminist activism:

> Welcome to the fourth wave of feminism. This movement follows the first-wave campaign for votes for women, which reached its height 100 years ago, the second wave women's liberation movement that blazed through the 1970s and 80s, and the third wave declared by Rebecca Walker, Alice Walker's daughter, and others, in the early 1990s.[62]

As Victoria Browne has pointed out, the narrative cited above corresponds to a linear unfolding of historical time that perpetuates the logic of succession and displacement. She writes:

> The dominant model of historical time within contemporary western historiography remains bound to notions of linear succession, teleological progress, and totality, and informs a hegemonic model of feminist history in the singular, presented as a progressive series of successive 'phases' or 'waves.' This hegemonic model severely curtails the ways in which diverse feminist histories can be mapped and understood, as it functions by blocking out or distorting trajectories which do not fit into the dominant frame.[63]

The wave metaphor is then bound by a particular temporal rhythm where time moves forward and generations are distinct from, and displace, each other. The tendency becomes particularly pronounced in the distinction between the so-called second and third waves, formed through a myopic narrative that has become part of the immediately-there: 'That shift from second to third wave took many important forms, but often felt broadly generational, with women defining their work as distinct from their mothers.'[64] Although it is important to not conflate wave with generation *per se*, waves are nonetheless stuck[65] to feminist generations and, at times, operate in synecdochical fashion, so much so that it becomes difficult to think feminist generations apart from waves. As Browne writes, 'like the phasic narratives . . . wave narratives unify "feminist history" into the collective singular, and classify feminist thought according to a developmental taxonomy, representing higher and higher levels of historical, moral, political, and aesthetic development.'[66] Waves act as both epistemological constraint and possibility within feminist theory, indicated by the names of feminist publishing series such as 'Breaking Feminist Waves' and 'Next Wave.'[67] They are established patterns that must be broken down or away from, or they enable the articulation of new departures. In either sense, it seems as if they must *always* be acknowledged (as I do here, without recourse to irony), *or* they are spoken of as if they are self-evident facts.

Reliance on self-evidence, however, impoverishes feminism's epistemic, conceptual and political imaginary, as Elizabeth Grosz writes:

> The less one consciously utilizes theoretical concepts, frameworks, and assumptions, the more one unconsciously relies on concepts nevertheless, but based on a philosophy of obviousness, of self-evidence, of the concepts supporting majoritarian interests and values. . . . The task of philosophy is to create concepts and, especially, to create new concepts, even if these concepts resonate with and recall other concepts, concepts inherited or given, but always made over again, always revived and created again *if the concept is to do the work of thought.*[68]

Deploying the wave metaphor, as we have seen above, does the work of thought so feminist activist and theoretical communities don't have to. And what does that work of thought do? Invoking the wave metaphor, and using it as support for knowledge claims, in fact makes it harder to access the diversity of resources within feminism's already-there. Despite theorists such as van der Tuin figuring the third wave as more open, more 'transgenerationally continuous, but not [more] reductively unifying'[69] than others, such a move still works to displace feminist generations, rather than activate them, and maintains classificatory operations that her project otherwise seeks to denounce.[70] Waves act as funnel and blockage, directing attention to certain places and times, while rendering certain forms of feminist activism conceptually unrecognisable within specific generational configurations. The waves, in other words, frame our knowledge of *what we think* is already-there, stabilise expectations and render static the categorisations used to make sense of feminist historical action that always exceeds any attempt to fix events in specific times and places.

Waves also define the origins and movement of feminist activism as a Western, and more specifically Anglo-American, phenomenon. This has serious implications for engendering any kind of feminist imaginary aiming to foster what M. Jacqui Alexander calls 'pedagogies of crossing,' points of contact where dialogue, discussion and learning *can* occur across differences of time and space.[71] Feminists from all over the world have criticised the colonising tendencies of Anglo-American temporalisations at length.[72] This means that feminist imaginaries, cultural practices and worlds that are vastly different from each other are pushed into the corner of the 'collective singular,'[73] rhythmically subjected to agendas, visibilities and historical trajectories that do not, necessarily, relate to them. Taking seriously the way temporalities act as framing devices that define what is visible and legitimate, and, crucially, enable access to the generational knowledge that is already-there, is part of what is at stake in conferring value on wave-based narratives that conceal other, more complex forms of generational transmission central to feminism as a philosophical, political and world-making project.

If waves are meta-narratives used to prop up feminist self-identity, would the organisation of feminist knowledge be undermined if their operability were refused? Is it possible to think of feminist generations apart from waves? My argument, of course, is yes. But it must be done by retaining emphasis on the generational composition of feminist worlds, foregrounding the *transmission* of feminist knowledge, practices and culture across different historical times and places, and being attentive to *how* this takes place. As I have already suggested, the aim of this work is not to *oppose* generation and transmission or even waves and transmission. Rather, waves are a symptom of the centrality of generational processes through which feminist knowledge is transmitted. To think of feminist generations dislocated from waves is to take seriously the *compositional* power of the already-there, feminism's diverse, differentiated, exteriorised inheritance, as underwriting conditions for feminist thought and action. It is to know that generational thought emerging from such exteriorised technical-memory must always be elaborated via transmissive practice, rather than accepted as mere fact. Feminism's already-there can never be self-evident—it *demands* to be thought, interpreted, activated. The formation of feminist generations cannot be taken for granted as if they were established fact; generational knowledge is always caught in the nexus of making and forgetting. It is a site of fragile contestation, tireless struggle and political transformation, and the question of *how* we access the knowledge *generated* by feminists across different historical times and spaces is one that is key, I shall argue, to pursuing a feminist politics attentive to processes of transmission.

Cultural Feminism

How then can generational orientations be used to elaborate a politics of transmission? What would it mean to understand feminist generations as composed of heterogeneous communities who have, in different ways, created *feminist culture* that different 'political generation[s]'[74] are responsible for transmitting? Is it possible to understand feminists as culture-producing historical actors who responded to feminism's already-there encountered in their own time—an already-there that often appears fragmentary amid the partial visibilities of the immediately-there, and sometimes not even discernible at all? These feminists who similarly expanded the resources of the already-there with their own actions, so that other generations of feminists may use them, differently? In the early twenty-first century, feminists are part of a community of interest that now spans centuries of activism and culture making. A breathtaking array of material has been created in connection to, and in the name of, feminism—a feminism that always changes when it is reinterpreted and redeployed according to context and political need. These heritages and traditions are internally diverse and different from each other— the culture of feminisms cannot be reduced to any one idea, expression or practice. This conception of feminist tradition emerges particularly from a 'relationship to time and history that has only recently become possible'; it is that which 'one can only experience *after one is both certain that they have history* (perhaps, only after one begins to feel the weight of such a history and at least some responsibility for its preservation).'[75]

If heritage value can then be ascribed to the cultural production of nations, places and communities, why cannot such a heritage correspond to particular ideas, interests and identities, like feminism? Heritage is, after all, not fixed in a material object or place. It is something actively created, as Laurajane Smith asserts: 'Heritage is a *process* or a performance, in which certain cultural and social meanings and values are identified, reaffirmed or rejected.'[76] To consider and discuss the heritage value of feminist culture is then to instigate a conversation about the cultural and social meanings we ascribe to the material and immaterial heritage that has been produced by feminists across varied temporal and spatial locations. It is a process of *identifying* value that is in no way guaranteed in advance, and remains open for contestation, reclamation and reappropriation. It is a process of *curation*, an orientation of care located in 'acts of gathering or bringing together'[77] materials, stories, practices, ideas and people.

An integral argument of this book is that in order to care better for cultural forms generated by feminists across historical time and space, it is vital to recognise the *heritage value* of feminist worlds. That is, rather than understanding feminist histories as being part of another story—a *history*— I argue here that feminist activisms have generated their own worlds, social relations, practices, representations and values—in short, their own cultures and *her*itage. These different cultures have produced certain kinds of feminist knowledges—feminist knowledges of how to live in the world, *techniques* to live feminist lives[78]—that cannot be subsumed into, or by, other forms of knowledge. Feminist traditions subtend dominant traditions but are not reducible to them. Crucially, the means of transmission also diverge, with feminist cultural heritage always filtered through inconsistent, precarious vectors, often making what is already-there truncated, disappeared and broken. With all this in mind, we need to consider how much of what is already-there it is possible to access. What would it mean to establish consistent, secured access with these diverse resources of feminism's already-there and use them as supports for the elaboration of feminist political, cultural and economic worlds? How is it possible to be oriented within these materials as more than 'just' archival evidence from a temporal zone that is always before or behind us (passed/the past)? Occasionally, materials from feminism's already-there generate astonishment because they present very different ideas to the received image of feminist culture, politics, history and theory.[79] 'It is precisely the unsettling consequences of reading a feminist text from the archive that gets us going for the feminist cause in all its *multiplicity*.'[80] What if contents composing feminism's already-there can be perceived as carriers of tradition and knowledge, whose transmission and re-elaboration has profound consequences for how feminist worlds are fashioned, understood, created and sustained in the long term? How can strategies be devised that create different orientations to the constitutive force of the already-there? These are questions that will be discussed in detail throughout the course of the book.

Clarifying the Double Meaning of Feminist Culture

While feminist cultures are distinct, they are not completely sealed off from, or unaffected by, other kinds of political ideas and social phenomena. Feminist cultures are always infused with various ideas from across the political

spectrum, from communism to imperialism, anarchism to fascism, liber-
tarianism to animal rights. In the discussion below, I use the term 'feminist
culture' in two ways. The first is fairly descriptive and straightforward: I use
it to refer to feminists who produced culture such as music, film, art, writing
and theatre to communicate and realise feminist ideas, values and philoso-
phies. These cultural experiments create time-limited, often ephemeral situations, where different relationships—social, aesthetic, political, sexual, and
so forth—are embodied and realised. Within my understanding of feminist
culture I also include discos, event nights, bookshops, parades, protest
camps[81] and skill-sharing workshops—any kind of social meeting where
feminists come together and attempt to create a different social, cultural
and political reality that challenges the exclusionary values of the dominant
(sexist, racist, transphobic, ableist, etc.) culture. These events facilitate the
expression of what Gail Lewis described, in relation to her participation in
the Black Women's Movement, as

> our *culture of being*, how we related to each other: were we just there really to
> always do organising and politics or should we also be doing something about
> providing a space in which we can kind of meet together with like-minded
> people in more recreational sociality, that was important because this was also
> part of consciousness raising in a way.[82]

In Amanda Sebesteyen's 1979 somewhat tongue-in-cheek chart 'Tendencies in the Women's Liberation Movement,' she describes a cultural feminist
as someone who understands that the 'revolution means *living as if* men
didn't exist (the future is Female, anyway).'[83] A cultural feminist revolution
will be achieved

> by putting all energies into women [building] an alternative society where
> women are not oppressed; housing networks, farms, businesses, busic [sic], art
> & therapy are all steps in the direction of women taking power. And the lesbian
> is the only woman who knows her full sexual potential.[84]

Of course, cultural feminism in the WLM was understood in a specific way,
and also needs to be differentiated from the *cultures of being* practiced within
the Black Women's Movement. I want to argue, however, that such world-
making activities, which attempt to create an alternative to the immediate
conditions of existence, premised within '*living as if*,' or even '*living as*,' are
present across feminist activist histories—although they are articulated differently according to locations, contexts, community needs and resources available to the actors involved in creating those cultures. These articulations of
other worlds become part of feminism's already-there, existing as 'potentiality

. . . [which] never completely disappears but, instead, lingers and serves as a conduit for knowing and feeling other people,' and other historical times.[85] The first point I want to make about *recognising* feminist culture, then, is that feminist activism has always provided *more than* critique, reaction and reform of the dominant hetero-patriarchal, capitalist system. It does not stop at equality and seek to adjust to the existing social and political imaginary. It is also characterised by invention, and the substantial elaboration of different worlds, worlds that are also, as a consequence, available and *already-there*.

The second way I use 'feminist culture,' then, refers to this more expansive understanding: how feminist activists create autonomous cultural forms that express and enact the *cultural values* of feminist worlds. Feminist cultures, feminist cultural heritages, are diverse and can often be ephemeral and temporary. Feminist cultures often strive to transform relational and social structures as much as they can generate intense feelings of inclusion and exclusion. The value of feminist cultures includes their suggestiveness, and how they encourage attention to the processes of social transformation rather than the end product, which can be mired in a sense of failure, exhaustion and hopelessness ('we' did not win, nothing has changed and in fact, it has worsened, *we have failed*). Feminist cultures are lived imaginaries, embodied collectivities woven by people that seethe desire, hope, anger and frustration. Their archive is predominantly one of 'feelings,'[86] as Ann Cvetkovich has argued, because the cultural worlds of feminism are patchily documented and often composed of intangible, rather than tangible, remains. In this sense they are akin to what Diana Taylor has called the 'repertoire,' which 'enacts embodied memory: performances, gestures, orality, movement, dance, singing—in short, all those acts usually thought of as ephemeral, nonreproducible knowledge.'[87] To access feminism's already-there we must therefore 'take seriously the repertoire of embodied practices as an important system of knowing and transmitting knowledge.'[88] A technical orientation attuned to the transmissive vectors of the repertoire, and the feelings embedded within feminism's already-there, is crucial if the heritage value of feminist worlds is to be recognised.

Of course, there is a risk in asserting that there is something called 'feminist culture' that I may be seen as making too general a statement about the diverse articulations of feminist politics in vastly different temporal and spatial locations. I am aware of this risk, but it is a necessary one to take it in order to widen conceptualisations of the political activities—the practical, creative, artistic, relational and economic imaginaries—that occur in the name of feminism. These practices not only talk about feminist ideas but also *use* them in order to reconfigure the world, to tinker with the world utilising feminist techniques. Such *application* can be both conscious and

unconscious, intentional or accidental, structured or unstructured, deliberate or after the fact. These degrees of motivation and realisation do matter,
but not as much as the resources available to activate feminism's already-
there through transmission, which demonstrate that other ways of thinking,
doing and being are possible, and, furthermore, they are not consigned to
some distancing categorisation often performed under the sign of 'the past/
passed.' This occurs on a practical level of being able to come into contact
with feminism's already-there (how visible, catalogued and financially accessible resources are), but also with being able to recognise the elaboration
of a different feminist world when we see it among the often fragmentary
remains of feminist cultural heritage.

My aim here, then, is to not collapse 'feminist culture' to any one thing.
I mobilise the term as an invitation to explore different feminist worlds according to the cultural materials they produce/d, invoke/d and imagine/d.
To say that 'feminist cultures' emerge and exist—no matter how temporary
they are because even the tiniest incision[89] can become part of feminism's
already-there—does not mean it is always *the same culture* across different
historical moments. Indeed, it is always different feminist cultures. Feminist
cultures cannot be understood by appeals to generality; they can only be
grappled with through engagement with (im)materials and suggestions of
worlds that can be glimpsed through exploring the unelaborated contours
of feminism's already-there. Working with feminist culture necessitates
proximity rather than abstraction. It is a slowed-down, interpretive *orientation within* feminism's already-there that does not know in advance the
encounters materials can yield, or the types of possibilities they foreclose
or enable. It meddles with temporalities and expectation, and it is capable
of exploding apparently stable categorisations. It is a risk, but also an adventure into the paradoxically unknown known, unregulated by the lure of
futurity because its resources are *already-there.*

Disavowal of Feminist Culture

To conclude this chapter, I finish with a specific example of how the failure
to recognise the culture heritage of feminism is entangled with normative
iterations of feminist generations predicated on the logic of succession and
displacement. In particular, I focus on assigning activist practices to particular cohorts and how this renders access to what is already-there difficult, if
not impossible. My concern here is US 'third-wave' feminism, particularly
those that arose vis-à-vis riot grrrl. As Julia Downes suggests, 'nostalgic and

romanticised interpretations of US riot grrrl undervalue the (sub)cultural resistance of girls and young women that span different locations and eras.'[90] As
a collection of activist practices, theorists have discursively produced 'third-
wave' feminism as *uniquely cultural*, and such a claim has been used in order
to distinguish between the so-called second and third waves of feminism. As
Mary Celeste Kearney wrote in 1997:

> The question is not so much 'Is the younger generation *feminist*?' as much as
> '*How* is the younger generation feminist?' Often highly critical of how 'second
> wave feminism' operated as a fundamentalist religion with prescriptions on
> how to behave, dress and think, young feminists such as riot grrrls are *infusing
> feminist politics with forms of confrontational cultural activism which rely less on
> exposing gender differences than deconstructing them.*[91]

Kearney's statement indicates the view, often repeated across critical literature about feminist generations, that prior to riot grrrl, feminist politics
were not infused with 'forms of confrontational cultural activism.' Yet such
claims are both conceptually and empirically false, and all the more surprising
within a US context given that the notion of 'women's culture' was developed
within the US WLM.[92]

Many women involved in the UK WLM created cultural forms and practices that expressed feminist ideas and elaborated feminist worlds. Women
were engaged in theatre, art, music, literature, film or printmaking and also
organised autonomous social spaces to hold political meetings and social
events. Some women's liberationists, such as the Northern Women's Liberation Rock Band (NWLRB), argued very explicitly that the root of women's
oppression lay in the patriarchal *culture* that surrounded them—the images,
narratives and representations that perpetuated unequal and exploitative
relationships between men and women. 'All music says something,' their
1974 manifesto declares. 'It is an expression of feelings, a powerful means
of communication, and contains a certain way of life, a certain order of
things.'[93] This kind of analysis—which was debated at conferences, among
groups, at discos, across kitchen tables and within periodicals—stated that it
was imperative for WLM activists to devise a cultural response to what was
deemed a cultural problem. This cultural revolution was realised in part by
the NWLRB's music-making and manifesto writing, as well as the actions
of many other women who produced feminist culture that carved out an
alternate social, political, cultural and economic reality. The political value of
creating a feminist culture was misrecognised within certain sections of the
WLM, perhaps in a fashion similar to what Kearney attributes as a *generational* difference between the 'fundamentalist' views of second-wave feminists

and the more progressive, culturally savvy riot grrrls. For example, Rosemary Schonfeld, member of lesbian feminist music duo Ova, explains that her decision to use music-making as a vehicle to express feminist ideas was not always approved of by fellow 'sisters' in the movement. In an interview I conducted with Schonfeld, she strongly emphasised that her feminist activism as a musician was always both cultural *and* political.

> The socialist feminists and left-leaning feminists dismissed us as cultural feminists and that used to annoy me because I felt it had a lot of relevance and it was a form of activism. We were not entertainment! We were challenging roles, singing about issues and empowering and all that kind of stuff. Most of the events had that kind of flavour. There was the women's monthly event and you'd get all sorts of different bands, duos, theatre groups performing. At the time we were just totally consumed by it, having political discussions about it all. Agit-prop, where the audiences wanted more than just entertainment.[94]

Music-making was thus not *merely* entertainment—it was, in fact, highly political for a woman to stand on stage with other women and play music.[95] It was also an activist statement when a woman played drums, plugged in an electric guitar, drove a tour van, carried amplifiers down the street and ran a PA system—WLM activists did all of these things. Through moving into a traditionally male preserve (whether that be music-making or manual trades) and exploring how these areas could be feminist—that is, not only *doing* activities but *also changing how they were done*—the archive of women's liberation culture offers extraordinarily rich alter-political realities that create, suggest and at times elaborate other worlds that were qualitatively different from the male-dominated world they wished to dismantle through their actions.

The Women's Liberation Music Project Group (WLMPG) further emphasised this point: 'We are involved in taking control over our own music, which means not only playing and singing, but also gaining knowledge about instruments, equipment, sound engineering and recording—usually a male domain, and having control over the distribution of our music, etc.'[96] To transform culture in the WLM was then to embody cultural practices that were always entangled with political, social and economic analyses that attempted to carve out a different, more feminist world where women were liberated from the constraints and expectations placed upon them by patriarchal values. And rarely, it has to be said, was that entertaining (as in escapist, perhaps, or fun), *even if* music was central to that vision. Whether it was defined as apolitical because it provided a distraction from the 'real business' of revolution, using culture politically in the WLM was unquestionably one of the many strategies women used to practice and realise feminist political ideas.

The WLM is not singular in the regard of feminist culture making. We might also reflect on the mass of cultural production generated by feminists at other historical moments. The UK suffrage movement, for example, generated a breathtaking array of culture, much of which was documented in Susan Croft and Irene Cockroft's 2010 exhibition, 'How the Vote Was Won: Art, Theatre and Women's Suffrage.'[97] On display there were board games, figurines, cards, classical anthems, images of theatrical processions, tea towels, scripts and costumes. The citation of a public exhibition here is very deliberate, as it draws attention to the sites where feminism's already-there can be accessed. Croft and Cockroft's exhibition was my first encounter with the cultural legacies of the suffrage movement, and the context of this encounter is as important as the content. The exhibition challenged me to revise the perceptions of suffrage activism that I had inherited from a range of sources that included popular culture, public history and academia. And as I have grazed through other suffrage histories that sometimes rise to the surface and become part of what is immediately-there through being featured in public lectures, archives, websites and exhibitions, I have learnt about tree planting, UK caravan tours, vegetarian tearooms, international lecture tours, newspapers and playful, gender-bending activist antics. These objects and images bring different worlds to life. They transmit the culture that emerged around suffrage activism. They are rarely, however, viewed as anything other than part of a wider narrative about women 'getting the vote,' despite how they elaborated a different social arrangement that rewrote the rules of what women could do and be, either as individuals or in relation to each other.

In these chapters I have begun a process of elaborating access to feminism's already-there. I have outlined what is immediately-there, and suggested the necessity to delve further and not assume that what is immediately-there is *all there is*. Through examining the generational narratives embodied by the wave metaphor, I have proposed that as a political project, generational thinking composes feminism's identities, but it does so within a restricted framework that is bound up with specific geopolitical and temporal locations. In lieu of such observations, I argue that it is important not to abandon generational thinking altogether, but that it is necessary for feminism as political project to reorient itself within generational knowledge, forged from the resources of what is already-there and apart from prescriptive narratives and temporalisations. As an alternative, I suggest a fruitful approach would be to consider the culture and world-making activities of feminists across generations, attending the material specificities circulating within the already-there. I argue that it is essential that we pay attention to how processes of transmission occur, and the implications this carries for knowledge politics, which I shall discuss in depth in the next chapter.

Notes

1. Jussi Parikka, *The Athrobscene* (Minneapolis: University of Minnesota Press, 2014).

2. Nicole Starosielski, *The Undersea Network* (Durham, NC: Duke University Press, 2015).

3. Browne, 'Backlash, Repetition, Untimeliness: The Temporal Dynamics of Feminist Politics'; Friedrich Nietzsche, 'On the Use and Disadvantages of History for Life,' *Untimely Meditations*, Daniel Breazeale, trans. (Cambridge: Cambridge University Press, 1997), 57–125.

4. Stiegler, *Technics and Time, 2*, 216.

5. See, for example, Jonathan Crary, *24/7* (London: Verso, 2013), and Manuel de-Landa, *A Thousand Years of Non-Linear History* (New York: Swerve Editions, 2000).

6. Andrew Hoskins, 'Media, Memory, Metaphor: Remembering and the Connective Turn,' *Parallax* 17:4 (2011): 19–31.

7. Transmission Control Protocol/Internet Protocol.

8. Stiegler, *Acting Out*, 75.

9. Stiegler, *Decadence of Industrial Democracies*, 5.

10. The category of the hyper-industrial should be understood in the context of Stiegler's desire to differentiate his understanding of society from postindustrial and postmodern theorisations. See Stiegler, *Symbolic Misery*, 46–47.

11. Stiegler, *Acting Out*, 53.

12. Theodor Adorno, *The Culture Industry: Selected Essays on Mass Culture* (London: Routledge, 2001).

13. Stiegler, *Symbolic Misery*, 13.

14. Stiegler, *Acting Out*, 68.

15. Stiegler, *Symbolic Misery*, 12.

16. Bernard Stiegler, *Taking Care of Youth and the Generations*, Stephen Barker, trans. (Stanford: Stanford University Press, 2010), 6.

17. Anna Reading also encourages a focus on the poisonous aspects of digital culture. Anna Reading, 'Seeing Red: A Political Economy of Digital Memory,' *Media, Culture & Society* 36:6 (2014): 749. Of course, Stiegler's formulation of digital pharmacological politics is an adaptation of Derrida's reading of Plato in Jacques Derrida, *Dissemination*, Barbara Johnson, trans. (London: Continuum, 2004).

18. Stiegler, *Symbolic Misery*, 47, italics in original.

19. Stiegler, *Taking Care of Youth and the Generations*, 128.

20. Stiegler, *Taking Care of Youth and the Generations*, 13.

21. Peter Gratton, 'Review of *Taking Care of Youth and the Generations*,' *Notre Dame Philisophical Reviews*, 2010, accessed 11 December 2013, http://ndpr.nd.edu/news/24441-taking-care-of-youth-and-the-generations/.

22. Stiegler, *Taking Care of Youth and the Generations*, 13, italics in original.

23. Stiegler, *Acting Out*, 78.

24. Stiegler, *Technics and Time, 2*, 65–97 and 176–187.

25. See also Kristina Lebedeva, 'Review Article: Bernard Stiegler: *Technics and Time, 2,*' *Parrhesia* 7 (2009): 81–85, accessed 11 December 2013, http://www.par rhesiajournal.org/parrhesia07/parrhesia07_lebedeva.pdf.

26. Sophie Fuggle, 'Stiegler and Foucault: The Politics of Care and Self-Writing,' in Christina Howells and Gerald Moore, eds., *Stiegler and Technics* (Edinburgh: Edinburgh University Press, 2013), 200.

27. Browne, 'Backlash, Repetition, Untimeliness.'

28. Margaretta Jolly, *In Love and Struggle* (New York: Columbia University Press, 2008), 20, italics mine.

29. Rosalind Gill, 'Postfeminist Media Culture: Elements of a Sensibility,' *European Journal of Cultural Studies* 10 (2008): 147–66.

30. Joan W. Scott, *The Fantasy of Feminist History* (Durham, NC: Duke University Press, 2011), 57.

31. Stuart Hall and Alan O'Shea, 'Common Sense Neo-liberalism,' *Soundings* 55 (2013): 7, accessed 24 March 2015, https://www.lwbooks.co.uk/journals/soundings/pdfs/Manifesto_commonsense_neoliberalism.pdf.

32. Stiegler, *Technics and Time, 2,* 241.

33. Judy Wajcman, *Pressed for Time: The Acceleration of Life in Digital Capitalism* (Chicago: University of Chicago Press, 2015), 14.

34. Consider, for example, what Alison Winch calls the 'emerging "girlfriend culture" with its . . . emphasis on peer control' to be found on pro-anorexia and 'thinspiration' community websites. The formation of female homosocial circuits, premised within 'an intimate friendliness with a mutual body regulation that is configured as entrepreneurial and empowering,' indicates how the immediately-there can be used to secure relational circuits that, if not harmful in themselves, affirm harmful bodily practices. Alison Winch, *Girlfriends and Postfeminist Sisterhood* (Basingstoke: Palgrave, 2013), 2.

35. Yula Burin and Ego Ahaiwe Sowinski, 'Sister to Sister: Developing a Black Feminist Archival Consciousness,' *Feminist Review* 108 (2014): 118.

36. Van der Tuin, *Generational Feminism.*

37. Rebecca Munford and Melanie Waters, *The Post-Feminist Mystique: Feminism and Popular Culture* (London: IB Tauris, 2013), 29.

38. This is not to say, of course, that there are no collections that contain histories of black British feminist movements. The Black Cultural Archives, Feminist Archives and local archives all hold significant collections relating these histories. The extent to which they are 'joined up,' and extensively and consistently interpreted, is limited. This impacts on the capacity for widespread recognition, for such perspectives to become 'normative.'

39. Terese Jonsson, 'White Feminist Stories: Locating Race in Representations of Feminism in *The Guardian,*' *Feminist Media Studies* 14:6 (2014): 1012–1027.

40. A play on Betty Friedan's *The Feminine Mystique* (London: Penguin, 2010).

41. See Niamh Moore, 'Eco/Feminism and Rewriting the Ending of Feminism: From the Chipko Movement to Clayoquot Sound,' *Feminist Theory* 12:1 (2011): 3–21.

42. Angela McRobbie, *The Aftermath of Feminism: Gender, Culture and Social Change* (London: Sage, 2009), 66.

43. Yvonne Tasker and Diane Negra, eds., *Gendering the Recession: Media and Culture in an Age of Austerity* (Durham, NC: Duke University Press, 2014).

44. Rosalind Gill and Christina Scharff, 'Introduction,' in Rosalind Gill and Christina Scharff, *Postfeminism, Neoliberalism and Subjectivity* (Basingstoke: Palgrave, 2011), 1.

45. Kristin Aune and Catherine Redfearn, *Reclaiming the F-Word: The New Feminist Movement* (London: Zed Books, 2013).

46. Kat Banyard, *The Equality Illusion: The Truth About Men and Women Today* (London: Faber, 2011).

47. Kira Cochrane, 'The Fourth Wave of Feminism: Meet the Rebel Women,' *The Guardian*, 10 December 2013, accessed 13 December 2013, http://www.theguardian .com/world/2013/dec/10/fourth-wave-feminism-rebel-women.

48. 'Here Is Julie Burchill's Censored *Observer* Article,' *The Telegraph*, 14 January 2013, accessed 5 November 2013, http://blogs.telegraph.co.uk/news/toby young/100198116/; Theresa O'Keefe, 'My Body Is My Manifesto! SlutWalk, FEMEN and Femmenist Protest,' *Feminist Review* 107 (2014): 1–19.

49. Mark Hansen, 'Memory,' in W. J. T. Mitchell and Mark B. N. Hansen, eds., *Critical Terms for Media Studies* (Chicago: University of Chicago Press, 2010), 65.

50. See, for example, the Mechanical Curator, http://mechanicalcurator.tumblr .com/, 'Randomly selected small illustrations and ornamentations, posted on the hour. Rediscovered artwork from the pages of 17th, 18th and 19th Century books.' An interesting note on the website in relation to the discussion of digital technics in this book: 'The pictures are chosen at random, selected by a computer algorithm and *their selection is in no way meaningful,*' as if an artifact selected by an algorithm could ever be meaningful.

51. Brian Massumi, 'Painting: The Voice of the Grain,' in Bracha Ettinger, *The Matrixial Borderspace* (Minneapolis: University of Minnesota Press, 2006), 204.

52. Yet the technical question of *discovery* for feminism's digital already-there within an internet designed to extract financial value from data commodities, rather than act as a publishing platform for subversive political ideas, remains a pressing question, and one that is beyond the scope of this book. See Sheenah Pietrobruno, 'Between Narrative and Lists: Performing Digital Intangible Heritage Through Global Media,' *International Journal of Heritage Studies* 20:7–8 (2014): 748, for a discussion of how user-generated content such as tagging, viewing, rating and commenting can influence the visibility of listed items on YouTube. See also David M. Berry, *Critical Theory and the Digital* (London: Bloomsbury, 2014), and the discussion of 'algorithmic cages' (6).

53. Stiegler, *Technics and Time, 2*, 117.

54. See Rob Coley and Dean Lockwood, *Cloud Time: The Inception of the Future* (Winchester: Zer0 Books, 2012); Ippolita, *The Dark Side of Google* (Amsterdam: Institute of Network Cultures, 2013); and Gilles Deleuze, 'Postscript on Societies of Control,' *October* 59 (1992): 3–7; Mark B. N. Hansen, *Feed-Forward: On the Future of Twenty-First-Century Media* (Chicago: University of Chicago Press, 2015), 4.

55. See also David Grubbs, *Records Ruin the Landscape: John Cage, the Sixties, and Sound Recording* (Durham, NC: Duke University Press, 2014).

56. See Elke Zobl and Ricarda Drüeke, eds., *Feminist Media: Participatory Spaces, Networks and Cultural Citizenship* (Bielefield: Verlag, 2012).

57. Clare Hemmings, *Why Stories Matter.*

58. Isabelle Stengers and Vinciane Despret, *Women Who Make a Fuss: The Unfaithful Daughters of Virginia Woolf* (Minneapolis, MN: Univocal, 2014), 43.

59. Van der Tuin, *Generational Feminism.*

60. See Browne, *Feminism, Time and Non-Linear History*, 154, n. 35.

61. Barbie Zelizer, 'Cannibalizing Memory in the Global Flow of News,' in Motti Neiger, Oren Meyers and Eyal Zandberg, eds., *On Media Memory: Collective Memory in a New Media Age* (Basingstoke: Palgrave Macmillan, 2011), 28.

62. Cochrane, 'The Fourth Wave of Feminism.'

63. Victoria Browne, 'Feminist Historiography and the Reconceptualisation of Historical Time' (PhD diss., University of Liverpool, 2013), 7.

64. Cochrane, 'The Fourth Wave of Feminism.'

65. Sara Ahmed, *The Cultural Politics of Emotion* (Edinburgh: Edinburgh University Press, 2004), 91.

66. Browne, *Feminism, Time and Non-Linear History*, 14.

67. These series are run by Palgrave Macmillan and Duke University Press.

68. Elizabeth Grosz, 'The Practice of Feminist Theory,' *differences: A Journal of Feminist Cultural Studies* 21:1 (2010): 96.

69. Van der Tuin, *Generational Feminism.*

70. Van der Tuin, *Generational Feminism*; and Clare Hemmings, 'Generational Dilemmas: A Response to Iris van der Tuin's "Jumping Generations": On Second- and Third-Wave Feminist Epistemology,' *Australian Feminist Studies* 24:59 (2009): 33–37.

71. M. Jacqui Alexander, *Pedagogies of Crossing: Meditations on Feminism, Sexual Politics, Memory and the Sacred* (Durham, NC: Duke University Press, 2005).

72. See Aili Mari Tripp, 'The Evolution of Transnational Feminisms: Consensus, Conflict and New Dynamics,' in Myra Marx Ferree and Aili Mari Tripp, eds., *Global Feminism: Transnational Women's Activism, Organising and Human Rights* (New York: New York University Press, 2006), 51–79; Agnieszka Graff, 'A Different Chronology: Reflections on Feminism in Contemporary Poland,' in Stacey Gillis, Gillian Howie and Rebecca Munford, eds., *Third Wave Feminism: A Critical Exploration* (Basingstoke: Palgrave, 2007), 142–55; Kanika Batra, 'The Home, the Veil and the World: Reading Ismat Chughtai towards a "Progressive" History of the Indian Women's Movement,' *Feminist Review* 95 (2010): 27–44; Pat Caughie, 'Theorizing the "First Wave" Globally,' *Feminist Review* 95 (2010): 5–9; Chandra Talpade Mohanty, 'Under Western Eyes: Feminist Scholarship and Colonial Discourses,' *Boundary 2* 12:3 (1986): 333–58.

73. Browne, *Feminism, Time and Non-Linear History*, 14.

74. Margaretta Jolly, 'Assessing the Impact of Women's Movements: Sisterhood and After,' *Women's Studies International Forum* 35 (2012): 151.

75. Eichorn, *The Archival Turn in Feminism*, 54, italics mine.

76. Laurajane Smith, 'The "Doing" of Heritage: Heritage as Performance,' in Anthony Jackson and Jenny Kidd, eds., *Performing Heritage: Research, Practice and Innovation in Museum Theatre and Live Interpretation* (Manchester: Manchester University Press, 2011), 69–81, 69.

77. Mike Rowlands and Beverly Butler, 'Conflict and Heritage Care,' *Anthropology Today* 23:1 (2007): 2.

78. As I write this, Sara Ahmed is finishing her book, *Living a Feminist Life*, which will no doubt have more interesting things to say on this subject. You can, of course, read her blog, http://feministkilljoys.com/about/, to get an impression of what the book may contain.

79. For example, following a recent screening of the film *Nightcleaners* (1972–1975) by Berwick Street Collective at Birkbeck University in London (29 November 2013), the panel reflected on how the film provided counterevidence to the narratives that claimed the WLM never engaged in class politics (even though the film also revealed the power dynamics between WLM organisers and the Nightcleaners). The rendering of class politics in the film was described by one presenter as painful because of how clearly it betrayed the middle-class bias of the movement. The presence of class politics in the film created feelings of incomprehensibility that were suggested, but not pursued. At workshops I have run about the Feminist Archive South, my colleagues have been shocked at how certain publications deeply engaged with the politics of race, class and anti-imperialism. Such moments present an aporia within feminism because they fundamentally question the terms of knowledge production on which feminism is built. However, the system itself is rarely transformed through an interrogation of discrepancy between evidence and secured narrative. See http://www.lux.org.uk/collection/works/nightcleaners-part-1.

80. Van der Tuin, *Generational Feminism*.

81. Sasha Roseneil, *Common Women, Uncommon Practices: The Queer Feminisms of Greenham* (London: Continuum, 2000).

82. Gail Lewis, interviewed by Rachel Cohen as part of *Sisterhood and After*, 2011. Transcribed by the author from the audio file, accessed 24 March 2015, http://cadensa.bl.uk/uhtbin/cgisirsi/?ps=dftkoGSvHL/WORKS-FILE/97220073/9.

83. Amanda Sebesteyen, 'Tendencies in the Women's Movement,' *Ms Understood: The Development of the Movement*, Exhibition Newspaper, 2012, London Metropolitan University: 45.

84. Sebesteyen, 'Tendencies,' 45.

85. Muñoz, *Cruising Utopia*, 113.

86. Cvetkovich, *Archives of Feelings*.

87. Diana Taylor, *The Archive and the Repertoire: Performing Cultural Memory in the Americas* (Durham, NC: Duke University Press, 2003), 20.

88. Taylor, *The Archive and the Repertoire*, 26.

89. Michel Foucault, *The Archaeology of Knowledge* (London: Routledge, 2002), 28.

90. Julia Downes, 'DIY Subcultural Resistance in the UK' (PhD diss., University of Leeds, 2010), 61.

91. Mary Celeste Kearney, 'Riot Grrrl—Feminism—Lesbian Culture,' Sheila Whiteley, ed., *Sexing the Groove: Popular Music and Gender* (London: Routledge, 1997), 224.

92. See, for example, Gayle Kimball, *Women's Culture: The Women's Renaissance of the Seventies* (Lanham: Scarecrow Press, 1981); Gayle Kimball, ed., *Women's Culture in a New Era: A Feminist Revolution* (Lanham: Scarecrow Press, 2005).

93. Northern Women's Liberation Rock Band, *Manifesto: Why Are There Hardly Any Women Rock Bands?* (1974), accessed 27 November 2013, http://womenslibera tionmusicarchive.files.wordpress.com/2010/10/northern-womens-liberation-rock -band-manifesto-and-lyrics-booklet.pdf.

94. Rosemary Schonfeld, interview with author, 18 December 2010.

95. Sadly, it still remains a political statement today.

96. Tierl Thompson, Andrea Webb and Janie Fairchild, 'Introduction,' *Sisters in Song: Collection of New Songs from the Women's Liberation Movement* (Only Women Press, 1978), 4.

97. 'How the Vote Was Won,' accessed 24 March 2015, http://www.thesuffrag ettes.org/.

2

Feminist Knowledge Formation
and the Already-There

THE PREVIOUS CHAPTER ELABORATED how the already-there, composed of exteriorised technical forms, *supports* the work of thought. Ideas arise from encounters with the im/material of the already-there—texts, moving and still images, sounds and other mnemo-technical forms embedded within its contours, gestures and depths. 'This initial situation of inheritance,'[1] within which the '*I* and the *we* are bound in individuation by the *pre-individual milieu*,'[2] is where human lives *as* technical lives are 'prosthetically supported and synthesized.'[3] The already-there is compositional rather than determinant, acting as the precondition for thought, feeling and orientation in and of the world. Emergent realities can always be woven from what is already-there—it does not simplistically duplicate sameness *ad infinitum*; it is composed by differences. It can, of course, regulate what is known as 'reality' in the decontextualised milieu of the immediately-there, and through transmission processes that promote 'mechanical re-comprehension' rather than 're-activation, the resumption or recovering of original opening.'[4] The already-there is *resourceful material*, more or less pliable, the stuff out of which worlds are (re)made and emerge.

Within such an arrangement there is already a strong relationship between what is already-there, what can be known, and perhaps most importantly, *how* it can be known. Exploring the relationships between knowledge and the already-there within feminist knowledge politics is the focus of this chapter. My aim is to draw out how access to the already-there is regulated by historical configurations of technical systems that produce temporal conditions of access to historical information, which, in turn, produces formations of historical knowledge. In other words, we are going to explore how historical temporalities *change* in accordance with technical forms used to *access* historical information or, to repeat the quote used earlier, to examine how 'transmission is determined by the explicitly technological forms recording forms of knowledge, by the conditions of *access* they provide.'[5] Technical conditions of access, which are also temporal conditions, are not insignificant to the transmission of information: They delimit the form of the knowledge encounter, quite literally, the time taken for the encounter to occur. Consider, for example, the difference between reading the same words in a handwritten letter, an ebook or a printed book anthology—the form transforms the content, how it can be read and what kind of historical knowledge it produces. Over the course of this chapter, we shall explore this issue in relation to feminist knowledge politics. In so doing we will try to understand how access to the already-there—so often *unmarked* as a constitutive force of knowledge-making—operates, emphasising the importance of understanding these *conditions of operation* for the emergence of (feminist) knowledge.

Debates about formations of feminist knowledge often focus on the content of discussions rather than the forms through which knowledge claims are transmitted. A thorough consideration of the technical composition of feminism's already-there is however crucial because feminism as a political, activist and epistemological project is self-referentially defined by generational thinking as such. That is, feminism is derived from the available form *and* content that composes the variegated fabrics of the already-there; it is reliant on technical supports for transmission and therefore meaning, intelligibility and effectiveness within the worlds it is seeking to intervene and/or create. As we have demonstrated in the previous chapters, such imagining of generation within feminism is subject to normatively linear and successive temporalities, which regulate the extent to which feminist knowledge *can be* transmitted across generations. It assumed that knowledge only moves through time in a unilateral direction: from 'the past' to 'the present' for 'the future.' We have to ask, then: What happens if generational transmissions are not understood within such rigid temporal frameworks? What happens to feminist knowledge when we explore the question of transmission as a technically composed political process that facilitates the emergence of temporal knowledge, which invites us to reconceptualise the political terms of feminist generations? It is this temporal issue I explore below because normative iterations of generation are neither natural nor inevitable. They arise from the techniques of organisation that condition access to feminism's already-there.

The Emergence of Academic Feminist Knowledge

An 'episteme' has come to index a scale, longevity, and hardening of thought formations that can set us astray.[6]

What happens when our knowledge systems lead us 'astray'? When what is *un-thought* becomes hardened 'thought formations' that appear self-evident, functioning as unspoken truths that everyone plays along with *without thinking*? And what happens when such sedimentations of thought are called into question for some reason or another, and knowledge emerges that strays from 'ways of knowing that are available and "easy to think,"'[7] and instead seeks to understand how knowledge *operates* and how it is produced? This is what occurs when we explore *access* to the already-there as an epistemological problem or, rather, when we decide that *how* we access the already-there *is* an epistemological problem. Feminism's evolution to the status of 'episteme' has occurred relatively recently. Juliet Mitchell's 1969 course, 'The Role of Women in Society,' in the student-led 'Anti-University' was deemed to be the first women's studies class in the UK.[8] Elizabeth Bird describes how women's studies classes burgeoned between 1972 and 1975 in 'extramural departments [which] in the 1960s existed in all the major civic universities throughout the United Kingdom, and, along with the Workers' Educational Association (WEA) and local authority community centres, they were to be crucial places for the first women's studies courses.'[9] Due to the extramural departments being 'outside the walls' of the traditional academy, it enabled greater participation from women, as both students and teachers.

Women's studies emerged as the 'academic arm of the women's movement.' Like other radical left, black and anti-imperialist activist groups of the 1960s and 1970s, education was deemed central to activist praxis. Gail Lewis, for example, reflects on her experience in the Black Women's Movement in the late 1970s and through the 1980s:

> Activism and writing and learning through writing and the different kinds of pedagogical strategy that alternative writings could produce, both in the fictional form and poetry, and the essay form and . . . research form were actually linked together. It wasn't an idea of somehow scholarly activity was devoid and separated from activist campaigning. . . . Writing was part of activism and campaigning was another part of activism and, you know, Audre [Lorde]'s stuff about poetry not being a luxury kind of captures that in a sentence really.[10]

Within the WLM, women's studies developed through 'learning from experience' that occurred within consciousness-raising groups. This conferred what we might call now, but certainly was not then, 'epistemic value' on the life-knowledge of women who actively created critical vocabularies to describe and analyse the political experience of women's liberation. As Pat VT West reflected in an oral history interview conducted in 2000, this language had to very much be invented anew:

> We decided after a few meetings [of the Bristol WLM], when we found it increasingly difficult to speak [that we would produce a magazine called *Enough*]. It's hard to remember now, but [feminism] wasn't talked about and it was hard to find the language. We didn't know how to voice the things we were feeling.[11]

The type of knowledge created in consciousness-raising groups is, of course, very different from conventional 'academic' knowledge built on peer-reviewed, 'citational' knowledge. As women's studies evolved into a set of distinct practices, the pressure to formalise its epistemic and pedagogical values in accordance with norms of the academy became stronger. Liz Bird describes how

> there were decisions about reading lists. What could be included, did it have to be 'academic' and what did that mean? Then there was the thorny problem of experiential learning: *what counted as knowledge*, how was an academic course different from a CR group? How did you run a group democratically—did everyone have equal space to talk?[12]

Anxieties about *how* to differentiate feminist knowledge, and what processes would be used to create that knowledge, characterised women's studies at its inception. As more courses were accredited in the 1980s, the emphasis shifted to make women's studies a 'legitimate field of study within higher education and giving it a voice, making it I suppose "respectable."'[13] Part of that respectability emerged by formalising assessment through written exams or coursework, a far cry from meandering journeys of thoughts, feelings and experience that was a key part of earlier feminist understandings of *collective* learning. Making feminist knowledge 'academic' undoubtedly transformed the status, aspirations and processes of feminist knowledge, and its modes of 'production.' 'To me it was all crushed up with . . . that awful word "critical" . . . taking what they already knew and just looking at it in a different way.'[14] Early women's liberation texts by writers such as Mary Daly and Kate Millett were weeded out for their partiality and lack of critical sophistication, completing a cycle whereby 'academic feminism . . . graduated from its lowly seventies' birthplace in adult education into professional status in the universities—promoting conceptual uncertainty, political indeterminacy and subjective fluidity.'[15] Within such a context black British feminist texts, perceived as too closely aligned to 'experiential' activist knowledge to become a staple part of women's studies reading lists, were denied credibility and respect. Gail Lewis explains:

> It was an important volume and what's interesting about *Charting the Journey* is, it's so little known in this country [UK], and yet in the States it was taken up much more, much more. . . . But I think that's absolute testimony to the ways in which, the limits to which black women's work could be seen coming out of Britain, was seen as central to feminist politics in this country by feminists, by white feminists and when they went into the Academy and formed all of this women's studies network, which of course is under siege and now very in demise in terms of independent departments or units within universities, when they went in there they looked to the US for their women of colour scholarship and not to Britain and they've not picked it up and I feel very resentful about it actually. Not so much on a personal level, but for it being a sign of the way in which the limits to which the Movement here could really take us on as part of the Movement, I think was shown in what happened in the Academy in this country. Because the fact that we're much more known, I mean all of us in all of our work, in the States, as a body of thought. *You got called out as voices and living examples of activism, you weren't called out as voices of and living examples of scholarship and theoretical development.* We just weren't given that kind of recognition and I think that's an example of it really.[16]

Lewis describes the uneven transmission processes that excluded key black British feminist texts from the formation of the feminist episteme at the historical moment when feminist knowledge emerged as an institutionalised mode of knowledge. The legacy of this exclusion—informed by white supremacist and colonial inheritances perpetuated within feminism—has created assumptions about what counts as legitimate knowledge, and legitimate knowledge *bearers*, which, in turn, impacts on perspectives foregrounded within feminism's already-there. While such marginalisation of black British feminist thought is certainly more than regrettable, it is important to remember that the epistemic conditions of feminism's already-there are not fixed determinably; they can change through practices of transmission that are, necessarily, *active processes of artificial selection from the already-there.*

Hardening the Episteme

The story of women's studies entering the academy is often simplistically framed as a tussle between activist and academic values in which the academic values won (and sold out the activists in the process). Yet the blaming and shaming of academic women is unfair. According to Bird, many of the

women involved in establishing women's studies in the academy felt they
were engaged in *acts of bravery*.[17] Their hard work went unrecognised by sus-
picious students and ambivalent colleagues, whose perceptions of women's
studies ranged from tolerance at best to ridicule at worst. 'I sometimes think
there isn't even the imagination to even imagine what women alone can be
getting up to, it's a bit like Queen Victoria and lesbianism, I mean you know,
what could a women's studies group be doing but making jam you know, so
long as they are happy and not bothering us, that's ok.'[18]

Accrediting feminist knowledge in the academy reveals how rules, prestige
and cultures establish standards of legitimation that tacitly recommend engagement with selected parts of feminism's already-there. These procedures
are not 'innocent' (even if no one person in particular is to blame for their
formation, although we might point out collective complicity with such operations), but are deeply conditioned by institutional structures of racism,
sexism and classism. This means that feminist knowledge *production* is still
waged 'against the odds,' and faces 'enormous obstacles,'[19] largely because
the wider academic culture sees no *economic* value in it. Yet the establish-
ment of women's studies, and the later integration of 'gendered perspectives'
into 'mainstream' disciplines like history, English literature or philosophy
within the rules designated by the academy, seems like a Pyrrhic victory
when the status of feminist knowledge, and feminist scholars, are taken into
account. Feminism continues to be perceived as 'not proper knowledge,'[20]
rather than simply *a different kind of knowledge* capable of elaborating different values and relations, as well as different epistemic and pedagogical practices. Where now is the type of feminist knowledge that flourished 'outside
the walls' of the academy, just as Plato and Socrates left 'the walls of Athens,
the proper place of *logos*, learning and the "Academy"' in order to 'take time
to waste time with each other, with enchantment and the light-play of air
and shadow'?[21] Can such an outside be accessed again, activated from within
feminism's already-there?

Following academic protocol meant feminist knowledge practices perceived to be less 'sophisticated' had to be consigned to an outside, a space
where the mad, bad, sad and brilliant ideas that emerged from social
movement struggles could not contaminate the serious, well-mannered
discipline of emerging feminist thought. Fitting in became more important
than 'rocking the boat,' while professionally it was imperative to 'challenge
without being seen as "difficult," "eccentric," "political" or "off the wall."'[22]
Within feminist knowledge politics lines were drawn in the sand between
acceptable and non-acceptable ideas. For feminist theory to be taken seriously, it was vital to protect itself from any critical position that appeared
naïve or could expose knowledge claims to ridicule. Enter the lofty battle

over 'woman' as figure, ground, concept, collectivity, identity or imaginary. 'Essentialism,' of course, was probably the worst intellectual crime one could commit within feminist theory during the 1980s onwards, and debates over whether an idea promoted anti-essentialist (read: sophisticated) or essentialist (read: retrograde) positions became the apex of feminist epistemology in this time, and its influence continues into the second decade of the twenty-first century.[23] The proliferation of such discourse often favoured anti-essentialism, and, as van der Tuin and Hoel argue, 'the notion of "essence"' itself became 'tainted.'[24]

Increased attention has been paid to affect, feelings and emotion within critical theory since the late 1990s. Yet, as Maud Perrier argues, the 'affective turn' is often criticised by feminists because of the fear it may result in the potential depoliticisation of feminist theory if critical thinking is (re)aligned with feelings and emotion.[25] The anxiety provoked by the anti-essentialism/ essentialism debates and concerns regarding feelings and affect are telling because they indicate feminist fears of being trapped by knowledges that emerge too directly from the body. The desire to assert that biology is not destiny, and that women's thoughts are not defined by her womanhood, can explain why essentialism generated so much dread, disparagement and loathing. It is not surprising therefore that feminists would treat affect theory with caution, because lending credence to emotions and invisible forces can only ever cloud the judgement of a hard-fought-for, detached and rational analysis. Feminism can ill afford to be seen pandering to the whims of feelings, particularly given the historical spectre of consciousness-raising that threatens to ruin the legitimacy of feminism as an intellectual project within the academy.

Taking Care of Abstractions

> Our duty is to take care of our abstractions, never to bow down in front of what they are doing to us—especially when they demand that we heroically accept the sacrifices they entail, the insuperable dilemmas and contradictions in which they trap us.[26]

As Isabelle Stengers suggests above, abstractions can be dangerous. Rarely is there time and space to consider 'what they are doing to us.' Abstractions can function as a trap, ensnaring knowledge and encouraging 'sacrifices' because of their ease of persuasion. Stengers suggests that the need to 'take care of abstractions' is a duty, as much ethical as it is intellectual. She underscores: Abstractions are *powerful*. We have to *notice* them and interrogate *how* they allow certain forms of access to knowledge, and by extension in this study, feminism's already-there. The most considered meditation on the problem of abstraction in feminist thought can be found in the work of Clare Hemmings, particularly her 2005 essay, 'Telling Feminist Stories,' and later her book, *Why Stories Matter: The Political Grammar of Feminist Theory* (2011). Hemmings's text is an exemplary investigation of how feminist knowledge communities emerge from the contours of a particular already-there, in this case the collectively iterated practices that occur within academic feminist journals. Through stripping texts of their individual authors and focusing on recurring tropes and common narrative 'glosses,'[27] Hemmings charts the trajectories of feminist knowledge production. The stories that emerge through her analysis operate as a series of narrative techniques that re-produce rigid temporalisations of feminist history and feminist theory. These align certain forms of knowledge within the parameters of particular decades—1970s, 1980s and 1990s. According to trajectories in these narratives, 'essentialist' feminist thought, often aligned with the 'primitive,' underdeveloped theory born of social movements, is an example of work produced in the 1970s. Black and lesbian feminist thought emerged in the 1980s, introducing difference into feminist debates, and the 1990s belongs to the sophisticated or depoliticised (depending on how you see things) activities of the post-structuralist, often queer, theorists. The abstractions feminist theoretical communities bow down before in this example are historically inflected epistemological statements. They suggest that people thought or did something at a certain point in time *historically unique* to, and could have *only* happened in, the 1970s/1980s/1990s, thus shaping the ways people can access feminism's already-there. These stories act out grand narratives of feminist self-identities, comparable in function to the wave metaphor because of how they strictly distinguish thought into temporal zones that do not overlap or converge. Hemmings's stories matter inasmuch as they regulate our access to feminism's already-there. They operate according to implicit consensus, as Hemmings shrewdly outlines:

> The shared terms and chronology underpinning these narratives allow for contests over feminist value to be resolved without having to revisit what we think happened in Western feminist theory in the recent past: we require only to value those shifts differently, not to abandon them altogether.[28]

A key point made here is that the collectively practiced stories announce knowledge as *already produced*, hardened by 'the shared terms and chronology underpinning these narratives.' This is partly the result of the temporal form of narrative that produces specific orientations in time, mechanisms that make it epistemologically possible for knowledge participants *to not have to* 'revisit what we think happened.' It is important to acknowledge here that Hemmings is not talking about feminist history per se in her arguments; she is discussing the history of feminist theory. Her interrogation of theoretical ideas, however, reveals the very complex relationship between historical ideas and the production of knowledge. Her analysis enables the articulation of critical attention focused on the 'dependency on universalising abstractions and towards an attempt to historicise abstractions in thought.'[29] Hemmings's work usefully indicates *how* the 'episteme' of feminist theory emerges through spectacularly generalised figures of thought embodied by the narrative announcements of the '1970s,' '1980s' or '1990s.' These somewhat arbitrary, and let's face it, convenient, temporal bookends come to synecdochically express the types of ideas in existence across vastly different historical moments. The temporalising narratives are precisely the forms of abstractions Stengers warns it is our duty to take care of, despite the challenge refusing such abstractions presents for making meaningful descriptive—yet performative— acts within our critical conversations. Of course, temporality and history are not the same thing, even if they entangle to produce specific configurations of knowledge.[30] Indeed, Hemmings's work outlines these entanglements, demonstrating how temporal statements produce ideas *about* history, which, in turn, create ideas about knowledge. This is, in part, how it is possible that knowledge comes to be based on 'what we think happened.' Furthermore, because these stories accord with the 'relentless persuasiveness of the presumed' and 'appeal the common sense of the reader without detailed discussion,'[31] they ironically become *more powerful* than the (im)material compositions of feminism's already-there. Consulting—that is, *transmitting*—materials embedded in the already-there is not to uncover 'what actually happened' in history, as if there was an authentic historical truth to be gleaned. Such consultations can, however, help to potentially undo the trap of abstraction by nurturing an epistemic culture of proximity to the materials used to construct knowledge claims. Such an emphasis allows understanding of the processes of *how* we say, rather than a mere focus on *what* we say. It is a temporal orientation to the middle of knowing, its doing, technique and constant (re)invention, creation and negotiation, rather than settling for a ready-made encounter with what we already know.

Hemmings's work offers tools to begin thinking through these very important processes within feminist knowledge politics. She demonstrates 'why and how'[32] narratives operate through common tropes, shared meaning and structures of feeling that regulate what is permissible within feminist theory. Crucially for our purposes, such narrative techniques direct those seeking feminist knowledge toward limited selections of the already-there, instilled with not-insignificant affective biases about what, and what not, to engage with. Hemmings argues that alternative strategies cannot simply be revisionist in approach, even though she acknowledges, in a manner profoundly congruent for this book, that epistemic strategies must make 'visible what is, importantly, already there.'

> For this approach not to be a mere prioritization of a different, but nevertheless singular, history, the attention needs to be placed on what happens when we fold what haunts these stories back into them, making visible what is, importantly, *already there*. To fold what is almost-but-not-quite forgotten back in is a process that inquires after obscured dimensions of the present, rather than one that seeks an alternative history to replace those that are dominant now.[33]

The problem with seeking out alternative histories for Hemmings, then, is that they can only ever produce singular versions of events. She retains far greater faith in the *stories* that haunt collective knowledge practices, and exploring other possible 'ways of thinking stories differently.'[34] Yet relying solely upon the techniques of stories and, by extension, narratives to communicate that there might just be something 'almost-but-not-quite-forgotten' within any normative story instates a singular technics of epistemic transmission. This move, I want to suggest, takes risks with the politics of memory that has not yet become a politics of transmission. It is to not think through how narrative is embroiled with temporality, *supported* through technical form as an expression of time, in such a way that can only ever locate our access to knowledge claims in a very singular way.

Epistemological Temporal Objects

In order to think through how theoretical narratives produce specific kinds of temporal knowledge, I now propose a modification of Stiegler's 'industrial temporal object.' My aim here is to draw our attention to how technical forms, such as a written, linear narrative, *formalise* certain temporal expectations of the reader, creating what I will call an *epistemological temporal object*. For Stiegler, the 'industrial temporal object' is exemplified by the unfolding of cinematic consciousness, which 'takes time, the time of the spectator's attention to its unfolding, a time invested in the promise of the experience offered and expected by the film.'[35] Watching a film at the cinema cannot be compared with reading an academic article. The understanding, however, of a technical object as something unfolding in a temporal manner is what I want to think through here, keeping in mind the 'promise,' 'expectations' and trust that are placed in academic journals as a form of *knowledge*. Within Western culture, it is customary to start reading something at the beginning and finish it at the end. Reading is a linear process that moves from start to finish, and when we finish a piece of writing, no matter how 'open' its closing remarks may be, or how invested we may be in the open play of signifiers and meaning, we attain the physical experience of the writing stopping when the text reaches the end. We close the book (or turn off the electronic reading device) and put it on the shelf. Within academic journal articles, or any kind of 'rational argument,' it is customary to offer a conclusion that neatly summarises the main points, perhaps making a tentative gesture towards a departure, so that the content neatly folds into the form.

Of course, academic articles are not necessarily read in a linear fashion. They may be reread compulsively, worked though slowly with pauses that last hours, days or even months before 'the end' is reached. Yet, as an epistemological temporal object, the journal article (and its sister technique, the book-length academic monograph) forecloses temporal possibilities because of how the form lays down the law of linear thinking. If the reader's thoughts scurry, become undone, collapse and reverse, it is despite, rather than because of, the conditions of knowledge the epistemological temporal object enables through its formal technical properties. The technical form of the article unfolds *more or less* logically from point A to point B, leaving the reader to *always move forward from*, or otherwise build upon, its insights. As such, the epistemological temporal object takes the time of the reader and produces the time of knowledge in quite a specific, positional-oriented manner, so that as readers *we always arrive after knowledge has been produced*. We are witness to the beginning, middle and end. We unfold in time with the presented ideas from the beginning to the end, from the past to the present to the future (yet to come). The orientations this produces are not incidental to the quality and tenor of knowledge created. Michelle Bastian has argued that normative conceptions of Western time (the linear unfolding of past, present and future) are deeply embodied. They are located within a certain positional logic that designates the past as behind, the present as now and the future as in front of us. As Bastian reflects, exposure to other cultural experiences of time that position bodies differently can be disorienting for those temporally regulated by the position/time of Western temporality.[36]

It follows, then, that when an epistemological temporal object unfolds in accordance with linear temporalities, the knowledge-experiencing subject is only ever granted a limited positional compass. That is, the 'when' of knowledge can only be accessed *after*, rather than during, or even as part of, its emergence. The epistemological temporal object therefore enacts a *specific kind of temporal knowledge* secured within the unfolding of linear time that performatively enacts the *experience* of pastness. This performative and everyday (re)enactment of pastness is embodied, and serves to create specific feelings that underscore normative relationships with what is already-there. Those feelings align with distance, a severing of relation, produced within 'the historical research process and in the historian's responses to "*pastness*," to the otherness of *historical distance*.'[37] Such an attitude produces a sense that something happen*ed* and is, unequivocally, *over*.

Finitude and Narrative Persistence

The deathly finitude of past-produced-historicity is similar in effect to Walter Benjamin's conception of the bourgeois novel within which 'the novelist . . . cannot hope to take the smallest step beyond that limit at which he invites the reader to a divinatory realization of the meaning of life by writing "Finis."'[38] Benjamin's essay 'The Storyteller' meditates on the changing conditions of cultural transmission within modernity. Within it he deeply mourns the disappearance of storytelling and its attendant temporalities. In contrast with the individualistic finitude enacted by the narrative techniques embedded in the novel, the stories of storytellers are kept alive so they can make 'peace with the power of death.'[39] He goes on to say that 'the listener's naïve relationship to the storyteller is controlled by his interest in retaining what he is told. The cardinal point for the unaffected listener is to assure himself of the possibility of reproducing the story.'[40] Benjamin's notion of storytelling contrasts sharply with the modes of storytelling Hemmings outlines as the basic epistemological foundations of Western feminist theory, which are more aligned in temporal effect with the 'finis' of the novel.

Yet it is the curious persistence of narrative's linear temporalities that I want to dwell on here, specifically how such temporalities have infected other techniques of expression, such as the critical essay. Why has the *techniqual form* of scholarly thought not been more experimental? Why has it not played with perspectives, structure, time and space—the very position of knowledge as a thing to be created, opened, moved around, mocked or destroyed? Why has it become largely static, monodimensional and standardised as a technique of knowledge *production*, despite the rapid innovation of other technologies and techniques of transmission? I am not in the position here to offer the detailed response these questions demand and deserve. My concern is to reflect upon Ann Laura Stoler's shrewd observation that '"epistemic habits" are steeped in history and historical practices,'[41] and that understanding how epistemological temporal objects *operate*, is to appreciate how knowledge-position-time are conjoined and configured within technical systems that transmit information in the process of becoming knowledge. Such processes, in turn, regulate conditions of access to the already-there.

What other techniques for transmission are available if we accept that historical thinking profoundly shapes the formation of knowledge *in general*? Stoler points to the power of 'archival events.' These are

> moments that disrupt (if only provisionally) a field of force, that challenge (if only slightly) what can be said and done, that question (if only quietly) 'epistemic warrant,' that realign the certainties of the probable more than they mark wholesale reversals of direction.[42]

The value of archival events resides in how they realign the field of knowledge, if not transform it altogether. Stoler suggests that archival events are provisional, slight and quiet, but can be used to hinder the pronouncement of *epistemic certainties* within the field of knowledge production. Archival events 'flash up,'[43] acting as evidence to contradict, contest and elicit doubt. They force people to think again, unlearn or revise what previously appeared probable or true. As an encounter they can reveal that knowledge is never *over completely*, but instead is an active process, created in proximity with polyvocal, contradictory and challenging voices embedded within heterogeneous archive material. Such encounters may not trigger *rewritings* of the historical record that would produce new stories to replace the old, but are an invitation and orientation to knowledge that moves 'along the archival grain.'[44] Archival events emit strategies that realign not just the end product of historical knowledge (because there never is one) but also the time of knowledge in the making. This is the realm of what Kate Eichorn calls 'archival time,'[45] when the archive *operates* as a 'historiographic *technology*'[46]—that is, a *technique* of knowledge opening—a tool to elaborate resources that are *already-there*. Such practical reworkings of knowledge/time are pursued 'not to follow a frictionless course but to enter a field of force and will to power, to attend to both the sound and sense therein and their rival and reciprocal energies.'[47]

To read along the archival grain is then a bumpy, *material* process that involves thinking with multiple others: those who produced the material (authors/publishers), depositors, archivists and other custodians charged with taking care of collections, as well as other readers or researchers whose eyes and hands have wandered over or across archival objects, tracing coarse and smooth surfaces in moments of interpretation. This process generates sensate awareness of knowledge emergence vis-à-vis the archive as messy, chaotic, invested, troubled, partial and significant, never representative or representable in a final form. The archive nurtures proximity, rather than distance, from the *acts* of knowledge created therein. We return to the objects, always, and objects 'speak' when they are operationalised. Not through obeying their authority, but as a means to care for the resources already-there and from which situated claims emerge.[48]

Generational Entanglements and the Challenge to Feminist Knowledge

I finish this chapter with some examples of materials encountered in feminist archives that stopped me in my tracks. Within an epistemological milieu where access to feminism's already-there is overdetermined, as we have seen, by powerful narrative techniques, these examples may seem like generational oddities or anachronisms. They are misplaced, rogue histories that 'stick out,' appearing like the bumpy surface of the archive's grain, incongruous in relation to currently available schema. How can archival techniques enable access to parts of feminism's already-there that lie buried in its deeper layers, and, crucially, put them into intensive rather than latent operation? Do I only insert these action/events as casual provocation, a titillating invitation to consider what is within feminism's already-there in a more thoughtful and careful way? What is to be done with the knowledge resources of feminism's already-there when they reveal epistemic certainties to be, in even the smallest bit, shaky?

How do we account for the male-to-female transsexual who played keyboards for the Northern Women's Liberation Rock Band from 1974 to 1976, when the WLM was supposed to be transphobic, only identified with biological females? Or what about Pat VT West and Jackie Thrupp's gender-bending antics at the 1972 national women's liberation conference in Acton, when they dressed in male drag in order to explore gender politics? How does such knowledge challenge the underlying conception of the 'second-wave feminism' as rigidly 'essentialist'? VT West explains that she and Thrupp

> were fed up with how women were looking so went as elegant men in drag. We drove up to Delamere Services and changed into drag in the women's changing rooms. We went in as women and came out as men. And drove into London. I looked particularly good. I did look very much like a man in drag. Jackie had a strange demeanour too. She could be very silly. I was more serious than her.
>
> *How were you received in drag? (interviewer)*
>
> We were turned away! We were told the conference was dealing with the issues of gender. *There were some real transgender people there. This whole issue was a burning issue at the conference.* They let us in in the end as someone knew who we were. We thought that was wonderful. We tried to bring out these issues. What does it mean to be a feminist anyway? Do you have to dress in dungarees, sensible shoes and not wear make up? We did loads of guerrilla warfare. *Questioning. The women's movement [was] all about gender.*[49]

Let us dwell within VT West's eloquent insistence that the discussion about gender was a 'burning issue' at the 1972 conference, rather than a peripheral one. Does her oral testimony, her voice, resound enough to profoundly challenge assumptions about what activities took place at national women's liberation conferences? VT West's relaying of events resonates with what we would probably call today 'queer politics.' Yet I do not want to suggest that contemporary queer politics were being practiced in the WLM, as this would elide the historical specificity of different historical times. My aim here is not to collapse distinct historical events in order to create an impression of illusory sameness. Part of the problem with normative conditions of access to the already-there is the assumption that generalisability is an acceptable principle of transmission. In a comparable spirit with Victoria Hesford's analysis of the US WLM in *Feeling Women's Liberation*, I wish to explore techniques to access historical events that attend to the contingency of their articulation, that effectively mess with and reorder expectations of historical time in order to *mobilise* the unruly forms of knowledge embedded within different moments of historical time.[50] This is a crucial shift in orientation—a technique—that resists perceiving historical events as inevitable or conclusive from the perspective of a now that can only look *backwards* toward the *past/passed*. Like Regis Mann, I want to create space for 'what could have been,'[51] and what will be, in historical relationalities, so that *temporal* access to feminism's already-there is widened and reconfigured.

A further, and related, consideration are transformations to the category of woman in the WLM. Is it possible to understand the desire to widen understandings of what or who a woman is, which were so often proclaimed in the publications and pamphlets of the WLM, as articulating a kind of trans-feminist politics—a politics that aims to challenge the idea that gender is inevitable because 'biology is *not* destiny.' Take, for example, the call for self-improvement proclaimed in *Shrew*, the collectively produced newspaper made by the Women's Liberation Workshop Group in London:

> I am becoming aware of my position as a woman, both in society and in my own personal relationships, but awareness and commiseration with other women are not enough. True sisterhood is not a mutual bargain to protect each other to the point of presenting growth. Solidarity must not become yet another enveloping blanket of security, but a framework for development.[52]

Political solidarity, understood here through the lens of sexual politics, is a transformative framework through which subjectivity is reconfigured across singular and collective identities. Of course, such a statement bears little resemblance to the practices and critical languages deployed by trans-feminist activists in the contemporary moment. I do, however, want to suggest that it is possible to detect in the WLM prefigurative political actions that aimed to transform gender by radically questioning and exploring what it meant to be a man or a woman. When the politics of the WLM are viewed this way, with a pinch of lateral historical generosity perhaps, it becomes a lot harder to make generic statements about the kinds of politics that were practiced within a so-called generation. There are always exceptions to any rule, and exceptions *undo* the rule. So where does that leave us, with such knowledge at our disposal? Do we carry on, repeating stories without thinking; what is at stake in how we transmit feminist knowledge?

This book poses the question: What does it mean to build an episteme on the assumption that what appears already-there—immediately-there—is *good enough* to act as self-evident ground from which theorisations are built? This chapter has stressed that *how* we access historical knowledge matters because of the way "'epistemic habits" are steeped in history and historical practices, ways of knowing that are available and "easy to think.""[53] Yet I hope that it is clear that what is already-there should not be easy to think at all. *Habitual* epistemic difficulty must instead be *elaborated* in order to explore the caverns, erasures, silences and multiple interpretations lodged within feminism's already-there. The question of a reactivation and reelaboration that can generate different forms of knowledge and orientation to feminism's already-there, rather than simply 'mechanical re-comprehension'[54] of the expected, received and normative, or what can be described as 'what we know already,' is precisely what is at stake in *processes* of transmission.

Notes

1. Stiegler, *Symbolic Misery*, 28.
2. Stiegler, *Symbolic Misery*, 51.
3. Stiegler, *Technics and Time, 2*, 243.
4. Stiegler, *Technics and Time, 2*, 240.
5. Stiegler, *Technics and Time, 2*, 210.
6. Ann Laura Stoler, *Along the Archival Grain: Epistemic Anxieties and Colonial Common Sense* (Princeton, NJ: Princeton University Press, 2010), 43.
7. Stoler, *Along the Archival Grain*, 39.
8. Anna Coote and Beatrix Campbell, *Sweet Freedom: The Struggle for Women's Liberation* (London: Pan, 1982), 17; Maggie Humm, ed. *Feminisms: A Reader* (Hemel Hempstead: Harvester Wheatsheaf, 1992), xvi.
9. Elizabeth Bird, 'Women's Studies and the Women's Movement in Britain,' *Women's History Review* 12:2 (2003): 265.
10. Lewis, interviewed by Rachel Cohen.
11. Pat VT West, Oral History with Viv Honeybourne, 2000, transcribed by the author. Feminist Archive South, DM2123/1/Archive Boxes 79. Italics mine.
12. Bird, 'Women's Studies and the Women's Movement in Britain,' 268.
13. Anonymous interview with Elizabeth Bird, 14 January 1999, Feminist Archive South, DM2123.

14. Anonymous interview with Liz Bird, 14 January 1999, 18.

15. Lynne Segal, 'Generations of Feminism,' 11.

16. Gail Lewis, 'Black Feminist Texts,' *Sisterhood and After*, 2013, accessed 25 March 2015, http://www.bl.uk/learning/histcitizen/sisterhood/view.html#id=143433 &id2=143140.

17. Bird, 'Women's Studies and the Women's Movement in Britain.'

18. Anonymous interview with Elizabeth Bird, 14 January 1999.

19. Gail Lewis, 'Against the Odds: Feminist Knowledge Production and Its Vicissitudes,' *European Journal of Women's Studies* 17:2 (2010): 99.

20. Maria do Mar Pereira, 'Feminist Theory Is Proper Knowledge, But . . . : The Status of Feminist Scholarship in the Academy,' *Feminist Theory* 13:3 (2012): 283–303.

21. Alex Wardrop, 'A Procrastination,' Alex Wardrop and Deborah Withers, eds., *The Para-Academic Handbook: A Toolkit for Making-Learning-Creating-Acting* (Bristol: HammerOn Press, 2015), 16.

22. do Mar Pereira, 'Feminist Theory Is Proper Knowledge,' 298.

23. See Toril Moi, *Sexual/Textual Politics* (London: Methuen, 1985); Naomi Schor and Elizabeth Weed, eds., *The Essential Difference* (Bloomington: Indiana University Press, 1994); Diana Fuss, *Essentially Speaking: Feminism, Nature and Difference* (London: Routledge, 1989); Gayatri Chakravorty Spivak, 'Feminism, Criticism and the Institution,' *Thesis Eleven* 10–11 (1984/1985): 175–187; Deborah M. Withers, 'What Is Your Essentialism Is My Immanent Flesh! The Ontological Politics of Feminist Epistemology,' *European Journal of Women's Studies* 17:3 (2010): 231–247; Lena Gunnarsson, 'A Defence of the Category "Women,"' *Feminist Theory* 12:1 (2011): 23–37.

24. Aud Sissel Hoel and Iris van der Tuin, 'The Ontological Force of Technicity: Reading Cassirer and Simondon Diffractively,' *Philosophy & Technology* (2012), accessed 25 March 2015, Philos. Technol. DOI: 10.1007/s13347-012-0092-5.

25. Maud Perrier, 'The Fear of Depoliticization in Feminist Critiques of the Affective Turn: The Necessity of the Unstable Psyche for Reframing Affect Debates' (paper presented at the 8th European Feminist Research Conference, Budapest, Hungary, 17–20 May 2012).

26. Isabelle Stengers, 'Experimenting with Refrains: Subjectivity and the Challenge of Escaping Modern Dualism,' *Subjectivity* 22 (2008): 50.

27. Hemmings, *Why Stories Matter*, 19.

28. Hemmings, *Why Stories Matter*, 133.

29. Hesford and Diedrich, 'Experience, Echo, Event,' 105.

30. Karen Barad, 'Quantum Entanglements and Hauntological Relations of Inheritance: Dis/continuities, SpaceTime Enfoldings, and Justice-to-Come,' *Derrida Today* 3:2 (2010): 240–268.

31. Hemmings, *Why Stories Matter*, 20.

32. Hemmings, *Why Stories Matter*, 17.

33. Hemmings, *Why Stories Matter*, 180–181.

34. Hemmings, *Why Stories Matter*, 22.

35. Patrick Crogan, 'Experience of the Industrial Temporal Object,' in Christina Howells and Gerald Moore, eds., *Stiegler and Technics* (Edinburgh: Edinburgh University Press, 2013), 102.

36. Michelle Bastian, 'Political Apologies and the Question of a "Shared Time" in the Australian Context,' *Theory, Culture & Society* 30:5 (2013): 116.

37. Emily Robinson, 'Touching the Void: Affective History and the Impossible,' *Rethinking History* 14:4 (2010): 505, italics mine.

38. Walter Benjamin, 'The Storyteller,' *Illuminations* (Glasgow: Fortuna, 1977), 100.

39. Benjamin, 'The Storyteller,' 97.

40. Benjamin, 'The Storyteller,' 97.

41. Stoler, *Along the Archival Grain.*

42. Stoler, *Along the Archival Grain*, 51.

43. Walter Benjamin, 'Theses on the Philosophy of History,' *Illuminations* (Glasgow: Fortuna, 1977), 257.

44. Stoler, *Along the Archival Grain.*

45. Kate Eichorn, 'Archiving the Movement: The Riot Grrrl Collection at the Fales Library and Special Collections,' in Liz Bly and Kelly Wooton, eds., *Make Your Own History: Documenting Feminist and Queer Activism in the 21st Century* (Los Angeles: Litwin Books, 2013), 25.

46. Eichorn, 'Archiving the Movement,' 30.

47. Stoler, *Along the Archival Grain*, 53.

48. Such points will be further elaborated later in the book, when we consider how such arguments transform orientations to knowledge within the digital environment.

49. VT West, Oral History with Viv Honeybourne.

50. Hesford, *Feeling Women's Liberation.*

51. Regis Mann, 'Theorizing "What Could Have Been": Black Feminism, Historical Memory, and the Politics of Reclamation,' *Women's Studies* 40:5 (2011): 575–599.

52. Women's Liberation Workshop Group, *Shrew* 4:1 (1972): 1.

53. Stoler, *Along the Archival Grain*, 39.

54. Stiegler, *Technics and Time, 2*, 40.

3

Generation and Conflict

I HAVE ARGUED SO FAR THAT feminism as a political, cultural and epistemic project is defined by generational thinking *as such*. Generational thinking, often narrated in terms of waves emblematising specific phases of feminist thought and action, are techniques that tacitly regulate collective orientations to feminism's already-there. Such normative iterations of generational logic are damaging because they limit access to the different resources within feminism's already-there. Due to the prevalence of such thinking, I argue it is essential that generational frameworks are not abandoned altogether within a feminist critical project deployed across varied contexts and locations. Instead I propose a shift of emphasis that pays attention to and understands the technical processes through which knowledge is transmitted across feminist generations.

Commonsense understanding of generational dynamics within feminism is often presented as follows:

> While it seems that generational accounts will always have a winner and a loser, it is worth remembering that generation *always produces a tension*. The young may inherit a feminist legacy (whether they want to or not), but they are also expected to learn from their elders, who may turn out to be right all along. Family dramas may be temporarily resolved, but they are also de facto bound to be replayed. The key here is that *generational accounts propose a dynamic*, and thus always hold the possibility of the 'return' of the cast-out family member.[1]

Here generations are fashioned as always already saturated by a particular tension—the dynamics of disavowal and rejection, framed as an irreconcilable family feud between old and young. Certainly, as we have seen earlier in this book, this is how generational thinking has been conceptualised, especially through differentiating the activism of so-called second- and third-wave feminism. Yet does generation always have to be understood in this way? What other resources are available to think of the 'dynamic' transmission of knowledge across feminism generations differently? Can alternative questions be posed, such as 'Have we made the crossing? In what shape have we reached the shore? In whose company? With what in hand?'[2] How can *the practice of generational transmission* be realised differently as a series of crossings, rather than simply reducing generations to a form of identity politics whose manifest effects are to contain, via a specific practice of categorisation, the vast multiplicities immanent to the actions embedded within all historical time?[3]

In order to respond to these questions, this chapter outlines how black feminist and women of colour thinking invokes the strength and presence of ancestors in order to create a mythographic historical-political consciousness. Such writing offers techniques for practicing feminist generation otherwise and, in so doing, elaborates alter-orientations to the already-there that can often remain hidden when the question of generation is prefigured by the expectation of inevitable conflict. I will then go on to discuss how the process of cultural transmission is understood within cultural anthropology and critical heritage studies, exploring how these theoretical and practical traditions can offer different tools for accessing feminism's already-there. I finish this chapter by seeking to understand the factors that shape the transmission of ephemeral cultural traditions such as feminism, whose transmissive trajectories are marked by short-circuits and traumatic vicinities. An appreciation of such dynamics is vital, I argue, for understanding how the transmission of feminism's already-there *operates*.

Bridges

Creating contexts where shared conversations can occur is central to reimagining generation and community within feminism as a cultural, political and epistemic imaginary, even when (especially when) those conversations are difficult. Bridge metaphors, as a means to bring the possibility of shared conversations into the world, were central to the theory produced by women of colour from the 1980s, particularly Gloria Anzaldúa, who coedited the 1981 collection of writings by radical women of colour, *This Bridge Called My Back*. Within *This Bridge*, bridges and bridging are deployed to explore the 'relationships *between women*'[4] whose cultural experiences and inheritances are different from each other, but who group together under the bridge-sign *Women of Colour*. M. Jacqui Alexander remembers that '*Bridge* was both anchor and promise in that I could begin to frame a lesbian feminist woman of colour consciousness and, at the same time, move my living in a way that could provide moorings for that consciousness. Neither anchor or promise could have been imaginable without the women in *Bridge*.'[5] Bridging, then, enabled Alexander to become moored within an emergent woman of colour consciousness. As a lived process, the book helped her take root in the world as part of a specific community enjoined through difference and cultural heterogeneity. Such lived applications are reflected in Anzaldúa's understanding of metaphor as something that can conjure images, feelings and sensations, world-making processes that are a 'simultaneously metaphorical and material practice.'[6] Metaphors are transformative for Anzaldúa because, as she argues, 'we preserve ourselves through metaphor; through metaphor we protect ourselves. . . . But we can also change ourselves through metaphor. And, most importantly, attempt to put, in words, the flow of some of our internal pictures, sounds, sensations, and feelings.'[7] Metaphors in Anzaldúa generate spatial orientations; they are the 'anchors' Alexander cherishes. Deployed with such intention, they link communities to what is already-there (that is, each other), but they are also reminders of 'la mierda between us, a mountain of caca that keeps us from "seeing" each other, being with each other.'[8]

Anzaldúa presents bridging as a difficult and disorienting process, because it 'enables individuals to connect to others so as to transform and shift the boundaries between self and other without effacing various histories, desires, and differences.'[9] Such forms of connection are necessary in the 'Earthquake country, these feminisms,'[10] in order to refuse the powerful fantasy of 'common ground,' and 'render perceptible the (linguistic) cracks existing in every argument while questioning the nature of oppression and its diverse manifestations.'[11] Let us follow Anzaldúa further into her elaboration of bridging:

> Bridges are thresholds to other realities, archetypal, primal symbols of shifting consciousness. They are passageways, conduits, and connectors that connote transitioning, crossing borders, and changing perspectives. Bridges span liminal (threshold) spaces between worlds. . . . *Transformations that occur in this in-between space*, an unstable, unpredictable, precarious, *always-in-transition space lacking clear boundaries*. . . . Though *this state links us to other ideas, people, and worlds, we feel threatened by these new connections and the change they engender.* I think of how feminist ideas and movements are attacked, called unnatural by the ruling powers, when in fact they are *ideas whose time has come*, ideas as relentless as the waves carving and later eroding stone arches. *Change is inevitable; no bridge lasts forever.*[12]

In this meditation, written as the preface for *This Bridge We Call Home: Radical Visions for Transformation* (2002), bridges are metaphorical techniques for thought that can facilitate shifts in consciousness. The bridge is the transitioning, transformative space that 'links us to other ideas, people, and worlds' and offers a way to think how feminist ideas and movements *can move* across generations, '*ideas whose time has come*, ideas as relentless.' The visualising, *bringing into the world* of the bridge, acts as a visionary portal, fusing ancestral knowledge with currents of immediate articulation, whirling, meandering and hurting. In this framing, the Anzaldúan bridge profoundly resists a futural logic—its operation and techniques of thought enable the realisation of ideas whose time *has come*. There is no plan *to build* the bridge that will be ready for ideas *to come*; the bridge *is for* those ideas that are ready, *now*. To write the bridge, think the bridge, be the bridge, take care of the bridge, destroy the bridge and so on, is to elaborate access to the already-there as an actively fashioned connection, made and remade amid inevitable change, vulnerability and loss that nonetheless foregrounds the centrality of transmission, what Alexander calls acts of 'crossing'—*pedagogies* of crossing, itself suggestive of the need to teach and learn such processes. *Using* the bridge is not easy—'unstable, unpredictable, precarious'—and the encounters made possible by its deployment are challenging and transformative because they can engender change, their watchword is *change*. 'Earthquake country, these feminisms.' Who goes there, who dares?

Have We Made the Crossing?

As we rethink the transmission of generational knowledge within feminism, and explore ways to escape truncated modes of exchange so often framed by disrespect, homogenisation, containment and disavowal, the bridge offers a crucial technique tenderly selected from the resources of feminism's already-there. For Alexander, bridging is the means to radically refashion the relation of self, other, community, history, time and desire in accordance with the deep recognition of difference:

> Remembrance is both individual and collective; both intentional and *an act of surrender*; both remembering *desire* and remembering how it works. Daring to recognize each other again and again in a context that seems bent on making strangers of us all. . . . All are part of this living memory, of moments, of imaginings which have never ended. And they will never end as long as we continue to dare yearning for each other.[13]

The daring act of crossing, which is an act of surrender, a means of saying 'I/we do not know (you),' is to honour the orientation within feminism's already-there as a live process continually made and remade through communicative acts grounded in desire. Crossing wards off estrangement and keeps yearning and curiosity alive. This elaboration of crossing would not have been possible without the bridge that makes permissible, renders visible—as image, symbol and transporter of feelings, information and knowledge—the *process* of transmission. The bridge is how we access '*transformations that occur in this in-between space*,' so often rendered invisible, unknowable, because our arrival usually takes place *after* the crossing has occurred, therefore making the journey itself irrelevant. But, of course, the journey, the crossing, is everything! We have to stay with the bridge even with its incommensurable difficulties: there is nothing outside the bridge, or the crossing. For Alexander, crossing is the site of profound, revolutionary change, 'not a transcendent vision, but one that was rooted in transforming the mundaneness of lived experience.'[14] Crossings are therefore immanent, of the world, capable of reworking the 'relationship to Time and its purpose.'[15]

Such a reworking of relation, time and purpose also informs the visionary activist work of contemporary black feminist Alexis Pauline Gumbs, which is similarly committed to 'an everyday practice of unlearning what we think we know and becoming present to how the miraculous future is already evident here.'[16] In projects such as the Eternal Summer of the Black Feminist Mind, Audre Lorde Resurrection Sundays, Juneteenth Freedom Academy (in honour of poet June Jordan) and the Mobile Homecoming, Gumbs draws on the power of black feminist ancestors to guide her political work, informed by the deep conviction that 'we cannot live without each other; our connections persist even across death.'[17] Like Alexander, Gumbs foregrounds relationality, interdependence, yearning and desire at the centre of engaged activist practices, although she arguably amplifies the spiritual, ancestral dimensions within black feminist and women of colour thought to new levels of noisy 'brilliance.'[18] Gumbs's invocation that 'Black feminism lives!' is as much a call to arms as it is a call to recognise the continuous presence of ancestors whose words, lives and actions still influence political imaginaries *despite* material death. This is precisely what happens when the 'relationship to Time and its purpose' is reworked: The dead become alive again as the *purpose* of their work becomes invigorated. Here black feminist ancestrality emerges from the deep and sacred respect for the work that women from different generations have created and struggled for.[19] The texts that Lorde and others like her wrote can be read, shared and studied *transnationally* across generations— they are a *resource* to be revived and resurrected. As Gumbs writes in a letter addressed to Lorde, 'It became clear that . . . "our Lorde," had a sacred role in the lives of our community. You became our Lorde of an awakened need and a renewed faith in the practices of gathering, breaking bread and turning over words in our open mouths and our outstretched hands.'[20]

Such reverence for Lorde is understandable given how the self-declared warrior poet took the invention, revival and resurrection of tradition very seriously. Her 'Open Letter to Mary Daly' was famously critical of how Daly 'dismissed *my heritage* and the *heritage* of all other noneuropean women'[21] by only focusing on the spiritual legacies of white European goddesses. In order to emphasise her point about the exclusion of African goddess traditions in Daly's book, Lorde signs off her letter in the 'hands of Afrekete,'[22] a figure that appears at the end of her 'biomythography,' *Zami: A New Spelling of My Name*, as 'mischievous linguist, trickster, best-beloved, whom we must all become.'[23] Afrekete acts as a reclaimed[24] tradition for Lorde, a mythological symbol capable of transmitting women's love for each other while also acting as canny protectress from evil:

> Afrekete Afrekete ride me to the crossroads where we shall sleep, coated in the woman's power. The sound of our bodies meeting is the prayer of all strangers and sisters, that the discarded evils, abandoned at all crossroads, will not follow us upon our journeys. . . .
> Zami. A Carriacou name for women who work together as friends and lovers.
> We carry our traditions with us . . . new living the old in a new way. Recreating in words the women who helped give me substance.[25]

Lorde's delineation of women's communities, arts and culture is coexistent with her elaboration, imagining and reinvention of *tradition*, whether that be the reclaimed legacies of goddess spirituality—'Yemanje, Oyo, and Mawulisa . . . the warrior goddesses of the Vodun, the Dahomeian Amazons and the warrior-women of Dan'[26]—or the heritages carried within 'ordinary' women's bodies, re-created by Lorde, who names them *as* tradition in order to give herself and others 'substance.' Lorde's writings offer a qualitatively different orientation to feminism's already-there, propelled by the poetic-spiritual techniques of black feminist ancestrality, grounded in the possibility and necessity of dialogue and shared conversations across generations. Such possibility is powerfully communicated by Gumbs's series of letters to her ancestors that are themselves a bridge or crossing over within the Eternal Summer of the Black Feminist Mind.

Although the examples above explore the traditions and practices of black and women of colour feminism from the United States, similar ancestral orientations exist in UK black feminist communities. Indeed, the use of 'wisdom circles' in contemporary British black feminist activism as a means to 'learn from each other how to survive, hope and dream' is testimony to the central role ancestors and respectful cross-generational exchange perform within the culture of black feminism transnationally.[27] In an interview conducted as part of the Black Cultural Archives' *Heart of the Race* (2009–2010) oral history project, Gail Lewis reflected on how we used to have a set of meetings, they were called the International Cross Cultural Black Women's Conferences. One happened in London, one happened in New York, one happened Aotearoa, Japan, Central or South America—there was so much going on, so much connection . . . especially when we were working with first nation women, indigenous women from Aotearoa, from North America then those women would come in and there was no divide between the secular and the spiritual for them . . . and then you realise 'oh, there's more of this going on in our communities than you realise.' Many of the women I was connected to are now involved in those forms of spiritual practice, both in this country and in the USA. . . . The roots of those religions and those practices are the continent, are Africa, so there's another way these visions of being, occupying different kinds of womanhood that came out of the movement. *Self-survival, re-making of the self and reconnecting the self to another set of heritages.*[28]

Black feminist ancestrality is articulated here as part of a wider grassroots political project that strives to liberate the self—a self that is always located in relation to others, both 'living' and 'dead.' Within such understanding the divisions between embodied warrior/ancestral force are porous: through active engagement with ancestors, expressed by processes of reactivating, re-interpreting and resurrecting, the dead *live again*, and those who are living become *more alive*.[29] Within the crucible of black feminism in the UK, refiguring the self is described as part of wider 'processes of migration. Migrations away from past social norms, from different realities, from petrified ideas, and from past selves.'[30] These are journeys that have no definite conclusion because liberation is continuous and non-linear, complicated by traumatic 'fits and starts' that constitute the lives of people imprinted with profound psychic, spiritual, emotional, physical, spatial and cultural violence, the unavoidable inherited legacies of displacement and colonialism.[31]

Such turning to ancestrality is, however, by no means equivocal across black feminist and women of colour thought. Another view suggests it is necessary to commit severance with traumatic legacies inherited from slavery and colonialisation, so that 'petrified selves' can *move on*. Saidya Hartman's *Lose Your Mother* (2007) articulates this will to forget as much as remember, while clearly demonstrating the devastating presence of traumatic legacies that shape the temporalities staged in the text: 'The smell hung in a black cloud over Accra. When I breathed deeply I swore I could discern the sulphurous odour of things dead and decaying.'[32] Hartman's auto/ethnography reveals, with piercing clarity, the *ongoing* temporal intrusion of slavery's olfactory, psychic and historical legacy. Within Alexander's meditations on memory she also foregrounds the pain that can arise from negotiating inheritances embedded within the already-there: 'How do we learn the antidote to barrenness? . . . Forgetting is so deep that forgetting is itself part of what we have forgotten. What is so unbearable that we even forget that we have

forgotten?'[33] Ultimately, for Alexander, the will to remember, as both political and spiritual act, prevails. After all, she notes, ancestral impulses have
strongly shaped the political project of black and women of colour feminism,
an alternative tradition outlining a different kind of rootedness in the world
and a different kind of remembrance.[34] It is a project motivated by the search
for and within mother's gardens, in order to find inspiration, sustenance,
wisdom and loss.[35] To sever the potential resources that sustain the eternal
summer of black feminism, therefore, would be to deny the heritage that ultimately 'was never meant to survive'[36] but persists nevertheless.

Black feminist ancestrality outlines bridges to the already-there, and
foregrounds processes of crossing as central to the project of collective and
individual transformation. Black feminist thought and activism has been
formed through direct confrontation with legacies that are simultaneously
destructive and nurturing, but necessitate the daily practice of 'remembering all the time' so that it is possible to 'recognise each other.' As a resource
for thinking more widely about how the feminist epistemic, cultural and
political project can undergo reorientation to its already-there, black feminist ancestrality can facilitate different affective registers, spatial-material
metaphors and temporal knowledges that invigorate the presence of generations, and the transmission of generational wisdom. Through figurations of
bridges and crossing, which are always both metaphorical *and* material, the
writings of women of colour have created practical tools that connect the
unmoored to what is already-there. Black feminist ancestrality takes care
of generations by foregrounding processes of transmission, learning and
exchange that infect knowledge and actions in the world.

Transmission and Crisis

I now focus on questions of transmission as they have been discussed within
critical heritage studies, cultural anthropology and popular culture. My
concern here is to highlight how processes of transmission *in general*—that
is, outside of feminist articulations—are often figured in terms of crisis.
This manifests in two ways: first through the historical category of 'the present' being *overwhelmed* by the sheer amount of memory resources available,
and secondly through anxieties about the *fragmentation* of transmissive circuits that were seemingly once whole but are now eroded due to the loss of
certain values, community formations and a general 'tradition.' Ultimately
I want to argue that both approaches are insufficient for understanding
how transmission practices occur across feminist generations, generations
that are always already characterised by fragmentary circuits formed within

'the vicinity of trauma.'[37] In the following section, then, we will examine how cultural transmission, and the 'presence' of cultural heritage from different historical times, has been understood as the mindless accumulation of materials, things and ideas *or* as the fragmentation of a once robust and resilient heritage. In so doing, we can better appreciate the differences and divergences at stake as we elaborate how feminism's already-there is accessed. The aim here is to understand *how* techniques of heritage-making occur so that it possible to become better custodians and curators (those that care for) the heritage we may *choose* to be responsible for across feminist generations.

Heritage as Social Process, Invention, Value

In the first chapter you will recall that, following Laurajane Smith, I introduced the idea that heritage was an active process through which the value of diverse cultural entities were identified, affirmed or rejected. I was keen to assert that there is nothing essential or inevitable about what becomes interpreted or defined *as* heritage; it does not simply appear, obvious and ready-made for touristic consumption (although it can so often seem that way). Heritage is a process of *valuation* through which parts of the already-there are *selected* by individuals, groups or organisations because they are seen to define, embody, symbolise, represent and transmit ideas or values that 'belong' to a specific community. Often heritage-community imaginaries are bordered within geographical space, thus reifying *belonging* to place and, in particular, nation-states. As Geoffrey Cubitt writes, 'Conceptions of collective identity have taken shape whose sustenance requires *organised accounts* of collective past experience—especially, in the modern period, of a community's experience as a nation.'[38] Such nationalist attachments, inherited from modernity, become even more problematic in the ways they bind the heritage imaginary to Western-centric colonial frameworks, underpinned by stereotypical perceptions of exotic 'other' cultures. Tim Winter explains that because the contemporary theoretical concept of heritage 'is written through and from the point of view of the West,'[39] it is structured by 'the grammar of colonial power centred on three key institutional concepts—the census, map and museum.'[40]

There is, however, a growing movement of theorists and practitioners who want to foster a 'critical' interrogation of heritage, and challenge the normative assumptions that underscore how heritage is understood, managed, created and interpreted. The Association of Critical Heritage Studies Manifesto, published in 2012, states, for example:

Heritage is, as much as anything, *a political act* and we need to ask serious questions about the power relations that 'heritage' has all too often been invoked
to sustain. Nationalism, imperialism, colonialism, cultural elitism, western
triumphalism, social exclusion based on class and ethnicity, and the fetishising
of expert knowledge have all exerted strong influences on how heritage is used,
defined and managed.[41]

It would be limiting, therefore, to assume that 'heritage' as a concept and cultural practice is fundamentally attached to Western modernity and its vestigial
representations, even if those representations remain unquestionably powerful in how they shape perceptions of heritage value and recognition. As a concept and practice, heritage *can be* reclaimed, rendered 'critical' and dislocated
from its normative attachments so that it can be understood, following David
Harvey, as 'a social process' available to those wishing to engage with it.[42]
Harvey argues that it is necessary to explore the 'historically contingent and
embedded nature of heritage' because it enables 'us to engage with debates
about the production of identity, power and authority throughout society.'[43]
Understanding that heritage emerges from contingent social processes may
therefore help us to sidestep (that is, *move alongside*) what is encountered
immediately-there—the heritage imaginary defined by the parameters of nation and other expressions of the 'Authorised heritage discourse'[44]—in order
to uncover different heritage imaginaries that exist within the already-there.
It may open up time-spaces whereby heritage produced across communities of interest, which can be transnational *and* trans-historical, are valued
and *organised* through long-circuits within which generational knowledge is
taken care of and transmitted.[45] How can heritages and traditions that seek to
unravel power, identity and authority be recognised and preserved? To what
means are they deployed, and how are their traditions kept alive, their value
elaborated, their urgent messages transmitted? How can unofficial communities of interest organise their long-circuits so they can 'intimate a range of
connectivities that allows for the passage of thought across time'?[46]
    There are practical as well as theoretical difficulties in pursuing such
questions, because such communities of interest rarely benefit from the
'communicative techniques that allow information to be transmitted over
lengthy periods,'[47] such as memorial days, large participatory celebrations,
extended airplay on television and radio, monuments or parades—events that
punctuate the temporal rhythm of daily, weekly or yearly[48] life through practices of observance, mourning and celebration.[49] The long-circuits of feminism's mnemo-technical resources, those *minor* cultural heritages,[50] function
somewhat differently: unofficial, opportunistic, accidental, broken, rotting,
disappeared, ephemeral, animate, found, lost, troubled and *already-there*;
working across different contingent gradations of activation, forgetting and

operationalisation. To imagine heritages and traditions in this way designates counter-orientations that necessarily elaborate different communicative *techniques* for the transmission of knowledge, practices, ideas and culture across generations. These techniques undo a common misconception that heritage-making is located in a constructed techno-historicity produced as 'the present,' constructing a relationship with 'the past' for 'the future.'[51] Within the variegated contours of the already-there these categories are nonsensical in and of themselves—there are only processes of transmission, operationalisation and activation. *Across. Down. Again. Through. Up. Diagonal. Everywhere.*

The organisation of feminist circuits needs to be capacious and flexible enough to cross borders of different historical times, but also that of space and location, because communities of interest can exceed the borders of nation/locality (they undo the logic of borders and nation if not locality *entirely*). This is not to say that a trans-national and trans-historical feminist heritage imaginary will be stripped of temporal and spatial specificity. Such factors are instead communicated as elaborations of difference, bypassing the risk of reducing all artifacts to the element of the same, flattening through the rugged, sharp and poisonous gradations of the already-there. On the contrary, within such circuits there is an invitation to become proximate with the mnemo-technical resources that compose feminism's already-there. To learn from the materials as a curator would, arranging material objects or digitised equivalents with care in order to generate experiences, collisions, conversations and emergent situations. What is already-there arranges the curator too, composing a web of relationships and circuits of transmission. Not merely instrumentalised nodal points through which the big data flows and calculations are measured, but occasions where knowledge can emerge and learning takes place-time, up-down, across-across, all because a conversation between entities is happening, desired to be happening and in the 'making,' which 'is, literally, about creating and maintaining relations and exchanges in proximity (not necessarily spatial or temporal proximity).'[52]

To perceive of heritage as a social process of value making is to highlight how communities can explore what is already-there and undergo processes of interpretation and amplification according to need, necessity and *survival*. In what ways then can heritage-making practices, grounded in an orientation to knowledge that can care 'for the continuity of generational (collective) individuation possible only through technics,'[53] be useful for rethinking about how feminism *operates* as an epistemic, cultural and political project? What tools and lexicons are available that can facilitate access to feminism's already-there, which can create emergent opportunities for the transmission of ideas *whose time has come*? As we have seen through the earlier discussion of black feminist ancestrality, selecting, claiming and establishing a heritage is vital for rooting groups of people in the world through means of objects, places or cultural practices that belong to them (that belong to an *us*). Heritage helps to imagine community because it establishes *an idea of value*; it emphasises that a community's practices, ideas and culture are *valuable*. Heritage, Elizabeth Crooke writes, only becomes meaningful through its relation with the communities it is part of, and which it in turn helps to shape: 'The community concept and the idea of heritage become intertwined with the lived experience and expression of community. The community group is defined and justified because of its heritage and that heritage is fostered and sustained by the creation of community.'[54] Indeed, heritage creates value for communities because as a concept and cultural practice, it suggests that some things (many things) are worth saving *and* transmitting across generations. It suggests there may be something called a tradition, woven from the scrappiest and most fragmented remains, but a tradition nonetheless—techniques of being, belonging and, sometimes, dislocation. After all, there are many different kinds of knowledge of how to live and be in the world, and keeping such knowledge alive is essential for the survival of multiple bodies, livelihoods and imaginaries.

Piling Up 'the Past' and Crisis in Value

Some heritage theorists have articulated a crisis within the social function of heritage, which, in the twenty-first century, is represented as being no longer capable of conferring value upon objects, practices, ideas and places. Mechanisms of 'heritage recognition,' such as the World Heritage Register, Rodney Harrison argues, deploy an 'increasingly broad definition of heritage,' which has led to 'the exponential growth of listed objects, places and practices of heritage in the contemporary world.'[55] Somewhat portentously he concludes that 'we risk being overwhelmed by memory, and in the process *making all heritages ineffective and worthless*.'[56] In this statement Harrison rehashes much of the postmodern gloom that populated the late twentieth century, which presented itself as an attempt to 'think the present historically in an age that has forgotten how to think historically in the first place.'[57] This sense of a global culture, steadily drowning in the glut of its own hyper-valuation, is a suffocating, and somewhat hyperbolic, image. It is the articulation of a space and time suffering from 'a heterogeneous piling up of disparate and conflicting pasts in the present as a "crisis" of accumulation of the past.'[58]

There are two principal ways it is necessary to respond to such diagnoses. The first is the concern about heterogeneous, disparate and conflicting 'pasts.' The use of such language is laden with value judgments about the ideal composition of heritage. If we invert the statement, presumably this may be read as a desire for homogenous, similar and harmonious heritages—a proposition that is both banal and problematic. Is the world not composed of heterogeneous, disparate and conflicting 'pasts'? Heritages are, after all, as complex as the societies from which they emerge. Heritages can also be *difficult*—a factor acknowledged by an increasing field of professional practice within the field that bears the name.[59] Heritages can be marked by the very worst catastrophes, violence, trauma and exploitation that have ever happened, and they are usually multifaceted, composed of plural voices and perspectives. These voices and lived experiences can be key parts of reconciliation processes as much as they can promote nationalist fantasies. Heritage can bear wounds openly, but can also help healing. Sometimes there can be no resolution, and often no one wins. Heritage tells us that certain experiences, historical events and legacies are unbearable and cannot be assimilated. It surmises that restitution may be impossible, and the effects of what happened keep happening—the conditions of inheritance are ongoing.[60] To honour the complexities of heterogeneous heritages is to respect their disparities and persisting conflicts. These are transmitted across generations and affect the lives of many people, often without their conscious knowledge. Such a conception of heritage is not attended to in the complaint that heritages are too disparate, conflicting or heterogeneous and arguably trivialise such experience out of a desire for ease and homogeneity.

Another response is to read Harrison's statement as Stiegler perhaps would: where this crisis emerges because the knowledge of *how* to value heritage has been short-circuited across generations. This does not result from a lack of contact with mnemo-technical resources—particularly relevant when we consider the case of digital technologies and the digital archive, which we will later in the book—but a lack of knowledge about *how to confer value* and *make decisions* about what memory resources should be kept and which ones should be discarded. Harrison suggests this when he states that contemporary society encourages us to 'stockpile the redundant, disused and the outmoded as potential raw materials for the production of memories that we feel we are unable to risk losing, *even when we are powerless to articulate what their possible value might be*.'[61] Reframed in this way, the problem refers less to the crisis of an oversaturation of memory resources that transmit the 'cultural wealth' of heterogeneous, disparate and conflicting traditions than to the very ability to distinguish between them, *to select* and manage them. Harrison is not alone in feeling swamped by the forces of heritage and the intrusions of memory resources that occlude a distinct sense of 'the present.' Popular culture commentator Simon Reynolds has argued that we are now living in an environment saturated by 'retromania'—an addiction to the incessant recir-

culation of popular cultural forms at the expense of genuinely new forms of
creativity and endeavour. He writes:

> The presence of the past in our lives has increased immeasurably and insidi-
> ously. Old stuff either directly permeates the present, or lurks just beneath the
> surface of the current, in the form of on-screen windows to other times. . . . Until
> relatively recently, one lived most of the time in a cultural present tense, with
> the past confined to specific zones, trapped in particular objects and locations.[62]

The contemporary subject rooting through the 'barely navigable disorder of
data-debris and memory trash'[63] is also afflicted by this crisis in value. Yet,
as with Harrison, such diagnoses of contemporary culture reflect an enduring postmodern malaise that, I want to suggest, simply cannot cope with the
emergent modes of access to the already-there made possible by digitisation,
the conditioning mnemo-technical context of the twenty-first century. *There
is* another way to be (re)orientated within the digital already-there, as this
book elaborates, that attempts to respond to the changing tenor of temporal-
historical experience emergent within the digital. To be reoriented, however,
requires thorough questioning of the brute facticity of the historical categories of past, present and future that are used to raise cultural anxieties and
diagnose social problems within the *transmission as crisis* discourse. Within
such discourses, acts of misrecognition are at work because past, present and
future—hereafter signaled in this book through the figure of ←P→P←F→—
are historical categories produced by dominant technical modes of transmission that no longer *exclusively* condition perceptions, orientations and experiences within a digital milieu. As Trinh T. Minh-Ha has written:

> What we are witnessing today . . . if we do not think in terms of linear progress,
> but rather in terms of a spiralling, multidimensional here-and-now—where
> everything in the present carries with it its past and future. The seed of the fu-
> ture is always already there, in the present, in the past. If we think of it in that
> way, inclusively rather than exclusively, spatially and spirally rather than only
> linearly, then the time we live (in) is rich and full of potential.[64]

FIGURE 3.1
←P→P←F→ is a means to signal the triadic, yet flat, directional-orientative-imaginary
of historical time when articulated in terms of ←P→P←F→, which can only imagine the
movement of historicity in restricted channels ←P, 'look backward'; →P←, contained
by P and F; also understood as a turning point between←P and F→; F→ 'look forward.'
This figure will be elaborated further as this book unfolds.

If we refuse to categorise greater access to the already-there as an indication of historical malaise, but rather as the demonstrable evidence of different historical temporalities pressing into and *operating* reality, the problems raised by commentators such as Harrison and Reynolds are significantly altered, and different questions arise. After all, as Stiegler argues, 'lettered, analog, and digital reproducibilities configure *heterogeneous* temporalities . . . these new *conditions of access* affect the transmission and elaboration of knowledge *in general*: cognitive, artistic, ethical.'[65] Integrating such insights would necessarily take account of how the digital mnemo-technical already-there operates in a manner that is continually rotting and regenerating, forgetting and remembering, organising and dis-aggregating terms of reference that once operated as the stable grounds of historical temporalities unthought: ←P→P←F→. It is vital, therefore, that a politics of transmission within the digital mnemo-technical milieu devises alternative concepts, orientations and practices through which the already-there, and different temporal knowledges it harbours, can be operationalised *and* cared for. We must think transmission, in other words, dislocated from ←P→P←F→. From now on this text attempts to enact such a practice.

Transmission and Crisis, 2—Fragmentation

Cultural anthropologist David Berliner reflects below on how discussions about cultural transmission have become mired in nostalgia, fired by longing to restore forgotten worlds and lost customs.

> Cultural transmission is a hot topic today. However, nowadays it is mostly understood through its so-called 'crisis.' I have heard so many times in the field, in West Africa first and more recently at UNESCO meetings, these nostalgic longings about cultural loss and forgetting, the necessity and the impossibility of transmitting.[66]

In such a context transmission becomes defined by its crisis and impossibility. The practice of transmitting culture is figured as a means of stabilisation 'deployed by ordinary men and women in a world seen by many as globalizing and uprooting.'[67] The fragmentation as crisis narrative mirrors the fear of *too much* transmission elaborated by Harrison and Reynolds. Either way, the concern is fixated upon circuits—broken, uprooted, animate, overloaded— that resound in lives of 'ordinary' people and yield influence on policy decisions made at an international level. Worries about loss and forgetting, and desperately legislating to ward off such occurrences, need to be understood within a cultural context that assumes circuits were once whole, or at least

operational. Yet, as Berliner advises, 'studying cultural transmission . . . requires that one acknowledges that concepts, practices and emotions from the
past do not suddenly "happen" in people. It entails that one looks for the *long
processes* through which these things circulate between generations and peers,
being appropriated by individuals who *actively acquire them in situations.*'[68]
It is essential, then, as I have argued throughout this book so far, to view
transmission as a material-technical process that emerges from engagement
with what is already-there. Because the scene of transmission exists as proximate potentiality underlining all possible knowledge, circuits can become
animated and broken in surprising, spontaneous, accidental and deliberate
ways. Transmission should never be mistaken, however, as a true, identical
copy. As a process, and always *as a process*, transmission is defined by modification. Noise, compression, blurring, tearing, fading, creasing, smudging,
mould-infestation, mangling, redaction, embellishment, representation, destruction and just plain old 'things going missing' all occur within the process
of transmission. Sometimes metadata, if it exists, can help reconstruct the
afterlives[69] of transmission, but this should not be confused with authenticity,
or an appeal to truth. Transmission always elaborates difference as it moves
across—an across that is not necessarily temporal or spatial—a circuit that
always has to be tended to, in one way or another.

The Cultural Heritages That Are Not One

What about those cultural heritages that 'belong' to revolutionary practices
like feminism, whose transmissive circuits of memory are always already fragmented due to the peculiarity of historical circumstance? How is it possible to
understand *how* transmission occurs within such situations, what conceptual
tools need to be developed, what techniques of imagining are necessary for
this elaboration? To begin to answer this question, let us finish this chapter
by considering Rachael House's 2011 art installation *Feminist Disco*, in which
the artist spatialises the cultural memory of queer feminist music as a series
of miniature islands. 'Island for the Slits to live on,' 'Island for Jayne County
to live on' and 'Island for Poly Styrene to live on' are singular places for these
emblems of renegade femininity to endure within feminism's already-there.
Each island has wheels on their base and a leash that enables them to drift
toward each other. Sometimes they come into contact as the artist takes them
on public parades. The islands are comical but oddly moving configurations—in their miniature form they enact (queer) women's place in popular
music history: remote, stranded and disconnected from the mainstream
music histories that predictably exclude them. The loving care used in the

FIGURE 3.2
Rachael House, 'Island for the Slits to live on' (foreground), 'Island for Jayne County to live on' and 'Island for Poly Styrene to live on' (2011).

construction of the islands contrasts sharply with the neglectful omission of radical women who refuse to fit in to the pedestrian narratives of popular music history. It does, however, visually demonstrate how the cultural work of women and feminists are *arranged* within the scene of transmission.

Desert islands occupy a unique space in the cultural imaginary.[70] Islands are places for castaways, the shipwrecked, the savage and the survivalists. To live on remote islands requires endurance and guile, a gritty resilience that can adapt to surroundings in order to just stay alive. For Anzaldúa, islands are one of the 'ways of being, of acting, of interacting in the world,' a form of withdrawal and protection from damaging situations: 'Being an island means that there are no causeways, no bridges—maybe no ferries, either—between you and whites.'[71] Yet 'being an island cannot be a way of life; there are no lifelong islands because no one is totally self-sufficient.'[72] The island is, then, a lonely place—remain and possibly perish, or be saved and return to 'civilisation.' Someone may remember your existence and send out a rescue party, or a benevolent passerby may collect you as they sail past through the unknown waters of the far-flung ocean. In either sense, the desert island is set apart from 'normal' culture and society, and its inhabitants are ultimately stranded, isolated and exceptional. House's fashioning resonates with Deleuze's figuring of islands as 'the second origin of the world,' emerging from the 'movement of the imagination that makes the desert island a model, a prototype for the collective soul . . . cosmic egg . . . separate, separated by the massive expanse of the flood,' emblematic of the *'survival . . .* in a world that is *slow to re-begin.'*[73] The 'Islands to live on' series creates the conditions for remembering *from the egg,*[74] taking note of the fact that women are always the forgotten ones in need of rescue and recovery, cultural-historical actors subject to *slow re-beginnings.* Women's achievements are usually retrieved; they are never simply present in the ways that men's are.[75] If House's islands are points in the transmissive circuit, it becomes clear the amount of work required if they are to become connected—they are defined by their distance and isolation *from each other* and 'the real world.'[76]

Here, islands are a useful concept to think about how women's musical achievements in popular music history *appear* exceptional because they are stranded from mainstream society and, crucially, other women musicians. Through the islands we may rebegin to think about how feminist cultural heritage—feminism's already-there—transmits by drifting, happenstance and determined rescue missions. After all, what is said on and from the island can only reverberate against the ocean expanse, leaving a tantalising echo, a residual disturbance in the status quo. It is very difficult for the voices and actions of the stranded to connect to what is immediately-there, which is often relayed by museums, archives, radio shows, TV, newspapers, monuments and, yes, even the internet. House's solution is to take her islands onto street parades, where they temporarily float into visibility and, occasionally, win prizes. There remains a melancholic and resilient humour to their movement, and the visualisation of the space created for them. Lonely and defiant, they are crucially not moored to one particular place. Such capacities for mobility and circuitry ward off forgetting while parading the necessity of (second) origins and inheritances located in the island-egg. House's installation therefore offers another different technique for understanding the arrangement of feminism's already-there and its modes of transmission, which we shall carry with us in the remainder of this book.

In the next chapter, we further explore why the transmission of feminism's already-there has been fragmented, partial and marginal with an in-depth consideration of the cultural practices of women's liberation music-making.

Notes

1. Hemmings, *Why Stories Matter*, 156.
2. Alexander, *Pedagogies of Crossing*, 275.
3. Van der Tuin, *Generational Feminism*.
4. Cherríe Moraga, 'Foreword,' in Cherríe Moraga and Gloria Anzaldúa, eds., *This Bridge Called My Back: Writings by Radical Women of Color* (New York: Kitchen Table: Women of Color Press, 1983), iii.
5. Alexander, *Pedagogies of Crossing*, 260.
6. Cathryn Josefina Merla-Watson, 'Metaphor, Multitude, and Chicana Third Space Feminism,' *ACME: An International E-Journal for Critical Geographies* 11:3 (2012): 504.
7. Gloria Anzaldúa, 'Metaphors in the Tradition of the Shaman,' in Gloria Anzaldúa and AnaLouise Keating, eds., *The Gloria Anzaldúa Reader* (Durham, NC: Duke University Press, 2009b), 122.
8. Gloria Anzaldúa, 'Bridge, Drawbridge, Sandbar, or Island: Lesbians-of-Color *Hacienda Alianzas*,' in Gloria Anzaldúa and AnaLouise Keating, eds., *The Gloria Anzaldúa Reader* (Durham, NC: Duke University Press, 2009a), 141.
9. Merla-Watson, 'Metaphor, Multitude, and Chicana Third Space Feminism,' 504.
10. Anzaldúa, 'Bridge, Drawbridge, Sandbar, or Island,' 141.
11. Pratibha Parmar and Trinh T. Minh-ha, 'Women, Native, Other,' *Feminist Review* 36 (1990): 70.
12. Gloria Anzaldúa, 'Preface: (Un)natural Bridges, (Un)safe Spaces,' in Gloria Anzaldúa and AnaLouise Keating, eds., *This Bridge We Call Home: Radical Visions for Transformation* (London: Routledge, 2002): 1.
13. Alexander, 'Remembering *This Bridge Called My Back*,' 278.
14. Alexander, 'Remembering *This Bridge Called My Back*,' 279.
15. Alexander, 'Remembering *This Bridge Called My Back*,' 278.
16. Alexis Pauline Gumbs, 'Eternal Summer of the Black Feminist Mind,' in Lyz Bly and Kelly Wooten, eds., *Make Your Own History: Documenting Feminist & Queer Activism in the 21st Century* (Los Angeles: Litwin Books, 2013), 68.
17. Alexis Pauline Gumbs, 'Eternal Summer of the Black Feminist Mind,' 68.
18. To learn more about Alexis's projects, visit her website at http://alexispauline.com/.
19. 'We would like to affirm that we find our origins in the historical reality of Afro-American women's *continuous life-and-death struggle* for survival and liberation,' wrote the Combahee River Collective in 1977. Combahee River Collective, 'The Combahee River Collective Statement,' 1977, accessed 25 March 2015, http://www.sfu.ca/iirp/documents/Combahee%201979.pdf.

20. Alexis Pauline Gumbs, 'Eternal Summer of the Black Feminist Mind,' 61.

21. Audre Lorde, 'An Open Letter to Mary Daly,' *Sister Outsider: Essays and Speeches* (New York: The Crossing Press, 1984), 68.

22. Lorde, 'An Open Letter to Mary Daly,' 71.

23. Audre Lorde, *Zami: A New Spelling of My Name* (Watertown, MA: Peresphone Press, 1982), 255.

24. I use this word deliberately here to refer to reclaiming movement.

25. Lorde, *Zami*, 252–255.

26. Lorde, 'An Open Letter to Mary Daly,' 71.

27. See, for example, the 2015 conference Black British Feminism: Past, Present and Futures, which used the method of wisdom circles in order to 'return to an activist-centred movement.' See http://bcaheritage.org.uk/black-british-feminism -past-present-and-futures/.

28. Gail Lewis, 'Oral Histories of the Black Women's Movement: The Heart of the Race Project,' ORAL/1, Black Cultural Archives (2009/2010).

29. There is much that could also be said here about how Afrofuturism reconfigures temporality and ancestral relations. For an excellent exhibition about Afrofuturist aesthetics, please visit http://shadowstookshape.tumblr.com/.

30. Gail Lewis et al., 'Preface,' in Gail Lewis et al., eds., *Charting the Journey* (London: Sheba Press, 1988), 4.

31. Avtar Brah, 'Journey to Nairobi,' in Lewis et al., eds., *Charting the Journey* (London: Sheba Press, 1988), 74–89.

32. Saidya Hartman, *Lose Your Mother: A Journey Along the Atlantic Slave Route* (New York: Farrar, Straus and Giroux, 2007), 47.

33. Alexander, 'Remembering This Bridge,' 276.

34. See also Cheryl Dunne's 1996 film, *The Watermelon Woman*, http://www .imdb.com/title/tt0118125/.

35. Alice Walker, *In Search of Our Mothers' Gardens: Womanist Prose* (London: Women's Press, 1983).

36. Audre Lorde, 'Litany for Survival,' *Collected Poems of Audre Lorde* (New York: W. W. Norton, 1997), 255–256.

37. Cvetkovich, *Archives of Feelings*.

38. Geoffrey Cubitt, *History and Memory* (Manchester: Manchester University Press, 2007), 176.

39. Tim Winter, 'Heritage Studies and the Privileging of Theory,' *International Journal of Heritage Studies* (2013), accessed 27 October 2013, DOI: 10.1080/13527258. 2013.798671, 5.

40. Lynn Meskell, *Archaeology Under Fire: Nationalism, Politics and Heritage in the Eastern Mediterranean and Middle East* (London: Routledge, 1998), 3.

41. Gary Campbell and Laurajane Smith, 'Association of Critical Heritage Studies Manifesto' (2012), accessed 1 April 2014, http://criticalheritagestudies.org.preview .binero.se/site-admin/site-content/about-achs.

42. David C. Harvey, 'Heritage Pasts and Heritage Presents: Temporality, Meaning and the Scope of Heritage Studies,' *International Journal of Heritage Studies* 7:4 (2001): 321.

43. Harvey, 'Heritage Pasts and Heritage Presents,' 321.

44. Laurajane Smith, *The Uses of Heritage* (London: Routledge, 2006), 29.

45. Bernard Stiegler and Irit Rogoff, 'Transindividuation,' *e-flux* (2010), accessed 26 March 2014, http://www.e-flux.com/journal/transindividuation/.

46. Stiegler and Rogoff, 'Transindividuation.'

47. Cubitt, *History and Memory*, 176.

48. Of course, it is important to point to the yearly recognition of International Women's Day (8 March, first observed in 1909) as a significant calendar event around which discussions, marches and women-focused politics are mobilised. It would be fascinating to investigate further how this event has enabled the persistence of feminist and women's focused activism across historical time by acting as a focal point for remembrance and activism.

49. Motti Neiger et al., 'Localizing Collective Memory: Radio Broadcasts and the Construction of Regional Memory,' in Motti Neiger et al., eds., *On Media Memory: Collective Memory in a New Media Age* (Basingstoke: Palgrave, 2011), 156–174.

50. Gilles Deleuze and Félix Guattari, *Kafka: Towards a Minor Literature*, Dana Polan, trans. (Minneapolis: University of Minnesota Press, 1986).

51. Rodney Harrison, *Heritage: Critical Approaches* (London: Routledge, 2013).

52. Dimitris Papadopoulos, 'Generation M: Matter, Makers, Microbiomes: Compost for Gaia,' *European Institute for Progressive Cultural Politics*, 2014, accessed 26 March 2014, http://eipcp.net/n/1392050604.

53. Bernard Stiegler, *Technics and Time, 3: Cinematic Time and the Question of Malaise*, Stephen Barker, trans. (Stanford: Stanford University Press, 2011), 226, n. 1.

54. Elizabeth Crooke, 'The Politics of Community Heritage: Motivations, Authority and Control,' *International Journal of Heritage Studies* 16:1–2 (2010): 17.

55. Rodney Harrison, 'Forgetting to Remember, Remembering to Forget: Late Modern Heritage Practices, Sustainability and the "Crisis" of Accumulation of the Past,' *International Journal of Heritage Studies* 19:6 (2013): 579.

56. Harrison, 'Forgetting to Remember, Remembering to Forget,' 580.

57. Fredric Jameson, *Postmodernism, or the Cultural Logic of Late Capitalism* (London: Verso, 1992), ix.

58. Harrison, 'Forgetting to Remember, Remembering to Forget,' 580.

59. William Logan and Keir Reeves, *Places of Pain and Shame: Dealing with 'Difficult Heritage'* (London: Routledge, 2008); Erica Lehrer et al., *Curating Difficult Knowledge: Violent Pasts in Public Places* (Basingstoke: Palgrave, 2011); and Jenny Kidd et al., eds., *Challenging History in the Museum* (Aldershot: Ashgate, 2014).

60. Anna Reading, 'Restitution Is Impossible' (keynote presentation at Memory and Restitution conference, 5–6 July 2013, http://www.memoryandrestitution.co.uk/).

61. Harrison, *Heritage: Critical Approaches*, 3, italics mine.

62. Simon Reynolds, *Retromania: Pop Culture's Addiction to Its Own Past* (London: Faber, 2011), 57.

63. Reynolds, *Retromania*, 27.

64. Trinh T. Minh-Ha, *The Digital Film Event* (London: Routledge, 2004), 21.

65. Bernard Stiegler, 'Programs of the Improbable, Short-circuits of the Unheard Of,' Robert Hughes, trans., *DIACRITICS* 42:1 (2014): 70–109, 71–72.

66. David Berliner, 'New Directions in the Study of Cultural Transmission,' L. Arizpe and C. Amescua, eds., *Anthropological Perspectives on Intangible Cultural Heritage*, Springer Briefs in *Environment, Security, Development and Peace* 6 (2013), 71.

67. Berliner, 'New Directions in the Study of Cultural Transmission,' 75.

68. Berliner, 'New Directions in the Study of Cultural Transmission,' 75.

69. Hito Steyerl, 'Politics of the Archive, Translations in Film,' *Transversal*, 2008, accessed 25 March 2015, http://eipcp.net/transversal/0608/steyerl/en.

70. Within the British literary colonial imagination, islands are figured as idyllic spaces where fantasies of conquest were played out in a distant setting. See Diana Loxley, *Problematic Shores: The Literature of Islands* (New York: St. Martin's, 1990), 3.

71. Anzaldúa, 'Bridge, Drawbridge, Sandbar, or Island,' 147.

72. Anzaldúa, 'Bridge, Drawbridge, Sandbar, or Island,' 148.

73. Gilles Deleuze, 'Desert Islands,' *Desert Islands and Other Texts 1953–1974*, Michael Taormina, trans. (Los Angeles: Semiotexte, 2004): 13–14.

74. See also Deleuze's discussion of eggs and individuation in *Difference and Repetition*, 249–252.

75. Think only of the recent turn to remember the life and work of electric guitar-wielding gospel legend Sister Rosetta Tharp. Tharp recorded seventeen albums, toured the United States with her female lover in a time of racial segregation, performed all over Europe and was cited as a major influence on Little Richard and Elvis; yet until recently she was largely forgotten. Tharp's grave was unmarked and overgrown as late as 2008—a staggering indication about the value placed on the achievements of such a genuine pioneer.

76. This viewpoint does, of course, perpetuate what Starosielski names 'the network versus island schema' within the Western imaginary that always figures islands as bounded entities and networks as connected spaces. This 'imagined geography,' she argues, eclipses our perception of how islands are, in a very material sense, vital connective points through which global information flows via the communications infrastructure of the undersea cable network. See Starosielski, *The Undersea Network*, 172–173.

4

Intangible Cultural Heritage, Transmission and Alternative Traditions

WITHIN THE CONTOURS OF the already-there we find interpretive tools that may help us further understand the forms and processes peculiar to the transmission of feminist cultural heritage. Within the first part of this chapter, I discuss the concept of intangible cultural heritage (ICH), an important aspect of international heritage management since the United Nations Educational, Scientific and Cultural Organization (UNESCO) introduced it in 2003.[1] The convention aims to safeguard a range of cultural practices including dance, storytelling and other forms of 'live,' performative heritage. I examine how the convention *text*, rather than its *application* by UNESCO in the context of international heritage management, offers useful tools for thinking about heritage traditions that are ephemeral, and whose loci of value and modes of transmission emerge through performative practices. I then explore the ways social movements grounded in leftist and anti-capitalist traditions, and the cultural forms generated by them, can be understood as examples of ICH. After all, the 'processes of globalization and social transformation' deemed to carry 'grave threats of deterioration, disappearance and destruction,'[2] outlined in the convention, may also relate to heritages whose *values* contradict the totalising economic procedures of neoliberal global capitalism.

While I do not want to make the argument that social movement cultures should be listed or even safeguarded by UNESCO, I *do* want to use the 2003 convention as a theoretical tool to think through how ephemeral forms of cultural heritage are transmitted across generations, and examine the ways such heritages are endangered by large-scale economic processes that effectively erode cultural, economic and systemic diversity. While ICH 'is most often associated with non-industrial societies, and its use seems to imply that "traditional" culture cannot exist except in such contexts,'[3] I want to mobilise the concept in a different way. My aim here is to expand the heritage imaginary *and* foreground the importance of 'tradition' in sustaining communities of practice that are seeking to resist the apparent inevitability of contemporary globalised capitalism. How can alternative traditions be activated to offer evidence to challenge this totalising picture, and highlight world-making practices and cultural techniques from which other ways of living and being can be sustained? Finally, this chapter will conclude with a case study of music-making communities connected to the UK WLM. This will demonstrate that thinking about social movement culture through the lens of intangible cultural heritage can help us understand how alternative traditions are, very pragmatically, *kept alive*.

Intangible Cultural Heritage

UNESCO defines ICH in the 'Convention for Safeguarding Intangible Cultural Heritage' as

> The *practices, representations, expressions, knowledge, skills*—as well as the *instruments, objects, artifacts* and *cultural spaces* associated therewith—that communities, groups and, in some cases, individuals recognise as part of their cultural heritage. This intangible cultural heritage, *transmitted from generation to generation*, is constantly recreated by communities and groups in response to their environments, their interaction with nature and their history, and *provides them with a sense of identity and continuity*, thus *promoting respect for cultural diversity and human creativity*.[4]

The 2003 convention followed previous safeguarding measures implemented by UNESCO, such as the 1972 World Heritage Convention, that focused on *tangible* cultural heritage, commonly understood as monumental architectural traditions such as ruins and historic buildings. The 2003 convention was an attempt to challenge Western-centric notions of heritage by recognising a wider breadth of heritage understood to have 'universal value' for global humanity. In practice, such distinctions tend to reinforce the idea that Western = monumental/non-Western = non-monumental. This is particularly evidenced by the UK government's decision to not, as yet, ratify the convention, as if to suggest that the UK does not have intangible cultural traditions such as dance, music and storytelling, despite clear evidence to the contrary.[5] The 2003 ICH convention has, however, influenced understandings of heritage and heritage practice in the UK, particularly within the context of 'live interpretation' and representing 'difficult' heritages.[6] Furthermore, communities of interest in the UK, with significant support from lottery funding, preserve and interpret many examples of what would be called, in a different geopolitical context, intangible cultural heritage.[7]

ICH is 'by definition people-orientated rather than object-centred.'[8] It is 'living' heritage, and the convention attempts to respond to somewhat slippery and diverse *processes of transmission*, the 'practices, representations, expressions, knowledge, skills' that are 'transmitted from generation to generation' via a range of different and 'locally' specific activities. As a concept, ICH is sometimes marked negatively because of its vague, imprecise and immeasurable namesake: intangibility, that which is 'unable to be touched or grasped; not having physical presence.'[9] Ironically, perhaps, the convention has also been critiqued for pinning down traditions that are necessarily live and changeable.[10] It has also been challenged for enforcing arbitrary and, for some, 'perplexing'[11] distinctions between tangible and intangible forms of cultural heritage. For Smith and Waterton, insisting upon the separation between tangible and intangible cultural heritages occludes a more significant understanding of how heritage functions in contemporary society, wherein it manifests as 'the performance and negotiation of identity, values and a sense of place.'[12] In practice the differences between these two 'types' of heritage are more fluid, as Arizpe notes: ICH is 'not an object, not a performance, not a site; it may be embodied or given material form in any of these, but basically it is an enactment of meanings embedded in collective memory.'[13] Many of the critiques of the ICH convention are valid. Nevertheless, I want to argue that the heritage formations the convention broadly recognises offer valuable tools for understanding the transmission trajectories of disjointed cultural traditions such as feminism. Feminism's already-there: fragmented, ephemeral, hard to grasp, yet nonetheless meaningful for communities and individuals for whom such an already-there resonates (and it cannot be known in advance who this will be, since belonging itself is selected, contingent upon exposure to what is already-there).

ICH, Transmission and Heritage Time

The ICH convention pays attention to how heritage temporalities are grounded in processes of transmission and reinterpretation that occur within marginal communities. These heritage temporalities are located in a range of 'living traditions' and therefore 'liveness,' heritages that become *operationalised* through their practice. As a temporal mode of transmission, it is congruent with Taylor's conception of 'repertoire' that 'requires presence: people participate in the production and reproduction of knowledge by "being there" . . . *the actions that are the repertoire* do not remain the same.'[14] Such temporalities cannot be understood within any temporal imaginary that contains the 'when' of heritage exclusively within ←P→P←F→, the containing figure of historical time we introduced in the previous chapter.[15] Undoing reliance on the self-evidence of ←P→P←F→, which operate as categories that essentially *manage* responses to heritage temporalities that are always different, processual, polluted *and* expressed, is key to taking 'up the baton'[16] relayed by the transmission of 'living' traditions. Like the digitised artifacts we will encounter later in the book, such traditions *enact* and *unleash* temporal differences.

Taking seriously the liveness of intangible cultural traditions, those modes of transmission located in the changeable repertoire, while seeking 'an integrated approach to heritage, where heritage is seen as an aspect of *everyday* life (that is, culture),'[17] my aim is to elaborate on the multiple yet singular, differential temporalities that infuse and spread within all transmission processes. When operationalised, they happen at no other time than the instances of their enactment, drawing the actions of *selected* traditions *into* and *through* the world. Already-there, all heritages are actually 'living,' or have the potential to be so, even if they are accessed and operationalised according to different degrees of organisation and intensity. Not all heritages, that is, can rejoin or animate long-circuits, circuits that can strengthen, weaken, break or rot in/as time, depending on their levels of concentration and singular or collective transmission. Exploring how such processes *operate* is key to the project in this book that seeks to articulate a politics of transmission without recourse to ←P→P←F→. Such a politics of transmission never looks *only* forward or *only* backward; it looks, feels and senses everywhere. 'Living' heritage. Take the tense of expression as a point of emergence: Living, not lived. Not will live, could live or can live; living, continuous and alive. Living but not 'not dead.' Living as proximate, unashamedly inauthentic, imitative and transmitting, those time-based cultural practices that *express* temporal difference, time as difference, time that is always changing as it moves across varying degrees of receptivity in circuits. When such modes of cultural heritage are practiced, traditions are alive and continuous, echoing Alexander's refiguring of the 'relationship to Time and its purpose.'[18] Examining cultural practices rooted in the temporal structures of do*ing* facilitates access to different spatial orientations available within scenes of transmission. *Across. Down. Again. Up. Diagonal. Everywhere.*

The arguments in this chapter draw upon and respond to a growing body of scholarly work exploring the intersection of performance theory and heritage studies. As Jenny Kidd and Anthony Jackson argue, performance theory is 'an important theoretical construct with which to analyse and understand a wide variety of social experiences' encompassing the production and reception of heritage across a variety of locations such as museums, archives and historic sites.[19] Performance theory also helps us to understand the significance and distinctiveness of live expressions as time-based phenomena.[20] Within such a schema performances embody durations of time, moments through which those participating—be they performers or audience members—experience temporal differences as unfolding in/of time that cannot be grasped simplistically as $\leftarrow P \rightarrow P \leftarrow F \rightarrow$. Time, in performance, is live—it is happening. It can be mediated, of course, and 'liveness' can also be simulated and constructed—synchronised.[21] As audiences we understand that performance is artificial, but such artifice is believed nonetheless because disbelief is suspended. For this reason, performance may help us to 'expand our concept of authenticity,' fostering a reexamination of the esteem bestowed upon truth, objectivity and the preference for 'critical distance.'[22] After all, the performative acting out of cultural forms has significant and enduring embodied legacies; they make the world through doing, as Judith Butler pointed out in her discussion of gender.[23] A similar orientation can be discerned in relation to time: transmission as a performative rendering of temporal difference that is operationalised through its doing—its announcement and enactment.

Rebecca Schneider has demonstrated how the performative cultural rituals of historical reenactment societies can create temporal contact zones within which 'the *feel*—the affective engagement [of] a physical collapse of time'[24] occurs. Although these different temporalities are amplified in deliberate moments of performative operationalisation (the reenacted Civil War battle, the medieval jousting contest), I want to argue that this is how time functions more broadly, even if it clearly manifests within transmissive iterations that appeal to performative liveness. As Schneider reminds us, 'Inside the archive *or* out, times touch,'[25] and within digital culture, as we shall explore later on, times are touching *all the time*. Performance theory offers then a series of very important openings for our further examination of how feminism's already-there can be understood to be transmitting. First, cultural formations are performative, emergent through processes of *doing* that bring them into action (operationalisation). Secondly, cultural forms are temporal phenomena—they are occasions in which to experience a deliberate organisation of time. In this sense, performative events are temporal objects capable of producing differential time consciousness. These are not reducible to consciousness, but also generate embodied techniques (the movement of the body with/in time) as a core part of the transmission process. Finally, authenticity doesn't matter—temporalities are expressed and composed by differences that bifurcate, distort, disappear, appear, restore and degrade the transmitted performative signal in organised, yet unexpected, ways.

Social Movements as Intangible Cultural Heritage

How then might the cultural heritage of leftist and anti-capitalist social movements be understood as intangible and in need of protection in the current economic context? Non-monumental, ephemeral and endangered, there is certainly an argument to be made for safeguarding cultural traditions that elaborate social values, ideas and cultural practices that offer alternatives to the homogenising cultural forces of globalisation, and its attendant capitalist hegemonies. Writing in 2001, J. K. Gibson-Graham observed:

> Fueled by the 'fall of socialism' in 1989, references are rampant to the inevitability of capitalist penetration and the naturalness of capitalist domination. The dynamic image of penetration and domination is linked to a vision of the world as already or about to be wholly capitalist—that is, a world 'rightfully owned' by capitalism.[26]

Despite Gibson-Graham's insistence that it is possible to intervene in the apparent inevitability of the 'globalization script,'[27] capitalism has, since the early years of the twenty-first century, expanded and contracted unevenly across locations across the world. *How then are alternatives and alternative traditions kept alive?* How do different ways of life become consistent, probable, realistic, shared and communicated beyond the realm of the individual? How do they become a resilient long-circuit? A key point about (feminist) social movements I want to make here, and it seems self-evident but nonetheless it must be stated, is that they do not merely articulate *opposition* to inequalities or injustices; they articulate different worldviews, relations and ways of being. Gail Lewis's insistence, quoted earlier in the book, that the 'culture of being, how we related to each other'[28] was an integral part of the black women's movement, is indicative of how social movements create cultural forms that bear the hallmarks of their identities, ideas, values and activities: '*practices, representations, expressions, knowledge, skills*—as well as the *instruments, objects, artifacts* and *cultural spaces.*' In this sense, social movement traditions bear remarkable affinity to the forms of organisation and transmission of cultural heritage imagined by UNESCO as pertaining to ICH, albeit in the context of indigenous and 'preindustrial' folk heritage. After all, UNESCO claims, 'Each people has a right to its own culture [because] adherence to that culture is often eroded by the impact of industrialized culture purveyed by the mass media.'[29] What, then, of the feminist people? Do *they* have a right to their culture? 'Local' and fragmented, connected through informal networks and ephemeral, improvised gatherings, social movement culture is rarely marked by monuments, buildings and enduring material remains. The cultural heritage of social movements is instead operationalised in times of need and possibility. It accrues meaning through the animation of ideas and action that form part of an explicit, or more likely implicit, circuit, forged with others striving for a similar goal. As Eyerman and Jamison write:

> The central social process is what we term . . . the mobilization of tradition: in social movements, musical and other kinds of traditions are made and remade, and after the movements fade away as political forces, the music remains as a memory and a potential way to inspire new waves of mobilisation.[30]

The extent to which 'music remains as a memory,' or can remain, is questionable given the unofficial, sometimes chaotic and unsupported nature of oppositional, grassroots social movements. As we shall see, the archiving and transmission of social movement cultures so often depends on a mixture of chance and determination at both ends of a circuit: *Labour* is required to organise a collection (deposit items in an physical archive, organise cataloguing or scan materials for digital dissemination). *Labour* is also required to *seek out* a collection so it can be operationalised as a 'potential way to inspire new waves of mobilization,' a point that will be further explored—and enacted—within subsequent chapters.

Feminist Social Movements and Intangible Culture

There is a modest collection of research that analyses the intangible aspects of social movement culture that we can learn from. Anna Feigenbaum, for example, has pointed to the importance of songs in fostering collective identities at Greenham Women's Peace Camp.[31] In a semiautobiographical article, Anna Reading writes about her experiences of Greenham Common (and subsequent reunions), examining the ways in which social movement cultures are embodied as living traditions among participants, often circulating within limited networks.

> The songs and the women who sang them . . . represent the living archives of nonviolent struggles. . . . While these were mediated at the time, in songbooks and pamphlets, their circulation remained largely limited to the community of women that created them.[32]

The wider focus in Reading's article is on how digital technologies widen the 'web of transmission' for ephemeral materials produced within social movements. Yet the way she describes how traditions of feminist nonviolent struggle are kept alive in the living memories of transmitters cannot be overlooked for the obvious convergence with conceptions of ICH. Reading clearly articulates how the culture of social movements is embedded in specific communities—that is, within specific circuits of transmission. Although limited to certain communities of interest (communities of consciousness, or of feeling?), they also had the capacity to traverse boundaries of location, as Reading reflects:

> The ripples from Greenham were far more internationalised in the 1980s than I thought. These globalised connections were woven at the time as part of the nonviolent struggle *well before digital connectivity*. Feminists moved around the world, nurturing links between and with other related struggles, with the international peace movement connected through its various camps at different global sites.[33]

As a complex set of ideas and cultural practices, then, 'feminism' can be used to connect people across varied locations. It '*provides them with a sense of identity and continuity*' that helps to foster meaning, purpose, a rootedness in the world. Feminism invents and transmits traditions that are diverse, multiple and more or less radical—after all, 'an inheritance is never gathered together, it is never one with itself.'[34] Feminism emerges around, and is operationalised by, communities of practice because it '*is constantly recreated by communities and groups in response to their environments, their interaction with nature and their history.*' It is therefore necessary to pay attention to the specific languages, symbolism and forms of identity deployed in the women's peace movement during the 1980s, and how they envisioned international connections, solidarity and 'webs' of resistance.[35] Or consider how the term 'sister' became a term of identification within the US WLM and travelled to other parts of the world, designating 'a relationship that either emerges or does not emerge out of certain actions and activist commitments.'[36] Note the significance of the Women's Social and Political Union (WSPU)'s gifts of small silver hammer brooches to members who carried out militant activities against property.[37] Or that 'riot grrrl' rapidly became a term for a set of specific cultural practices related to punk feminism that resonated with feminists outside of Olympia, Washington, and Washington, D.C., who were hungry for rebellious modes of political resistance. These are all examples (and there are, of course, many others) of how feminist cultural practices were *constantly reinterpreted* by groups interacting with the reconfiguration of women's 'nature' and history—history being here the *local* historical context in which activation of feminism's already-there occurs. Yet there *is* a common thread that links these diverse manifestations and expressions emergent from within feminism's already-there. If organised, they could form a consistent, concentrated long-circuit without losing any of the material, practical and interpretive specificities of generational locations. This is what is *politically* at stake in transmission—these different expressions of feminism do not merely outline *identities*. They correspond to sets of everyday cultural practices that remake the world through collective operationalisation that mobilises techniques of creative resistance that exist within *feminism's already-there*.

UK Women's Liberation Music—A Case Study of ICH

Women's liberation politics in the UK came in many different forms. Activists published newspapers and books, lived in squatted separatist communities, ran taxi companies and set up women's refuges; they campaigned to transform policy and the law, established community nurseries and did many other things that redefined the parameters of the political. Collectives were part of the wider UK and international movement, but they also formed specific networks of interest, focusing on areas such as manual trades, theatre or publishing. Music-making in the WLM functioned in a number of different ways. Bands would play at fund-raising benefits, socials and marches, and songs were used partly to create the collective 'identity' of the movement. Women's liberation music was also a microcosm of the movement, a movement within a movement. Women developed theories and practices about how to make music in a feminist way, and these interventions existed alongside other politicised discussions in the movement about health, child care, domestic labour, sexuality, war, internationalism, anti-imperialism and many others. The politicisation of music resulted in running skill-sharing workshops, carrying all the equipment to shows, learning how to work the PA and sound desks, playing certain instruments, creating women-only discos, making new instruments, writing songs in a particular way or adopting a genre as it was apparently more 'feminist.' Through the exploration of these practices, the feminist musical movement created its own specific networks and ways of doing things. These can be identified as the '*practices, representations, expressions, knowledge, skills*'—as well as the '*instruments, objects, artifacts* and *cultural spaces*' associated with the music-making of the WLM.

Feminist music-making was also independent of other radical music initiatives of the 1970s, such as punk and do-it-yourself, even if there were crossovers in terms of the strategies used, such as setting up record labels or organising independent cultural spaces. An important thing to understand about the music-making communities of the WLM is that they were activist *and* theoretical communities. Theorising emerged, of course, from women's lives ('the personal is the political'), but also as women engaged with institutions and representations that were part of the everyday oppressions they sought to deconstruct. Commercial popular music, culture and the leisure industry were for women's liberationists a key area where women were 'kept in their place.' 'With the growth of mass media and popular music, women are subjected to a barrage of songs, on radio and on television, which belittle them by describing them as babies, chicks, dolls, which reinforce all the stereotypes about us,'[38] members of the London-based Women's Liberation Music Project wrote.

The newsletters and discussions relating to women and music record the infiltration of mass-media culture and its increased influence on everyday life. Written mainly between 1974 and 1978, key documents, such as the Northern Women's Liberation Rock Band's Manifesto (1974), the publication *Women and Music* and the *Sisters in Song* songbook (1979), suggest that the media industry was young enough for women's liberation music-makers to view it as a contingent rather than inevitable part of cultural life, and thus it was therefore possible to envision concrete alternatives to it. 'We need to evolve an autonomous music that reflects who we are, that speaks to women where they live that cannot be co-opted by the leisure industry.'[39] Such statements were inherent to the feminist challenge to the capitalist music *industry*, which located the systemic exploitation of women in all areas of culture. Dispelling the dominant sexist, capitalist culture required a complete overhaul of economic and personal relations—and music was a vital part of that process of transformation. Women's liberation music was therefore highly *un*popular in relation to the commercial values of the 1970s music industry. They did not want to be part of the mainstream industry and actively sought to create an alternative to it. Resisting co-option was key to the WLM music's unpopularity: creating independent women-only networks across the UK, Europe, the United States and beyond that circulated 'women's music' to likeminded 'sisters.'[40]

Women's Music

Part matriarchal myth-making, part 'bloodless revolution' and a kind of total, cultural warfare, 'women's music' emerged from the United States with acts such as Meg Christian, BeBe K'Roche, Cris Williamson, Holly Near and Alix Dobkin. Olivia and Redwood Records are two of the most well-known examples of women-run, women-only record labels from the United States, and they were used as a blueprint for feminists in the UK seeking autonomy from male control. As a concept and activist strategy, 'women's music' travelled to the UK, often via British women who had been to the United States and had witnessed the development of an autonomous women's scene. Alison Rayner (Jam Today, the Guest Stars), Teresa Hunt (Jam Today), Jane Boston and Tash Fairbanks (Devil's Dykes, Bright Girls and Siren), as well as traditional folk singer Frankie Armstrong,[41] had all visited the United States in the early 1970s prior to the development of 'women's music' in the UK that blossomed towards the end of the decade. Perhaps most significantly, Caroline Hutton, who ran the feminist record distribution service Women's Revolution Per Minute (WRPM) from 1979 to 1999, had also visited the United States. The connections she made there with 'women's music' communities were crucial for the dissemination of women's music through the WRPM.[42] This excerpt from an early WRPM catalogue (1977/1978) clearly describes the emerging influence of US women's music on feminist communities in the UK:

> We were originally called the Olivia Records Collective, but now we are stocking other women's records. . . . We want to set up as widespread distribution of feminist music as possible, reaching women in many areas around the country. Hopefully we will not only supply women with music they have been wanting, but also stimulate interest and confidence in producing more music. So far there has been no such network of women's music, and only women in London, or a few with contacts in the States, have been able to get hold of records by women, that have a self-defined feminist or lesbian/ feminist identity.[43]

Of course, highlighting the importance of the US women's music scene is not to suggest that women were not exploring how to combine music and activism before the 'American invasion.' There were a number of collectives in the UK who began to play music together and perform at activist events in the early 1970s. The London Women's Liberation Rock Band (1972–1974) began after women discussed playing music together at the Third National Women's Liberation Conference in Manchester, 1972.[44] Frankie Green, original member of the London Women's Liberation Rock Band, Jam Today 1, and co-founder of the Women's Liberation Music Archive (WLMA), describes how

> we placed a notice in the London Women's Liberation workshop weekly newsletter and lots of women responded who wanted to play, discuss and develop feminist music; they got together at Hazel Twort's council flat in Peckham and from that grew the London Women's Rock Band. At the first practice our instruments were acoustic and I was drumming on saucepans with chopsticks. Later, helped by donations from other women, we acquired some instruments and a primitive PA

system, and played at the next national WLM conference at Acton Town Hall in
October '72, handing out songsheets and inviting women to join in.[45]

The London Women's Liberation Rock Band practiced many of the
values that would be so important to the development of 'women's music'
as it ebbed and flowed with the movement: demystifying music-making,
sharing skills with other women and using music as a 'practical expression
of our politics' fuelled by 'not wanting only to be involved in theoretical
debate' but also 'challenge conventional splits between political theory and
real life, activism and culture.'[46] Other feminist initiatives at the time had
similarly catchy names such as the Women's Street Theatre Group (who
collaborated with members of the London Women's Liberation Rock Band
on the 1974 film *The Amazing Equal Pay Show*). The Manchester-based
Northern Women's Liberation Rock Band (1973–1976) was the next major
known band to emerge from the WLM, followed by the East London–based
Stepney Sisters (1974–1976).

What is striking about the names of these bands is how they wear their
regional affiliation firmly on their sleeve. While the WLM was certainly a national movement, supported by national conferences throughout the 1970s,
the importance of decentralised regional networks, which sustained the
movement, cannot be underestimated. These early bands helped to develop
'women's music' in the UK. They turned to each other for mutual support—
the Northern Women's Liberation Rock Band and the Stepney Sisters, for
example, had a weekend skill-sharing session where they stayed in a country-
side barn and jammed together.[47] The equipment acquired by feminist music-
makers was used in workshops and at benefit events, such as the Women's
Monthly Event held in London. Women's music definitely developed in the
UK at a grassroots level throughout the 1970s; yet very little of it was recorded
'on tape.' Even in 1980 the WRPM catalogue included this telling note: 'Most
of the records we carry are imported from the USA, as that is where the vast
majority of feminist music has come from so far.'[48]

Recovery and Tradition

Emerging from the second British folk revival, Frankie Armstrong was a significant reinterpreter of women's folk traditions. Alongside Peggy Seeger and
Sandra Kerr, Armstrong was part of the Critics Group who released *The Female Frolic* in 1968, an album of songs that focused on women's experiences.
This record included songs such as 'The Doffin Mistress,' 'The Factory Girl,'
'Miner's Wife' and 'The Whore's Lament.' Armstrong describes the emerging
feminist consciousness that informed this work:

In 1966, the men in the group were invited by Argo record company to do al-bums on sea songs and shanties, so off they went to research Ewan [MacColls]'s books. Sandra, Peggy and I were left, and the obvious thing for us to do something around women and women's history through songs. That was when we started researching. That's how come we put together *The Female Frolic*. We toured it and found poems, proverbs, contemporary accounts of women's lives and what was said about women by women. We would have called ourselves Socialists, I guess. We looked at it from that perspective. That certainly laid the ground for what happened to us a few years later when we got more caught up overtly in the women's movement.[49]

Armstrong, Kerr and Kathy Anderson later published the book *My Song Is My Own: 100 Women's Songs*, accompanied by an album of the same name in 1979, which continued the documentation and recovery of women's musical heritage that began with *The Female Frolic*. 'Women's music,' as a cultural practice that emerged in the UK WLM, was therefore about the recovery *and* invention of tradition. Consider this excerpt taken from an A4 pamphlet-magazine *Women and Music* (1978) that indicates how strong emotional attachments to the *practice* of rediscovering cultural traditions circulated among certain parts of the women's movement:

> These songs are one way of partially rediscovering our hidden history. If art is about trying to express the truth as we see it, making sense and shape out of the chaos and complexity and trying to make us more whole as people in a society that fragments, stereotypes and divides us, then the best of the tradition can be said to stand alongside women artists. The creators of these songs were our ancestors—all those grandmothers and great-great-grandmothers forced into service or the mills and finding comfort in the old and new popular songs.[50]

The search for musical legacies mirrored wider historical work conducted by women in the movement—the most well-known example being Sheila Rowbotham's seminal text *Hidden from History* (1975), which sought to render visible women's political struggles from the seventeenth to the early twentieth century.[51] 'Hidden from History' was also the title of a song by the Brighton-based women's band Bright Girls. The song's lyrics explore the 'women unknown to me,' challenging listeners to look beyond 'what we learnt in school.'[52] Outside of music-making, women's liberationists set up publish-ing houses such as Virago and the Women's Press, whose Modern Classics se-ries republished 'lost' feminist authors such as George Egerton, Sarah Grand, Rebecca West, Marge Piercy, Maya Angelou, Kate Chopin, Antonia White, Zora Neale Hurston and many others.[53] Women's liberationists acted, there-fore, on a deeply cultural level, retrieving and disseminating the memories of women's political struggles and their cultural achievements as part of wider strategies to restore pride, confidence, equality and legitimacy to women's place in history. In the process, their activist work helped furnish feminism's already-there with greater concentration of both resources *and* circuitry.

Practices, Knowledge, Skills

Women's liberation music-making created cultural practices through which feminist techniques, and ways of doing things, were enacted in the world. These cultural practices were not simply about getting more women to play music, but about changing the way music was played. Mavis Bayton, member of Oxford-based melodic pop-rock band the Mistakes (1978–1983), writes that women's liberation music-makers created an 'alternative musical world of their own'[54] that sought to remove itself from the shackles of male dominance and corporate control.

Making music accessible to all women, and creating spaces where women could 'try out' different instruments and playing styles, was then a central part of the cultural practice of women's liberation music-making. The 1981 short film *In Our Own Time*, made by the Bristol-based film collective Women in Moving Pictures (W.I.M.P.S), documents the practices of women-only music-making, and how this translated as a cultural politics that empowered *womyn*'s social and political voice. *Practices* are politically significant: applied concepts, they are the *techniques* and supports that enable the possibility of collective worlds in becoming.[55] Practices are the processes put into bodily-active-motion, relations moving together, through which knowledge can emerge. The film is a documentation of such processes: women sat in a circle playing the pennywhistle and singing, *appropriating* the musical *savoir-faire* that had been denied to them; two women perform experimental saxophone while another makes abstract strokes on a canvas with a paintbrush, demonstrating the coexistence of older techniques and emergent cultural forms; in a darkroom a group learns self-defence to the soundtrack of 'Women of War' performed by the artist Jo Chambers,[56] evoking the fierce tribal spirit of Monique Wittig's poetic novel *Les Guérillères*; as Chambers sings, eyes closed, with her guitar, the close-up from the camera lingers, dwelling on the intensity of her delivery; women discuss the importance of music in their lives as they take their children to the playground; women perform a song they had collectively written that explores feelings, frustrations and elaborates experiences.

'I feel it's really important that women create their own songs, their own culture, musical culture,' one of the participants states during a consciousness-raising cum skill-sharing session.[57] The closing scene of the film depicts women organising a performance space, carrying huge amplifiers up a set of stairs—a potent symbol of women's autonomy and strength—before the

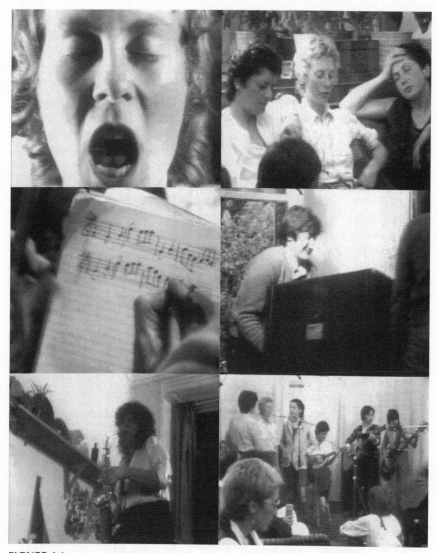

FIGURE 4.1
In Our Own Time (reproduced with permission from Women in Moving Pictures,
collage selections made by author).

group of music-makers performs a song for the women in their community. They sing, 'The time is here, the time is now, the time to find our anger.' The collective articulation of ideas 'whose time has come,' time performatively enacted as urgency, presence, action and realisation: here-now; a time whose intelligibility is operationalised through the reinvigoration of its place within a circuit—the time of women's liberation culture, grounded in and emerging through distinct techniques and practices.

Women's liberation music-making practices reappropriated musical techniques from the already-there, using them to further women's liberation. Both *In Our Own Time* and *Rapunzel, Let Down Your Hair* (which will be discussed later in the chapter) present women writing musical notation as part of the documentation of women's culture, leaving deliberate traces for subsequent activations of feminism's already-there. The notations indicate that this is music to be performed, interpreted and operationalised rather than simply *consumed*. We see such notations in the *Sisters in Song* songbook (see figure 4.2). Carefully marked out in black ink, the songbook was a means to archive, transmit and mobilise the songs of women's liberation among communities. Recording the music exactly is a performative mark of respect and esteem, a feminist reappropriation of male-dominated musical form.

FIGURE 4.2
Maggie Nicols, 'Changing,' *Sisters in Song* (1979) (Feminist Archive South, DM2598/5).

In other instances, the modes of documentation are not deliberate and less exact. Scrawled letters, representing which chords are to be played, can be found above song lyrics. From this evidence melodies can be reconstructed in any number of ways that may not be 'faithful' to the original. In the absence of alternative technics of transmission (i.e., an exact tape recording), how it is 'supposed' to sound can only ever be an approximation, a guess.

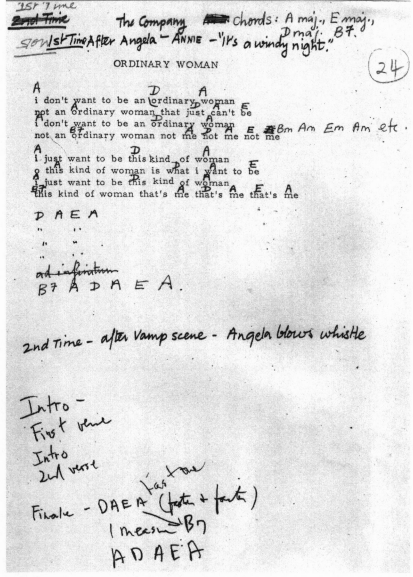

FIGURE 4.3
'Ordinary Woman,' Sistershow Revisited (Feminist Archive South, DM2606).

There were also attempts to deconstruct music-making practices, knowledge and skills, as an article written for *Shocking Pink*, a feminist publication aimed at younger women, demonstrates: 'Don't be intimidated or put off by boys who might try and make fun of you. Remember, that's *their* problem, *not* yours.'[58] (See figure 4.4.)

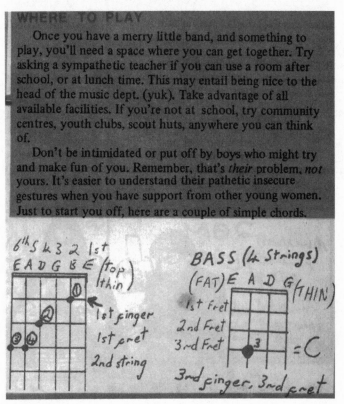

FIGURE 4.4
Excerpt from *Shocking Pink* (Feminist Archive South, DM2123/5).

There was not, in other words, one way to define the practices of women's liberation music-making, and as more women began to play music in the movement, the question of what women's music 'is' was debated time and time again. 'We don't pretend to know what women's music is, it is only the beginning'[59] was a common perspective, suggestive of openness, rather than outright conceptual confusion. The WRPM catalogues stated that 'women's, or Feminist music is woman-identified, it is about women's strength and caring, our experiences in a male-owned and identified society, and our struggle for change both in that society and in ourselves.'[60] The lack of firm definition is also talked about in the introduction to *Sisters in Song*, written in 1979 by Tierl Thompson, Janie Fairchild and Andrea Webb, who were members of the Women's Liberation Music Project Group.

> While there is still an ongoing debate as to what 'women's music' really is, we feel we must challenge all aspects of music making. This means challenging not only the words of the songs, but how we present them, avoiding male-defined styles such as 'cock-rock,' looking critically at what different styles of music represent and helping each other with criticism. We don't want to encourage stars and we feel that performing is not more important than other activities. We want to encourage women to have expectations of themselves musically, either as listeners, players, or whatever. Not only are we not encouraged to play, but we are encouraged to listen in a passive way.[61]

The key point to grasp here is that women's liberation music-makers were not solely concerned with writing and performing feminist music; this was 'no more important than other activities.' They wanted to transform the whole culture of music-making from top to bottom, and make something new in its place. As the tone of this quote indicates, these practices were never easy. Criticism—of both self and others—is emphasised, and the multiple interpretations and so-called openness of women's music could lead to heated conflicts among women in the movement.

Representations, Expressions

> [Commercial pop] songs help to keep women in their accustomed role of wives and mothers, dependent on men, because they hide the real conflicts in women's lives and relationships with men and so prevent them from understanding their oppression.[62]

> Popular music pours out endless, unrealistic clichés about love and relationships which are of course exclusively heterosexual. These ideas about relationships limit us all.[63]

For women's liberation music-makers, culture was, quite simply, a battlefield peppered with numerous examples of 'the mighty male wielding his instrument like a weapon.'[64] Dominant representations of women as weak, ornamental and dependent acted as sites of profound cultural-symbolic violence that had intense effects on the lives of women. They limited perceptions of what women could do, and the kinds of intimacies that could be imagined within society. To challenge this situation, women's liberation music-makers created an array of counterrepresentations that elevated women's independence, autonomy and strength. 'We want freedom, changes, power,' sang Jam Today 1, 'realise our dreams/change our lives in every way' because 'revolution is on its way right now.'

This song, and the band Jam Today 1, are featured in the celebratory closing sequence of 1978 feminist film *Rapunzel, Let Down Your Hair*, in which members of Jam Today gather a gang of women to watch them perform in a pub.[65] In a moment of exuberant collective liberation, women sip ale from pint glasses and marvel at the performance of female strength and independence. In the context of the film as a whole, a rewriting of traditional fairy tales that inculcate heterosexist, gendered behaviours in innocent children, it is a moment of cunning subversion. Similar to *In Our Own Time*, there is a convergence of cultural forms in the women's movement, as films acted as a platform to express the different aesthetic possibilities of women's culture. Theatre and music shared an equally hybrid relationship, as modes of improvisational techniques influenced groups like Contradictions, Clapperclaw and the Feminist Improvising Group (FIG). Former FIG members Sally Potter and Lindsay Cooper collaborated on the 1983 film *The Gold Diggers*, a film that similarly combines music, dance and the moving image to express an anti-capitalist feminist aesthetic.[66] 'Seeing Red,' the song that opens the film, criticises the images usually encountered on trips to the cinema: 'please please give me back my pleasure/please give me back my big night out/please give me back my leisure time'[67] is the demand, phrased within Cooper's lurching, anti-chorus score. Brighton-based Siren Theatre Company used music within their plays to express ideas, atmospheres and feminist values. The persistence of narrow representations is ironically played with on the only release by Jam Today (3), 'Stereotyping.' The cover depicts members of the band dressed in stereotypical women's roles (as a secretary, housewife and prostitute), while the lyrics unfurl a list of ways women can be insulted—gossip, witch, 'she'll give you the itch,' 'a good lay'—and singer Barbara Stretch melodically huffs that she is 'totally sick to death with' the limitations placed on women's lives.

The feminist critique extended to challenge the very fabric of 'man-made' linguistic representation itself: 'Your language has left me in limbo,' Siren sang in 'Language' from the self-released tape album *In Queer Street* (1985). The song also contains the following lyrics:

> In the beginning was the word
> and the word was always he
> He is me
> Its semantics
> But I'm not fooled by the royal we . . .
>
> I'm lost for words
> None of them are mine
> Your words fail me
> Every time.[68]

Women's estrangement from the communicative and meaning-making tools of the already-there meant that the cultural strategies of women's liberationists were a mixture of rewriting, subverting and reappropriating older forms and techniques, as well as inventing new forms, symbols, languages and expressions from which to express women's 'liberated' experiences. Songs such as Ova's 'Rainbowomon,' 'Lesbian Fighting Song' and 'Neither Gives In' extolled the pleasures, pains and possibilities of lesbian feminist relationships, while the Stepney Sisters' song 'Sisters' encouraged women to 'find their *true natures*/Hidden under cover.' Women's liberation culture charted, invented, named and practiced transformations in women's nature and history. The Northern Women's Liberation Rock Band's 'Matriarchy,' which survives in lyric form as it was distributed alongside their manifesto, evokes this sense of recovering and reconnecting with a deeper, mythical tradition of women's strength.

> Ponder the long time in between
> Down underground, quite rarely seen,
> Maintaining a guerrilla in the heart,
> A secret angry heart.
> *We took care to choose our ground,*
> *Left few records, smothered sounds.*
> Witches only came out at night,
> Pain in every fire flame bright.
> Coming out in a new way,
> Beginning to taste the day.[69]

The ephemeral, 'secret,' yet resilient notion of 'women's culture' is described in these lyrics, a series of knowledges 'quite rarely seen' but nonetheless 'coming out in a new way.' This intangible culture that 'left few records,' only 'smothered sounds.'

Instruments

Are instruments gendered? What role does amplified music have in 'women's culture'? How can a song be written in a 'feminist' way? What is the sound of women's liberation? While there is anecdotal evidence that women discussed making their own instruments—unique, feminist instruments, or their own versions of 'male' instruments like guitars (Deirdre Cartwright allegedly cried when she was told she had to do this by fellow women in the movement[70])—no remains of such materials have so far been discovered. Questions of song-writing process (collective, ideally) and aesthetics became prominent. The Northern Women's Liberation Rock Band, for example, described their sound as 'strong but not heavy.'[71] Nottingham-based band the Fabulous Dirt Sisters were aesthetically influenced by the peace movement, and wanted to create music that could express the *values* of feminist non-violence, but also embody these principles through instrumentation. Such eschewing of heavier sounds (if not amplification entirely) meant that, on the whole, women's liberation music-makers avoided the aggressive sound of punk music, opting instead for music that women could 'bop' to, often fusing genres such as funk, blues, soul, rock and jazz.

'Lead' guitars were uncomfortably looked upon. If women chose to play extended solos on the electric guitar, it was seen a political choice that perpetuated certain cultural formations. 'Cock-rock' was to be avoided at all costs because of how it imitated the styles, gestures, codes, performances and structures of masculinity that fundamentally oppressed all women. Terri Quaye stated that 'women who go into music want to create their own sound, it's not to *impersonate the male sound*.'[72] On the other hand, some women felt learning to play instruments that had been coded masculine in a proficient manner was a powerful feminist act: 'There was the expectation from the world that we weren't going to be any good, so it was important that you should be as good as you could be.'[73] Women's liberation music-makers *instrumentalised* cultural forms that were already-there in order to express a different, women-centred culture in which 'new feelings, relationships and attitudes towards each other'[74] could emerge. This different instrumentalisation was also reflected in the organisation of music, as Ova explained in an interview on the radio show *Inside London*: 'Our music is political because we don't have a standard line up. Neither one of us is a lead singer for example, we both sing. We don't believe in hierarchy, which makes it difficult to break into a hierarchical world.'[75]

Objects, Artifacts

As the Northern Women's Liberation Rock Band state in their song 'Matriarchy,' women's cultures *'left few records, smothered sounds.'* Part of what makes the cultural heritage of women's liberation music-making so intangible for later generations is its lack of material remains. Significant amounts of women's liberation culture were not recorded in a tangible form, and there are very few 'finished' pieces of musical work such as an album or seven-inch single. This means we encounter the already-there of women's liberation musical memory as scraps of reproduced photocopies, recordings of live performances and practices, photos, newsletters, manifestos, posters, magazine listings, fliers, films, TV documentaries and appearances, songbooks and sheets. The legacy is fragmentary, partial, dispersed, improvised and largely disorganised, mimicking the 'smothered sounds' of matriarchal memories—intangible traditions that cannot be grasped entirely. Like the song sheets and musical notations discussed earlier, this aspect of feminism's already-there necessitates decoding and interpretation. It cannot be *consumed* in a straight-forward way; it has to be *practiced* in a committed and creative manner if the cultural forms are to come *alive* (operationalised) through acts of trans-mission. In order to activate legacy and tradition, work is required so that a meaningful circuit can be created.

A lack of knowledge, money, time, resources and confidence impacted the extent of recorded music we can access today. After all, recorded musical artifacts are what we expect to find in the (popular) music archives. This is not to say that there are no recorded artifacts of women's liberation music. Yet the musicians may not see the recordings we can access as an adequate representation of their music or sonic identity, as we shall discuss in depth in later chapters.[76] The technological environment women's liberation music-makers were situated in was also significant: Although becoming amenable to low-financed recording ventures in the late 1970s, home recording remained inaccessible for many music-makers, and recording studios were often finan-cially prohibitive. Yet these 'unfinished' remains also present an opportunity because they help communicate temporalities embedded in process, action and doing, the temporalities of intangible transmission. The theoretical im-plications of this point will be explored in more detail in later chapters.

Cultural Spaces

Too often the sexism of popular and progressive music invades and insults the occasion, marring the experience of just being with other women. We felt the need to use music as a force for us to express new feelings, relationships and attitudes to each other that we are trying to create in the Women's Movement.[77]

[Women's discos] were a crucial space for women's to socialise in, and for lesbi-ans to interact and have a social and romantic space, where they wouldn't be at-tacked, where they could feel relaxed, and not be subject to people's judgement. At the worst end attacked, but at least being stared at.[78]

I remember on the inside of the disco it was absolutely fantastic. The bonding of women together, they were dancing and throwing their tops off. It wasn't like an average disco. There was real self-discovery and recognition. It was very excit-ing. I loved it! But the energy on the outside was very threatening.[79]

[Performing on the street was about] the unexpected. There was no set script. We were trying to be a breath of fresh air by surprising people who passed by.[80]

This selection of quotes from women's liberation music-makers demon-strates the different ways that autonomous cultural spaces accrued significance for women in the movement. Whether that was in terms of feminist space being 'invaded' by the artifacts and symbols of male culture (the moment when 'Under My Thumb' by the Rolling Stones is played at the feminist disco, 'insulting' the occasion), or the sanctity of 'self-discovery and recognition' described by Jana Runnalls, cultural spaces in the women's movement were ephemeral sites where the culture of women's liberation was expressed. *Where* such events took place is less important than what happened within them: the energetic secretions they emitted, which now operate as residual tremors of possibility within feminism's already-there. These sites where feminist culture was made emerged out of nothing, often located within temporary accommodation such as squatted buildings or community centres. It would be hard, therefore, to place a plaque to mark where such events took place, an increasingly common practice acknowledging sites of popular musical memory.[81] Most likely the physical space has long been transformed through redevelopment and gentrification, bearing no trace of the radical cultural politics that were temporarily housed there.

Ultimately cultural spaces acted as platforms for creating 'new feelings, relationships and attitudes to each other.'[82] Music was a crucial part of these emergent social formations, as the NWLRB reflected after their performance at the 1974 National Women's Liberation Conference in Edinburgh: 'After the first number, we could really feel the audience with us. . . . The music was no longer ours as a group, it was everybody's and we all wanted it.'[83] This loss of boundaries between performer and audience was the political ideal of women's liberation music-making: It was the moment when hierarchies were overturned, and a different social relationship was realised, no matter how ephemeral that moment was. Yet this act of memorialisation, written by the band weeks after the event, vividly immediate in its intensity, affectively conveys the practice of women's liberation music-making. It demonstrates a moment when the theory of the movement became practice, as a glimpse of a different social organisation was enacted through a collective experience of music. These 'archives of feelings,' notoriously difficult to document and transmit, even as they appear as fragmentary moments, or 'incisions,'[84] within feminism's already-there, are documented by this extraordinary piece of collective writing by the NWLRB.

It would, of course, be unwise to idealise the cultural spaces created in the WLM. In the WLM, politics punctured all aspects of life, including those designated for 'fun.' Forms of social violence and exclusion unique to WLM culture shaped social relations at discos and other musical events. Participants in the movement hurtfully questioned the politics of women who wore certain kinds of clothes, had long hair or wore makeup. Ruth Novaczek, member of the avant-garde band Abandon Your Tutu, described what she experienced as the 'whole mess' of class and cultural politics in London's lesbian feminist cultural spaces in the late 1970s and early 1980s.

> The Feminist, or lesbian feminist scene was a bit conservative, and that was a bit shocking. . . . And the whole class thing, you know everyone was pretending to be working class. I wanted to do something scholarly and broad without being about just one kind of politics. It was the first time I experienced racism and anti-semitism. I used to DJ a lot of Latin music which would get an awful lot of anger. I often had threats of violence and actual violence. I was always encountering angry women telling me I was playing crap music.[85]

Feminists also reclaimed public space by performing on the street. Performing on the street sidesteps traditional structures of gatekeeping that have implicitly refused women the permission to pick up an instrument and perform on the stage. The York Street Band (1978–1982) and the Fabulous Dirt Sisters (1981–1989) created joyful encounters for passersby, guided by chance and surprise. Both bands used instruments such as saxophones, violins, flutes, accordions, percussion and double bass and combined theatrical movement to capture the attention of audiences. The Fabulous Dirt Sisters always wore vibrant colours to affirm their group identity. If the autonomous cultural spaces of the WLM were marked by a certain ideological seriousness, the street performances of the York Street Band and the Fabulous Dirt Sisters were informed by the avant-garde happenings that sought to disrupt the everyday rhythm of 'business-as-usual.'[86] The performances aimed to make audiences question what they were seeing: Is there really a group of five women wearing bright colours, jigging together on the street? Such performances disappeared as quickly as they appeared.

While it is hard to pin down the impact of street performances on audiences, it is clear from the photographic evidence of both bands that they engendered a politics of spontaneity, improvisation and the unplanned. Nothing captures this better than a photograph of the York Street Band taken by John Walmsley.[87] Walmsley told me he had taken a train ride to York as part of a special offer he had seen in a newspaper. While walking around, he encountered the York Street Band on one of their regular self-selecting Saturday residences in the city centre. As the band strikes up, Nelly appears, an older woman who shops in York on a Saturday morning. She has seen the band perform on a number of occasions and always enjoys it. As John surveys the scene, Nelly puts down her shopping bags and moves toward Ros Davies. The two begin to dance together in a rapturous, yet rough-and-ready waltz. Nelly doesn't always feel moved to dance with the band, but today she does. John clicks his camera and light hits the film. Nelly and Ros are smiling—through the infinitely grainy gradations of analogue grey, the photographer captures the energy of the utterly singular moment, a moment that looks outrageously fun and wonderful. Through the photograph the unbridled, spontaneous joy is announced, and, with a lucky accident, turn of fate or both, it transmits the intangible heritage of street performances that were part of the varied fabric of women's liberation culture.

Why Fragmentation?

I close this chapter exploring the intangible quality of women's liberation music-making by focusing on the affective issues complicating the transmission of feminist cultural heritage. A key characteristic of ICH is that it is located in the live time of transmission, often embodied by people who operationalise mnemonic forms through dedicated practice, which results simultaneously in a transformation and preservation of 'tradition.' As outlined in previous chapters, feminism as an epistemic, cultural and political field is defined by generational thinking *as such*. It follows, therefore, that a far greater understanding of the formation and organisation of feminist knowledge-producing communities, which could account for material, economic, social and cultural factors shaping processes of transmission, is required. The question I want to dwell on is why the transmission of WLM music-making has been so fragmented across generations despite being part of relatively recent history—indeed, within 'living memory.' As Nina Power reflected in a review comparing music from the women's liberation movement and contemporary queer/feminist music:

> [T]here are intriguing continuities between the topics of the releases—gender, sexuality, queer politics, squatting/homelessness, among others—but what drops out in the twenty or so years . . . is as instructive as it is revealing: the knowing timidity and embracing of parochialism and marginality of the latter release, and a relative lack of musical inventiveness, is put into sharp contrast with the variety, strangeness and anger of many of the tracks by women's liberation music makers.[88]

How, then, can 'what drops out' be accounted for? Why is it that *long-circuits* have not been established across feminist generations, not quite composed by feminism's already-there? Such long-circuits foster

> less a perception of historical change, than a feeling of temporal depth rooted in the continuities of practical experience. But tradition is not to be understood as mindless persistence. Generally it involves at least a measure of social reverence—a disposition to *value*, rather than simply to repeat, the ways of one's ancestors or the established usages of one's community.[89]

Establishing disposition to value is crucial for the creation of a long-circuit that will enable cultural traditions to be kept alive, not simply as 'mindless persistence,' but as a means to nurture practical knowledge *and* the rooted-ness of being in the world *differently*. The connection enabled through the intersection and concentration of a circuit is not simply a relationship with 'the past,' but a means to activate techniques and operationalise modes of world-making that are ongoing and *already-there* in the 'internally complex, "composite" time, generated through the interweaving of different temporal layers or strands.'[90] Yet this process is endangered when 'the disposition to value' is already a contentious or fragile field (or at least such dispositions are not yet recognised *as* valuable), or when communities are fragmented and dispersed. In such occasions the circuits that made animated activity possible become thin or are broken.

Traumatic Vicinities

The WLM is often mythologised as a tumultuous relational space where women came together with dramatic, politicised intensity and fell apart with equal fervour. Within such an affective social environment it is important to emphasise Cvetkovich's observation that activists who participate in feminist and queer social movements operate within 'the vicinity of trauma.'[91] That is, even if women do not experience trauma directly (in the form of rape, childhood sexual abuse, il/legal abortion or domestic violence), the unbound forces of trauma nevertheless can *press against* relationships in the move-ment, and do so 'largely beneath conscious awareness.'[92] This lack of *con-scious* awareness, coupled with how difficult it can be to express, let alone communicate, traumatic experience in itself within language,[93] made such unresolved traumatic dynamics 'difficult to assimilate and address,' and sub-sequently 'exert[ed] pressure on the movement's existing customs, routines, systems, rituals, procedures.'[94]

Within the context of the WLM, traumatic experiences bound women together: '*I remember on the inside of the disco it was absolutely fantastic. The bonding of women together, they were dancing and throwing their tops off. ... But the energy on the outside was very threatening.*' For women who took social risks in pursuit of greater gender and sexual freedoms, trauma was *always there*, lurking in the background, haunting meetings and conversa-tions between activists, threatening to erupt, unexpectedly, as trauma can do. Within such an unstable relational space, establishing a long-circuit is difficult because it is prone to sudden, abrupt and *incommensurable* rupture. Indeed, traumatic experience has the potential to *rewire the circuit*.[95] For this reason, it may be instructive to think the quality of circuitry in line with Marian Hirsch's 'structure of postmemory,' which is composed of 'multiple ruptures and radical breaks introduced by trauma' that 'inflect intra-, inter- and trans-generational inheritance.'[96]

The affective intensities within feminist communities placed extraordinary pressures on the circuit-connections that relay feminism's already-there. Furthermore, as with most 'living,' ephemeral heritage, the capacity for transmission is embodied in the memories of *transmitters*. When the person 'carrying' such heritage is removed from the circuit, through disaffection, excommunication, exhaustion or disbelief, it is therefore weakened, thus undermining potential to endure across generations. Consider, for instance, the illustration from the *Sisters in Song* songbook shown in figure 4.5. The caption reads, in an almost joking manner, 'Sisterhood has taken a short break.' Yet the image illustrates the interruptions that punctuate the practice of feminist politics, which, in turn, has an impact on processes of transmission. Quite simply, if the door is shut, then so is the potential for communication and participation across circuits. Such affective ennui prevents what is already-there from moving across, to become a wider, more extensive circuit. This is a major issue that has an impact on how feminism's already-there is transmitted across generations.

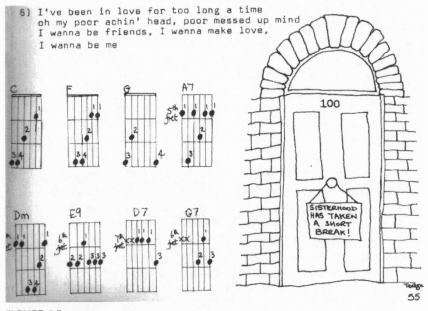

FIGURE 4.5
'Sisterhood has taken a short break' (image from *Sisters in Song* [1979], Feminist Archive South, DM2598/5).

Feminist social movements can be difficult to participate in. They experiment with forms of sociality that can be risky, transgressive and, in terms of normative cultural values, socially unacceptable. In such an experimental environment, people often require breaks in order to manage the intensities that arise from participation. There is the need to shut the door, regroup and sometimes have nothing to do with feminism ever again. Such acts of retreat and self-preservation create significant dropouts in long-circuits; consequently, the transmitted signal dwindles as energy and commitment wane. Sometimes the possibility of one circuit is shut down entirely, but this does not mean others cannot emerge. Circuits are prone to *divergence* rather than total destruction:

> Long circuits of transindividuation assume that each individual participating in the circulation of a circuit—that is, in its facilitation [frayage], its trans-formation, its expression—is a point of origin of this circuit, capable in principle (if not in fact) of re-initializing it, of re-individuating and of re-appropriating it each time as their own, that is, as an irreversible moment of *their* individuation.[97]

Long-circuits have multiple origins, which participants can reactivate and reintialise when they facilitate the movement of knowledge as part of the process of transforming that knowledge. No one person, state or corporation can 'own' a circuit entirely because of the inevitable alterations that occur in the process of transmission. These can distort or amplify information, as well as muffle or quieten it. This is especially true of feminism's already-there: a political, world-making tradition that emerges around a set of *ideas* and *practices* that enact a motivated heritage of interpretation. That is, there are many aspects of feminism's already-there, and therefore many potential ways to emerge within, through and across its circuitry.

Circulating Feminism's Already-There *Across*

Affective insecurities are not the only means to render circuits fragile and sometimes inoperable. For example, in an insightful article Krista Cowman explores how *Spare Rib*, the UK-feminist 'newstand' magazine, 'published history from the outset, reflecting the broader desire of second-wave feminism to historicize its activity.'[98] While 'the magazine connected feminist historians to a non-academic readership,' the demand for 'attractive copy' meant the 'complex nuances of historical research were not easily conveyed in the small space of a few columns.'[99] This led to the

> *retention* of key aspects of the non-feminist narrative (a small number of charismatic leaders; a campaign largely restricted to London) within features whose

stated aim was to challenge this says much about the *pervasive nature of mainstream history*. With *limited resources* in the form of *available primary material*,
it was hard to escape existing paradigms.[100]

Accessing what is already-there, and reinitialising it within a circuit, is then
compromised by the mnemo-technical forms of transmission-interpretation
(the popular magazine format), which are further undermined by the dictates of capitalist publishing norms and perceptions of the reading market
('attractive copy,' *read* simplified, sensationalist journalism). Furthermore,
Cowman points out that even when the much-needed primary sources were
already-there (in the sense that they were written, in existence), they were not
always accessible to women wishing to reconstruct feminist histories. This
meant these resources could not be *operationalised* within the already-there,
a process that would make them available as part of a transmitting circuit.

For example, Cowman reflects on Barbara Miller's *Spare Rib* feature about
sixty-eight WSPU members who were imprisoned in Holloway Prison after an
action in March 1912. The militants embroidered a handkerchief that was later
found in a jumble sale in Sussex, demonstrating 'the fragility of feminist knowledge and the speed with which critical events could be forgotten.'[101] Cowman
states that while Miller managed to retrieve biographical details of twenty-one
women who left their mark on the handkerchief, she used her *Spare Rib* article
to appeal for further information about the other women who were missing
from her reconstructive account. The telling point is that in her research Miller
did not encounter an important piece of primary source material: an autobiog-
raphy published in 1960 by Zoe Proctor, which also gave details of the life of her
'companion,' Dorothea Rock. Both women left their traces on the handkerchief.
Cowman concludes, 'Miller's ignorance of its existence suggests that *even when
women recorded their own activism such texts were so marginalized that they
could be overlooked even within the context of feminist research.*'[102]

Cowman's article is a rare example of detailed historical research that
examines the complex processes through which feminism's already-there is
transmitted, accessed and operationalised.[103] Fragile, forgotten and found
again, *sometimes accidentally*, the materials composing feminism's already-
there can be redistributed in ways that compromise their complexity and
re-enforce established narratives. These re-enforced narratives then become
the transmissive architecture around which circuitry is built and information channelled. The need to be 'accessible'—that is, 'popular'—within a
capitalist marketplace dictates how feminism's already-there *can be* transmitted. Cowman's analyses clearly indicate that the existence of primary
sources *alone* is not enough to ensure that diversity of resources within
feminism's already-there is utilised. Writing, publishing or putting a copy
in an archive is not enough. Feminism's already-there—its circuitry—needs

to be both organised *and* actively transmitted. As a circuit formed in a fragile and volatile context, such transmission practices need to be *tended to* with care and conscientiousness. Perhaps the mnemo-technical conditions that organise resources are different in the contemporary digital culture? This will be the concern of the next chapter, which examines how digital technologies have offered different tools that can redistribute the quickly forgotten and marginalised knowledge, practices and techniques embedded within the traditions of women's liberation music-making.

Notes

1. UNESCO, 'Text for the Safeguarding of Intangible Cultural Heritage' (2014), accessed 24 March 2014, http://www.unesco.org/culture/ich/index.php ?lg=en&pg=00006.
2. UNESCO, 'Text for the Safeguarding of Intangible Cultural Heritage.'
3. Rodney Harrison and Deborah Rose, 'Intangible Heritage,' Tim Benton, ed., *Understanding Heritage and Memory* (Manchester: Manchester University Press, 2010), 242.
4. Harrison and Rose, 'Intangible Heritage,' 242.
5. See Rob Young, *Electric Eden: Unearthing Britain's Visionary Music* (London: Faber, 2010); Michael Brocken, *The British Folk Revival: 1944–2002* (Aldershot: Aldgate, 2003).
6. Anna Farthing, 'Authenticity and Metaphor: Displaying Intangible Human Remains in Museum Theatre,' Anthony Jackson and Jenny Kidd, eds., *Performing Heritage: Research, Practice and Innovation Museum Theatre and Live Interpretation* (Manchester: Manchester University Press, 2011), 101.
7. Although it should be noted that many examples of intangible cultural heritage are funded by the Heritage Lottery Fund (HLF), which privileges activities that empower communities to learn the skills to interpret their own heritage across a range of different expressions. The influence of the HLF, established as a grant-giving body in 1994, in shaping conceptions of value and what constitutes heritage in a UK context has not been sufficiently investigated. See http://www.hlf.org.uk/HowToApply/ whatwefund/Pages/whatwefund.aspx#.U1t6jih8sfM.
8. P. J. Boylan, 'The Intangible Heritage: A Challenge and an Opportunity for Museums and Museum Professional Training,' *International Journal of Intangible Heritage* 1 (2006): 54–65.
9. 'Intangible,' 'Oxford Dictionaries,' accessed 26 March 2015, http://www.ox forddictionaries.com/.
10. Denis Byrne, 'A Critique of Unfeeling Heritage,' in Laurajane Smith and Natusko Akagawa, eds., *Intangible Heritage* (London: Routledge, 2009), 229.
11. Sara Cohen and Les Roberts, 'Unauthorising Popular Music Heritage: Outline of a Critical Framework,' *International Journal of Heritage Studies* 20:3 (2014): 241–261.

12. Laurajane Smith and Emma Waterton, '"The Envy of the World?" Intangible Heritage in England,' Laurajane Smith and Natusko Akagawa, eds., *Intangible Heritage* (London: Routledge, 2009), 291–292.

13. Lourdes Arizpe, 'The Cultural Politics of Intangible Cultural Heritage,' *Art, Antiquity and Law* 12 (2007): 361–362.

14. Taylor, *The Archive and the Repertoire*, 20.

15. Of course, in practice, the listing of intangible cultural heritages by UNESCO has been argued to freeze the dynamic quality of traditions. Pietrobruno, 'Between Narratives and Lists,' 4.

16. Stengers and Despret, *Women Who Make a Fuss*, 68.

17. Harrison and Rose, 'Intangible Heritage,' 247, italics mine.

18. Alexander, *Pedagogies*, 278.

19. Jenny Kidd and Anthony Jackson, 'Introduction,' in Anthony Jackson and Jenny Kidd, eds., *Performing Heritage: Research, Practice and Innovation Museum Theatre and Live Interpretation* (Manchester: Manchester University Press, 2011), 2.

20. Taylor, *The Archive and the Repertoire*; Peggy Phelan, *Unmarked: The Politics of Performance* (London: Routledge, 1993).

21. See Esther Weltevrede et al., 'The Politics of Realtime: A Device Perspective on Social Media Platforms and Search Engines,' *Theory, Culture & Society* 31:6 (2014): 125–150. We will discuss in more detail the question of real-time and synchronisation in later chapters.

22. Farthing, 'Authenticity and Metaphor: Displaying Intangible Human Remains in Museum Theatre.'

23. Judith Butler, *Gender Trouble* (London: Routledge, 2006).

24. Rebecca Schneider, *Performing Remains: Art and War in Times of Theatrical Reenactment* (London: Routledge, 2011), 50.

25. Schneider, *Performing Remains*, 35.

26. J. K. Gibson-Graham, 'Querying Globalisation,' in John C. Hawley, ed., *Post-Colonial, Queer* (New York: SUNY Press, 2001), 240.

27. Gibson-Graham, 'Querying Globalisation,' 243.

28. Lewis, *Sisterhood and After* transcript, 95–96.

29. UNESCO, 'Recommendation on the Safeguarding of Traditional Culture and Folklore' (1989), accessed 26 March 2015, http://portal.unesco.org/en/ev.php-URL_ID=13141&URL_DO=DO_TOPIC&URL_SECTION=201.html.

30. Ron Eyerman and Andrew Jamison, *Music and Social Movements: Mobilizing Traditions in the Twentieth Century* (Cambridge: Cambridge University Press, 1998), 1–2.

31. Anna Feigenbaum, '"Now I'm a Happy Dyke!" Creating Collective Identity and Queer Community in Greenham Women's Songs,' *Journal of Popular Music Studies* 22:4 (2010): 367–388.

32. Anna Reading, 'Singing for My Life: Memory, Nonviolence and the Songs of Greenham Common Women's Peace Camp,' in Anna Reading and Tamar Katriel, eds., *Powerful Times: Cultural Memories of Nonviolent Struggle* (Basingstoke: Palgrave, forthcoming).

33. Reading, 'Singing for My Life.'

34. Jacques Derrida, *Spectres of Marx*, Peggy Kamuf, trans. (London: Routledge, 2006), 18.

35. Anna Feigenbaum, 'Tactics and Technology: Cultural Resistance at the Greenham Common Women's Peace Camp' (PhD diss., McGill University, 2008).

36. Agatha Beins, 'Sisterly Solidarity: Politics and Rhetoric of the Direct Address in US Feminism in the 1970s,' *Women: A Cultural Review* 21:3 (2010): 229.

37. See http://collections.museumoflondon.org.uk/Online/object.aspx?objectID =object-65680&start=20&rows=1.

38. Women's Liberation Music Project, 'Introduction to Sisters in Song.'

39. *Women and Music*, Feminist Archive South, DM2123.

40. Agatha Beins argues that the use of 'sister' and 'sisterhood' as 'a form of direct address and a rhetorical structure' was an important concept to 'demarcate an identity, a relationship and organizing praxis' of a decentralised movement. See Beins, 'Sisterly Solidarity,' 292.

41. For more information about Frankie Armstrong, visit her website: http://www .frankiearmstrong.com/ (last accessed 22 December 2014).

42. Caroline Hutton, interview with author, 2009.

43. Women's Revolution Per Minute catalogue (n.d.), Feminist Archive South, DM2123.

44. For a useful and detailed chronology of the WLM, please visit http://www .feministarchive.org.uk/chronology/contents.htm.

45. Frankie Green, 'London Women's Liberation Rock Band,' Women's Liberation Music Archive, 2010, accessed 19 December 2012, http://womensliberationmu sicarchive.wordpress.com/l/.

46. Green, 'London Women's Liberation Rock Band.'

47. Caroline Gilfillan, interview with author, March 2012.

48. Women's Revolution Per Minute, January 1980 catalogue, Feminist Archive South, DM2123.

49. Frankie Armstrong, interview with author, April 2012.

50. *Women and Music*, 1.

51. Sheila Rowbotham, *Hidden from History* (London: Pluto, 1975).

52. You can download the song from the Punk Brighton website: http://www .punkbrighton.co.uk/brightgirls.html. Last accessed 22 December.

53. Rachel Cooke, 'Taking Women Off the Shelf,' 2 April 2008, *The Guardian*, accessed 28 October 2014, http://www.theguardian.com/books/2008/apr/06/fiction .features1.

54. Mavis Bayton, 'Feminist Music Practice: Problems and Contradictions,' Tony Bennett et al., eds., *Rock and Popular Music: Politics, Policies, Institutions* (London: Routledge, 1993), 179.

55. As Stiegler writes, individuation, 'a transformation which is also the becoming of the world,' *'rests on and is constituted by the fabric of savoir-faire and savoir-vivre, for which the object is a support of practices.'* Bernard Stiegler, *The Lost Spirit of Capitalism: Disbelief and Discredit, vol. 3*, Daniel Ross, trans. (Cambridge: Polity, 2014), 31.

56. From her 1979 album, *Every Woman Will Be Free*.

57. Women in Moving Pictures, *In Our Own Time*, 1981, Feminist Archive South, DM2123/1/Archive Boxes 35.

58. *Shocking Pink*, 2, n.d., Feminist Archive South, DM2123/5.

59. *Women and Music*.

60. Women's Revolution Per Minute, January 1980 catalogue.

61. *Sisters in Song*.

62. Northern Women's Liberation Rock Band, 'Manifesto.'

63. *Sisters in Song*.

64. *Women and Music*.

65. The film has recently been available to watch on the on-demand BFI player service: http://player.bfi.org.uk/film/watch-rapunzel-let-down-your-hair-1978/.

66. For information about *The Gold Diggers*, see http://www.screenonline.org.uk/film/id/453393/.

67. Lindsay Cooper/Sally Potter, 'Seeing Red,' *The Gold Diggers*, 1983, Sync Pulse 0617.

68. Siren, 'Language,' *In Queer Street*, 1985.

69. Northern Women's Liberation Rock Band, *Manifesto*, 6.

70. See Alison Rayner's interview for the *Sisterhood and After* project: http://cadensa.bl.uk/uhtbin/cgisirsi/x/0/0/5?searchdata1=CKEY7563683%20&library=ALL.

71. Northern Women's Liberation Rock Band, 'Women Together: Edinburgh Sixth National Women's Liberation Conference,' *Spare Rib* 27 (1974), accessed 26 March 2015, http://womensliberationmusicarchive.files.wordpress.com/2010/10/nwlrb-article-spare-rib-27-1974.jpg.

72. Terry Quaye in Chris May, 'Step Forward, Daughters,' unknown publication, Feminist Archive South, DM2123.

73. Teresa Hunt, interview with author, 2012.

74. Northern Women's Liberation Rock Band, 'Women Together.'

75. Jana Runnalls, interview with author, 2012.

76. This issue is discussed, with different emphasis, in Grubbs, *Records Ruin the Landscape*, when he explores how experimental musicians and free improvisers expressed dissatisfaction with commercial recorded artifacts, and highlights how problematic it is that many people access the legacy of these artists through recordings (rather than, say, performances).

77. Northern Women's Liberation Rock Band, 'Women Together.'

78. Caroline Gilfillan, interview with author, March 2012.

79. Jana Runnalls, interview with author, 2012.

80. Stella Patella of the Fabulous Dirt Sisters, interview with author, 20 May 2010.

81. Cohen and Roberts, 'Unauthorising Popular Music Heritage: Outline of a Critical Framework.'

82. Northern Women's Liberation Rock Band, 'Women Together.'

83. Northern Women's Liberation Rock Band, 'Women Together.'

84. Foucault, *The Archaeology of Knowledge*, 28.

85. Ruth Novaczek, interview with author, 2012.

86. Gillian Whiteley, '"New Age" Radicalism and the Social Imagination: Welfare State International in the Seventies,' in Laurel Foster and Sue Harper, eds., *British*

Culture and Society in the 1970s: The Lost Decade (Newcastle Upon Tyne: Cambridge Scholars, 2010), 35–51.

87. For copyright reasons we could not reproduce the image John Walmsley took in this book, but you can view it on the *Music & Liberation* website, as we used it as the cover image for the exhibition: http://music-and-liberation.tumblr.com/. To see more of John's photos, please visit http://www.educationphotos.co.uk/.

88. Nina Power, 'Why Diet When You Could Riot,' *Riots Not Diets Compilation*, Tuff Enuff Records, LP, *Music & Liberation: A Compilation of Music from the Women's Liberation Movement* CD, 2012, accessed 23 December 2014, http://music-and-liberation.tumblr.com/post/35555849335/nina-power-reviews-music-liberation-compilation.

89. Cubitt, *History and Memory*, 181.

90. Browne, *Feminism, Time and Non-Linear History*, 2.

91. Cvetkovich, *An Archive of Feelings*, 3.

92. Deborah M. Gould, *Moving Politics: Emotion and Act Up's Fight Against AIDS* (Chicago: Chicago University Press, 2010), 270.

93. Cathy Caruth, ed., *Trauma: Explorations in Memory* (Baltimore: Johns Hopkins University Press, 1995).

94. Gould, *Moving Politics*, 270.

95. Catherine Malabou, *The Ontology of the Accident: An Essay on Destructive Plasticity*, Carolyn Shread, trans. (Cambridge: Polity Press, 2012).

96. Marian Hirsch, 'The Generation of Postmemory,' *Poetics Today* 29:1 (2008), accessed 26 March, DOI: 10.1215/03335372-2007-019, 111.

97. Bernard Stiegler, *States of Shock: Stupidity and Knowledge in the 21st Century*, Daniel Ross, trans. (Cambridge: Polity, 2015), n. 38, 265.

98. Krista Cowman, '"Carrying a Long Tradition": Second-Wave Presentations of First-Wave Feminism in Spare Rib c. 1972–80,' *European Journal of Women's Studies* 17:3 (2010): 198.

99. Cowman, '"Carrying a Long Tradition,"' 202.

100. Cowman, '"Carrying a Long Tradition,"' 202, italics mine.

101. Cowman, '"Carrying a Long Tradition,"' 203.

102. Cowman, '"Carrying a Long Tradition,"' 204.

103. See also Laura Mayhall, 'Creating the "Suffragette Spirit": British Feminism and the Historical Imagination,' in Antoinette Fraser, ed., *Archive Stories: Facts, Fictions and the Writing of History* (Durham, NC: Duke University Press, 2005), 232–251.

5

Digital Technologies, Transmission and Long-Circuits

To state that digital technologies have radically increased the number of vectors through which information can be distributed will seem for anyone who has lived through the analogue/digital transition—a period 'indissociable from a new temporality of technics, from another rhythmics'[1]—a banal proclamation as much as an obvious one. Yet it is an important starting point for this chapter that aims to further understand a central question of this book: how mnemo-technical *conditions*, which underpin widespread digitisation, facilitate the distribution of historical information *differently*. Furthermore, this book seeks to understand how these technical changes shape both how knowledge is encountered and what can be known through accessing what is *already-there*. This chapter is strongly informed by my experiences constructing a digital 'archive' to document women's liberation music-making at the end of the first decade of the twenty-first century. I deliberately immerse you, reader, in my personal recollections of how events unfolded over the course of several years, including various false starts and detours, in order to underline how my '*quest* for history [w]as a psychic need.'[2] In adopting a more intimate tone in contrast to other parts of the book, I want to emphasise the contradictory mixture of empowerment and disempowerment woven from the '*affective* fabrics of digital culture'[3] that propelled my digital archive making. Feelings such as desperation, frustration, confusion, joy, disorientation and excitement were an intrinsic part of how I engaged with digital technologies, feelings that were entangled with the kinds of knowledge they could facilitate and the modes of transmission they enabled.

Reflecting in this personal manner is my way of creating space for the emergence of *temporal* knowledges 'open to the contingencies'[4] of practices *in the making*. Such practices, and the knowledge arising from them, risk being eclipsed by the mechanisms of displacement and obsolescence, the drives that sustain the hollow 'heart' of the innovation-driven digital economy. As Stiegler observes, 'The question of innovation . . . is not only a matter of conception and production as entrepreneurs transfer technological inventions and scientific discoveries onto their business: innovation is also and before anything else the *socialization* of innovation—that is, the transformation of society.'[5] Innovation, as a temporal dynamic and mode of social operation, does not apply then to the sphere of business alone; it impacts the whole of society. Within a context of constant and rapid change, incisive and contingent knowledge composed within specific technical configurations are not lost as such, but rather become *obsolete*. Obsolescence is the means by which the deeply 'socialised' innovation-driven market economy *voids* certain kinds of knowledge by rendering them *socially inoperable* and therefore *useless*. My intention within this chapter is to focus on how the socialisation of innovation impacts wider dynamics that exceed purely economic imperatives, focusing on an area that has relevance to this study: digital information, its creation and mismanagement.

To reflect quite personally on my experience of working to create a digital archive is then an attempt to inscribe such experiences before it is *too late*, before the epistemic insight gained from technically composed experience is forgotten because irreversible obsolescence has taken hold. I want to enable readers to dwell in the provenance of ignorance and mistake-making as a source of wisdom in a technological context that continually demands users to 'up-skill' and adapt to new techniques. Within this exhausting process of *'perpetual training'* where 'one is never finished with anything,'[6] which holds little promise of gaining any of the *actual* techniques necessary to operate within the digital milieu with longevity and grace, the '"human" individual exists here as a cell . . . literally *de-brained*. Exteriorized . . . superfluous and fallen into obsolescence.'[7] Rather than accelerate madly into the spectral future,[8] I intend therefore to dwell carefully in the obsolescent wasteland wrought by perpetual innovation in order to consider what remains there. On a more pragmatic level, emphasising the affective dimensions of digital archival material is also done to counter the idea that these unique forms of historical information cannot generate attachment, alienation or belonging because of their supposedly poor, imitative quality in relation to historical 'originals.'[9] This chapter is then largely affective and re-enactive. It reflects on the collection, transformation and transmission of digitised information, while self-consciously drawing attention to the performative aspect of language and its capacity to bring worlds into being. Before this process begins, I will further reflect on the difference the 'intrinsically contributive . . . digital stage of grammatisation' makes to the organisation and transmission of information.[10]

Digital Archives in the Twenty-First Century

The early twenty-first century has witnessed an explosion of self-documentary practices, commonly understood as a born-digital 'memory boom.'[11] Concurrently, analogue technologies are given a 'second life' through digitisation. Pierre Nora argued that 'modern memory is, above all, archival.'[12] Yet the archive in the twenty-first century, as both concept and practice, has transformed in ways that move beyond Nora's pre-digital summations. David Grubbs writes:

> The rapidity with which the category of the archive is undergoing change is striking. In the case of many of these [digital] online resources, the appropriation and transformation of the term 'archive' bespeaks a certain hubris—as if the category no longer implies aspiration toward permanence and no longer functions as boundary with regard to past, present and future. . . . The issue is not whether proliferating online resources are to be counted as archives but rather what these collections, and our unprecedented access to them, does to the category of the archive.[13]

Furthermore, Jussi Parikka suggests that archival practices, language and logic underscore normative orientations to all kinds of information, least of all those that we may call 'historical.'

> Suddenly archives are popping up everywhere. A lot of our software-based interaction online now has to do with archival metaphors. We see this in ways ranging from the replacement of 'Delete' or 'Trashcan' on our email screens with 'Archive' to attempts to offer new kinds of storage space—mistakenly conflated with 'archives'—for numerous traces we leave of our personal lives— photographs, sound files, videos, documents. We are miniarchivists ourselves in this information society, which could more aptly be called an information *management* society.[14]

Within such a context, the normative experience of historicity in digital culture, I want to suggest, *emerges through* encounters with archival information, as the archive is also changed as it moves through the digital. Wolfgang Ernst describes this as the dislocation from a spatialised 'narrative memory' to a time-based 'calculating memory.'[15] These changes are not incidental, as

Daniel Ross reminds us: 'All perception and knowledge arises, for the individual as for the collective, from technically "over-determined" processes of transmission and mediation, that is, that secondary and therefore primary retention always occurs within the *conditioning context* of the current mnemotechnical epoch.'[16] Digital technologies—their modes of storage, transmission, organisation and calculation—act then as conditioning context for our knowledge and perception of historicity in the early twenty-first century. The digitised condition of historicity is composed via the circulation of images, ephemera, text, sound and film, expressive of discrete fragments, rarely the narrative whole. This fundamentally shapes the ways 'history is encountered, *how it enters our lives*, and in what forms of consciousness and experience it does so.'[17] Whereas written, narrative historicity 'integrates what in the original may have been divergent, synthesizes different classes of information . . . [creating] a consecutive narrative out of fragments, imposing order on chaos, and producing images far clearer than reality could be,'[18] the unruly artifactual temporalities embedded within digitised historicity are subject to a different kind of lossy compression, the specificity of which needs to be elaborated, as I will attempt to do in what follows.[19] Key to such endeavour is to appreciate how digitised archival fragments bear the acute temporal marks of their own historicities. As fragmentary carriers of temporal difference, the *potentials* of these distinct temporal knowledges may be released through dissemination, interpretation, discussion, curation, organisation or excavation—operationalisation.

The singular, yet radically differentiated, temporality of digitised historicity is then a significant transformation of *how history enters our lives*, experienced *expressively* as a temporal phenomenon. Theorists have begun to give form to these changes in a number of ways. Katie King, for example, has conceptualised these temporal transformations as '*pastpresents*, run together all in one word, in which pasts and presents very literally mutually construct each other,'[20] while Vivian Sobchack has talked of the circulating 're-presence of the past.'[21] The apparently indiscriminate manner digital technologies transmit what has long been buried deep within the already-there can also be viewed dismissively. Digital technologies are often blamed for circulating heterogeneous masses of historical information that drown out the distinctiveness of the so-called present, as archive materials from *Other* historical times protrude and invade a cultural reality unable to mark out its unique—that is, memorable—quality. 'Everything happens now'[22] is the cry, including ancient and long-forgotten histories. This results, supposedly, in the 'flattening out' of historicity, as the radical and very obvious simultaneous circulation of different historical times is theorised as information overload, the collapse of historical narrative and so forth.[23]

Yet, I want to suggest, what is occurring is not a flattening of historicity, but rather a profound infusion by irrepressible temporal differences—an infusion that must be conceptualised, interpreted and elaborated.

A key point we will explore in the final parts of this book is whether this supposed 'crisis of historicity,' wrought by the transmission of archival fragments, can be viewed differently if we refuse the generalisation of historical experience it announces and presumes. It cannot be forgotten that amid all this nonconsensual remembering, history does not and has not always happened in the same way for everyone. Histories are famously partial, motivated and, until relatively recently *in* history, told from the perspective of the rich and powerful, which has mostly showcased the male, white, Western version of events. The same can be said, of course, for the collection, care and transmission of archives and their contents, which have similarly, until relatively recently, reflected the interests of those with power and resources. To make claims, therefore, that there is a *generalised* crisis of history resulting from greater access to archival material enabled by digitisation is to ignore the uneven distribution of historical materials that occur in the transmission process. We may not, as I have emphasised elsewhere in this book, always be the immediate recipients of inheritances that are meaningful to us. Instead of feeling overwhelmed by greater access to archival forms within the digitised historical condition, therefore, perhaps we can understand the *increased contact* with different historical times as a point of emergence. In this way it may be possible to not decry the collapse of historical narrative, which itself is a form of historical transmission arising from specific mnemo-technical conditions, but examine the possibilities offered by digitised historicities.[24]

In the next two chapters, we shall examine these propositions using the digitised remains of women's liberation music-making and their dissemination on a free blog, a particular mnemo-technical subconstellation enabled by early twenty-first-century 'prosumer' digital technologies. Namely, we shall explore whether the low-financed, yet widespread, distribution of digitised historical information creates possibilities for diverse inheritances to emerge and become communicable as they enter into a long, connective circuit. Do archival historicities generated by digital technologies enable an *arrival* of ideas *whose time has come*? Or should the fragilities of digital technologies—their instability and tendency to upgrade, migrate or disappear, as well as the kinds of technical deficiencies of highly compressed audio files or low-resolution images—encourage us to 'grasp a present that is always degenerating [and confront] the ways in which ephemerality is made to endure'?[25] There are also pressing questions emerging from the political economy of digital culture that will be attended to. Despite the faith,[26] euphoria and excitement that characterised early popular and theoretical responses to the everyday ubiquity of digital technologies, increasingly there is the sense that the 'net blues' are catching.[27] Moreover, as we witness the increased marketisation of *knowledge as archive* in the *information economy*, does this render the kinds of archival interventions suggested by digital technologies ineffective, as all kinds of information become subsumed by the voracities of capitalism (and therefore abnegate their possibility to become knowledge)?[28] As Stiegler advises, digital technologies are *pharmaka*; they are both poison and remedy. The therapeutic *and* destructive potential enabled by digitised archival historicity will therefore be explored in what follows.

Coming into Contact with Women's Liberation Music-Making: The Digital Archive to Come

The main focus of this chapter is a collection of digital artifacts assembled using a variety of low-/no-budget technical and software tools that have enabled the organisation and distribution (if not necessarily the preservation) of the marginal cultural histories of women's liberation music-making. The Women's Liberation Music Archive (WLMA) documents the histories of music-making in the UK Women's Liberation Movement (WLM) from 1970 to 1989. Launched in May 2011, it contains digitised music, film and photographs; oral history excerpts; written personal narratives; songbooks; fliers; and other ephemera from a wide range of bands and solo artists connected to feminist political communities during the 1970s and 1980s. For many of the acts documented on the blog, it is the only evidence that they ever existed, even if that was only for one spontaneous performance at an agit-prop cabaret event in Hackney, London, 1981.

On the WLMA's homepage, it is described as follows:

> This project documents and celebrates the wealth and diversity of the feminist music-making of the 1970s and 80s and demonstrates its importance in the political and social context of that era. As in other social movements and political struggles, cultural activism was a major part of the Women's Liberation Movement that began in the late 1960s. In a great burgeoning of creativity, feminists fused artistic activities with politics to develop and express feminist ideas. Women's music, film and theatre groups, art and theatre proliferated throughout the 1970s and 80s.[29]

Like other community heritage projects that emerged in the first decade of the twenty-first century,[30] the WLMA took advantage of a range of freely available software-tools (namely, Wordpress, SoundCloud and YouTube) to make visible a community of feminist music-makers whose acts of culture making had effectively slipped out of the operational circuits, trans-mitting—and therefore creating access to—feminism's already-there. Sarha Moore, who played in women's bands from the 1970s onwards, told me, 'I thought everyone "just knew" about all these bands, that their names were written in neon lights somewhere, and then I met you and I realised that it was just me and my circle of friends who remembered them.'[31] As we learnt in the previous chapter, women's liberation music-makers developed com-munities of *practice* that used music in order to establish, communicate, share and interpret *the culture* of women's liberation. 'Feminist music-making was not purely about providing great entertainment but embodied a world-changing commitment to putting politics into practice.'[32] The docu-mentation of such practices is uneven, partial and fragmentary, which in turn has radically impacted the *consistency* and *concentration* of transmitted signals across feminist generations. Women's liberation music-makers did, however, leave some traces in physical feminist archives, those *few records, smothered sounds.* Such resources are vital for feminism's already-there to be operationalised, to 'begin again.'[33]

My own discovery of women's liberation music emerged from an encoun-ter with such deposits. In 2007 I regularly visited the Feminist Archive South (FAS) in Bristol. The archive was then based in the back room of a public library. Posters hung on the walls, and the periodicals protruded invitingly for visitors. The material was as accessible as it could be; it was largely an 'open archive.' I arrived at the archive in 2007, because at that time I was very in-volved in feminist cultural politics, particularly music-making, and I needed to know more about my activist inheritance. I played guitar and sang in the queer feminist punk band drunk granny alongside my best friend, who played drums.[34] Together we produced an intense, if often shambolic, cacophony. We performed at events in the UK that took place under the Ladyfest and Queeruption monikers that broadly espoused a d.i.y/anarchist/riot grrrl in-terpretation of feminist/queer politics. This influenced the kind of music we typically performed: loud, fiercely angry, deconstructed and mostly guitar-led. As a political music-maker, I was very interested to learn more about the 'cultural' legacies of the WLM because I knew how important such articula-tions of feminist politics were in the communities I participated in. Music was part of how we expressed the values of the worlds we wanted to bring into being, as much as our songs were a platform to scream out our utter frustra-tion with everything. There was a gaping disconnection, however, between the cultural legacies of the WLM and what I had encountered, even within fairly alternative, feminist and queer subcultures. Before stepping across the FAS's threshold, I could not name one band or performer from the UK WLM whose feminist music-making preceded mine. I found this odd because the picture of the WLM I had somehow acquired from popular culture and academia was of a far more wide-ranging activist movement. Surely, then, there must have been music, culture and other kinds of artifacts that could transmit to me the expressions, skills and representations created within the WLM? With these feelings propelling my actions, I booked an appointment to consult the archive's materials. My search proved fruitful, yet frustrating.

The FAS did indeed have a reasonable collection of tapes and vinyl, but there were no facilities to play the items. I desperately wanted to play the vinyl copy of the Fabulous Dirt Sisters' *Flapping Out* (1986); the pictures on the back of the album showed a group of nerdy queer women, people who could conceivably be my friends (later on we did become friends). *Here We Go*, a cassette of working-class feminist music by Sheffield-based Flamin' Nerve, also caught my eye. You know that story about feminism being white and middle class? In a moment of 'archival proximity,' other (feminist) worlds were 'opened up,'[35] and established narratives and stereotypes were pushed aside. With my desire to access feminism's already-there partially realised, I scrawled down the names of bands in my notebook and later conducted an internet search. This also yielded no results. Where *were* they and how could I find them? After all, if you weren't on the internet, I thought at that time, you might as well be dead.[36] What followed were several years of searching for the ghost of feminism's musical past, a ghost that possessed me with the impulse to get to any collections of music I could find and *digitise them*. It was crucial, I felt, that this music be heard, and heard widely. It was important people knew about the existence of what was *already-there*, and that the hard work done by women in different historical moments was not lost forever. I possessed a keen appreciation of 'the fragility of feminist knowledge and the speed with which critical events could be forgotten,'[37] largely because of the profound lack of access I had to such legacies. If the feminist musical knowledge was more robust, if it had entered into a long-circuit, rather than being severed prematurely, surely we would have been listening to that music at the feminist disco in 2007 *as well as* US West Coast riot grrrl from the early 1990s? I thought that maybe *I* would feel less fragmented about my place in the world, as both female music-maker and feminist, if I was connected to a meaningful tradition, an '*aesthetic apparatus of socialization*' that would enable feminists to 'live together . . . feel together, to share in sensitivity, and say "we."'[38] Maybe others would too.

What followed such stirrings was a trip to the Women's Revolutions Per Minute Archive (WRPM), then based at Birmingham Central Library. Previous owner Caroline Hutton had deposited the WRPM archive at the library at the turn of the twenty-first century. Caroline had been the longest custodian of the WRPM business, acquiring it in 1979 after the initial founders, Nicolle Freni and Tierl Thompson, could no longer run it because of health problems.[39] The WRPM held many of the exclusive UK distribution rights for US labels such as Olivia and Redwood, and also distributed the work of British-based performers. The collection, which included one copy of every record, tape or CD that Hutton sold, as well as accounts, correspondence, minutes, fliers and newspaper clippings, was stored in the basement of the library. On a grim January day in 2009 I ventured deep into the bowels of the library to view (and, crucially, not listen to) the collections. Chaperoned by library employees, *there* my cultural heritage was—ordered in boxes but still maddeningly out of reach. A few months before my visit, and with a certain evangelical zealousness, I had arranged a meeting with the library managers in an effort to convince them we should digitise the tape collections because of the threat to the analogue format. I wanted to create a large website that would include scans of artwork, interviews, reviews and copies of the recordings. It seemed to me, at that time, that a digital archive was *the only way* people could access the material, and in the process rectify the profound lack of knowledge about music-making in the WLM. As Kate Eichorn shrewdly observes:

> The creation of archives has become integral to how knowledges are produced and legitimised and how feminist activists, archivists and artists, and scholars make their voices audible. Rather than a destination for knowledges already produced or a place to recover histories and ideas placed under erasure, the making of archives is frequently where knowledge production begins.[40]

While the WRPM archive did exist already—it sat, all ready to go, in the basement of the library—it was, I perceived, profoundly *inoperative*. This point was exacerbated by the archive's content: recorded music. The futility of a record without a player, a cassette without a tape deck, was galling. The inactivity of the archive objects, and the pressing need for their activation, was all the more striking. Yet, in the wake of the 2008 credit crunch, the library staff diverted me with talk of copyright issues and other practical considerations. It was clear that digitising a collection of tapes because an overenthusiastic scholar-cum-activist wanted it, was not high on the priority list. I left the meeting not without hope, however—namely, because later that day I had an appointment with the woman responsible for creating the WRPM collection: Caroline Hutton (who in my mind at that time had acquired mythic proportions). After we had conducted an oral history and shared a simple supper of soup, cabbage and toasted seeds, I slept contentedly in the loft of Caroline's house, situated just outside Birmingham city centre.

To move the WRPM digitisation project forward, the staff at the Birmingham library told me I needed to contact the current custodian of the archive,

Hilary Friend. Friend, who had bought the business from Hutton in 1999, agreed to meet with me to discuss my ideas. A few weeks later, on a grey day at the Southbank Café in London, we met. After she listened to my proposal, she told me, in no uncertain terms, that she was not willing to help me realise my plans to create a digital WRPM archive and accessible website. I felt utterly crushed after our conversation, not only because it seemed to be a brutal refusal of my plucky ideas, but particularly because I felt women's liberation music heritage *belonged* to me and I wanted to care for it. [41] Not belonged, you understand, as in wanted to *own* it (or make money from it), but belonged because it felt crucial to my sense of well-being and rootedness within the world. I felt responsible for it and responsible for helping others access it. I strongly felt that if one is not born, but rather becomes, a feminist, the process is unlikely to occur without access to the diverse forms of culture heritage produced by feminists. It is not impossible, of course—many people have managed to become feminists without access to feminism's already-there. Yet having access to materials, artifacts and techniques—the tools through which scenes of transmission are practiced—is crucial for supporting the formation of identities, ideas and actions. Carly Guest, who has conducted research about how young feminist women who weren't independently active in 1970s and 1980s feminist activism narrate and remember 'becoming feminist,' argues:

> Objects provide a 'relative stability' in our engagement with the past. Apparently durable over time they offer a point of reference amidst changeable relationships and the instability of remembering. . . . Objects give access to affective relationships. The books Jenny brought to the interview were worn, having been read and re-read, and were a testament to the long and enduring relationship she had with feminism. They had adorned the bookshelves of her childhood home and, having been passed onto her by her mother, now sat on Jenny's shelves in her own home. [42]

Yet such relative stabilities were simply not there for me as a feminist musicmaker when I needed them to support my practices and sonic sensibilities. Such an absence, rendered within the transmissive circuitry, was, of course, a void and a wound, but it was also a point of animation. The silence did not shut down the search for the circuit; it was also a point of emergence within it. Other fates and caricatures could have befallen the transmission of women's liberation music-making. After all, access to feminism's already-there can so often be mediated by one-dimensional 'screen' and 'image' memories that serve as 'shorthand notation,' which can prevent access to contingency, possibility and multiplicity. [43] Yet not even perverted soundings were possible; there really was nothing—the record remained unplayed; the cassette tape ribbon wrinkled within its shell.

Downgrading Operations

After my deeply disappointing experience with the WRPM, I downscaled my grand ambition to recirculate WLM music for all and sundry in the newly digital generation. A year passed, and in that time I became increasingly interested in the Fabulous Dirt Sisters. I decided to focus my attention on the Nottingham-based band whose endearing, eclectic music warmed my soul. I had already met Kaffe Matthews, who, post–Dirt Sisters, had achieved considerable success as a sound artist.[44] She was by far the most visible member of the band and was therefore easy to contact. Matthews's skillful recounting of the band's busking 'world tours,' performed irreverently on the streets of Europe, enchanted me. Her connections also led me to the other Dirts—Deb, Stella and Karunavaca—who still lived in Nottingham and continued to play music together in Salmagundi—a slightly more grown-up, mixed-gender version of the Dirt Sisters. I met the other Dirts in May 2010, when we reconstructed a history of the band over a potluck dinner. We watched videotaped performances, listened to the music and marveled at both how little and how much people could remember. The Dirt Sisters were enormously generous with their time and archives. They made it very easy for me to conduct my adopted role as transmitter 'participating in the circulation of a circuit—that is, in its facilitation [frayage], its trans-formation, its expression.'[45] They were happy for me to construct a blog, write biographies, and distribute photographs and other digitised images, album covers, films and even the music across the internet.[46] With the help of the Dirt Sisters, I had achieved modest success in my desire to create circuitry, connection and visibility for a largely forgotten part of feminist music history. Through their history I was sure other musical stories could be told, and they would be the lenses through which I would come to understand music-making in the WLM. All was not lost, like it had previously seemed to be.

Then the unforeseeable happened. Gail Chester,[47] a stalwart of feminist activism since the WLM and compulsive networker, put me in touch with Frankie Green (whom we have already encountered in the previous chapter through her accounts of being in the London Women's Liberation Rock Band). Green was also a founding member of Jam Today 1, and she had been keen for some time to record the musical histories of the WLM, which, she felt, were in real danger of being forgotten. It seemed as if the grand and systematic vision might just happen after all.[48] The rest, as they say, is history. Or is it transmission? Green and I decided to work together to establish what became the WLMA. We aimed to achieve a similar degree of visibility for women's music-making in the UK compared with what already existed in the US context.[49] We began working on the project in September

2010, organising the information alphabetically (A–Z), creating entries for performers but also for activities connected to music-making, such as workshops and distribution, and key projects, such as the Women's Liberation Music Group. No matter how long a project or band existed, whether it was for one day or ten years, an entry was created for them. Women were invited to write or record their own memories, and the testimonials complemented the images, video, photos, ephemera and music. There were limited attempts to offer overarching narratives for entries, and collected artifacts were roughly organised. Frankie solicited content through her networks (which were extensive), and when that failed, the wonders of Google and Facebook opened up a world of connections. I uploaded materials I had photocopied from research in the FAS, which, as already intimated, has an impressive collection of material relating to culture, music and the arts. When the online site was unveiled on the symbolic date of 1 May 2011, it already included a substantial amount of material.

Blogging

We had no funding for the project initially, so using a free blog seemed a sensible way to make the venture possible. I had already used a blog for a public history project conducted in 2010/2011,[50] and I wanted to continue using the medium to organise and publish marginal cultural histories. Furthermore, there was a whole range of synchronic Web 2.0 technologies such as YouTube, SoundCloud and Flickr that I wanted to explore. My interest in blogs was affirmed by research I had conducted with Ana Laura Lopez de la Torre. Ana Laura had been a driving force in setting up the *Do You Remember Olive Morris?* blog,[51] the internet presence of a project that explored the memory and life of Olive Morris, an inspiring community activist instrumental in the British Black Panthers and Black Women's Movement, but who died at the age of twenty-seven in 1979. Ana Laura told me:

> Because it was totally un-funded and it was a good way for putting the call out for people who wanted to be involved, and at the same time as information was coming in to publish it straight away so it is very immediate and that really appealed to us, because the main thing was that there was nothing on the internet about her, you know that was the first thing that was quite significant. . . .
>
> We always get a report on the blog on the search strings that people are using to look on the blog and we get people who are not necessarily looking for Olive Morris and they come for all different reasons. There is some information there we publish that is not published on the internet at all. There is nothing, for example on the British Black Panthers, and if you type 'British Black Panthers' we

come on top so I think it has been really instrumental in contributing to filling a gap about information online about this. . . .

    The thing about blogs is that they are quite viral things. They just get picked up and re-published.[52]

Ana Laura's enthusiasm for the hi-fi/lo-fi aspect of blogs was infectious, as was the promise of an immediate repatriation for feminist music's already-there that I so desired. The Remembering Olive Collective (ROC) was a shining example of what could be done with Web 2.0. They exploited blog's smart interfaces, predesigned templates and font choices by filling them with radical and marginalised content. This information was then pinged to all corners of the planet, and in the process connected diasporic communities with the heritage they needed: 'We are geographically quite dispersed although a few of us are from Brixton there is a lot of members in East London, a lot of us are immigrants so we spend a substantial part of the year abroad, maybe visiting our families or for work, so it helps us also to gather around this space and you can always check what is going on by looking at blog and contributing when you are away.'[53] I could see that blogs were a significant communication platform that effectively guaranteed new forms of connectivity and visibility for forgotten histories and knowledge.

    Another key inspiration for the WLMA was the *Unfinished Histories: Recording the History of Alternative Theatre, 1968–1988* project.[54] *Unfinished Histories* offered a different template for a digital resource, but was similarly concerned with the collection and publishing of oral histories, images, music, film and ephemera. Jessica Higgs and Susan Croft were experienced curators as well as community activists, so they approached the organisation of information and collecting practices differently from the ROC collective. Crucially, their website included templates that were used to collect information about theatre companies. Frankie and I downloaded and reformatted these sheets to reflect the needs of our project. From my perspective, the initial infrastructure of the WLMA was adapted from examples of similar projects I was inspired by. An important point to note about setting up the WLMA was that neither Frankie nor I were archivists or even historians by trade. We were passionate, organised and committed people, examples of what Andy Bennett has termed 'DIY preservationists.'[55] Do-it-yourself preservationist practices, he notes, are 'becoming increasingly common, to the extent that they can no longer be regarded merely as isolated incidents of fan innovation, but they constitute a globally connected informal network of activity orientated towards a re-writing of contemporary popular music history.'[56] Although digital technologies were by no means the sole reason the WLMA was created, the tools they provided, particularly Web 2.0, had (for a brief time perhaps) a wonderfully equalising effect on what amateurs could create and mass-circulate within culture. Quite incredibly, digital technologies gave people who had absolutely no knowledge or experience of creating archives the sense not only that they could do it but also that it was both possible *and* desirable to do so. No one was, in other words, *expert* in using these technologies because they were so new. Everyone was learning, up-skilling (whether they liked it or not). These conditions, for the most part, enabled the emergent amateur digital archivist to create, organise and distribute archival content. This digital amateur archivist acted without permission or training, she operated within the mnemo-technical conditions she was inserted into, putting them to work in inventive, opportunistic ways. The WLMA emerged, then, amid diverse and opportunistic communities practicing heritage and transmission in a previously unprecedented manner. The WLMA drew on the political urgency of the *Remembering Olive Morris* project, the curated examples of *Unfinished Histories* and the sophisticated way digital platforms could organise, disseminate, *transmit* and *connect* diverse mnemo-technical artifacts. It would be the first time women's liberation music-making produced in the UK was placed in such a circuit, an animate part of feminism's already-there.

Digitise Them

What followed were several years of searching for the ghost of feminism's musical past, a ghost that possessed me with the impulse to get to any collections of music I could find and digitise them.

The notion of digital imperative refers to the belief that the future is digital and that current practices need to digitise in order to make this future a reality.[57]

It is hard to convey the strength of my feeling that digitisation was both compellingly urgent and, quite frankly, *the answer* to the problematic and resounding absence of feminist musical memory within the circuits I participated in and was shaped by. The spectre of analogue disintegration hung close to me, despite my knowing very little about the durability of analogue magnetic tape. By digitising the music of the WLM and uploading it to our new blog archive, I knew, however, it would become *operationalised as mass media*—rendered synchronous inside the multivalent, increasingly proximate, connective beast of digital culture that swarmed through my consciousness, day and night. I was not the only one who felt like this about digital technologies. As Bas Van Heur suggests in the epigraph to this section, in the first decade of the twenty-first century the digital imperative worked widely throughout society via the promotion of this very simple message: digitise or be damned. Such an imperative affected a wide cross-section of organisations and people who were differently (yet connectively) invested in the creation, organisation and preservation of digital archives. These included large archival institutions such as the British Library, who led the way, in 2002, as an early adopter of digital technologies,[58] funding distributors such as Jisc, who helped organisations create digital collections,[59] countless businesses seeking to monetise their information assets, as well as the everyday, micro-archival practices that propelled initiatives like the WLMA.

Eichorn has argued that cultural initiatives within feminism are often very much a 'here and now' affair. They draw on readily available tools, while making the best out of the resources underfinanced, and often unskilled, projects can muster. She writes:

> The stock and trade of feminist publishing has long been in documents that can be produced quickly, inexpensively, and, most notable, *without vetting from outside publishers or the potential censorship imposed by commercial printers*. In short feminist publications have favoured accessibility over durability, resulting in a legacy of highly ephemeral documents. As Wooten emphasizes, regardless of the era, most feminist publications have been made 'with materials at hand.'[60]

The digital tools on offer in the everyday milieu of the twenty-first century, as publishing mechanisms, were potent, extensive and instantaneous in impact and reach. Furthermore, the early work of the WLMA seized upon the self-authorising quality of digital archival culture to produce a collection that bypassed the conventional gatekeeping decisions within professional archives. Little did I know, however, that the digital materials I was creating were equally, if not more, ephemeral than the analogue originals I 'venerated.'[61] At one time I scanned a thick folder of photographs and ephemera using my domestic scanner at a low resolution (72 dpi) because I did not know the implications of using particular resolution settings, or even at that time, the difference between a JPEG and a TIFF. Revealing this may very well be an admission of my stupidity and carelessness as I went about my digitisation work. Yet it also indicates how the digital technologies at my immediate disposal enabled me to create media forms without knowing why or how they worked, let alone having any insight about the preservation implications of my actions. After all, the difference between a 72 dpi and a 300 dpi scan on the computer screen appears minimal. It is only when the images are blown up that the varying quality becomes apparent. To my untrained digital eye, the scans looked right—good enough[62]—a faithful electronic version of the photographic paper I held in my hand. In reality the copy was extremely flimsy—in the preservation sense—but ideal, of course, for internet distribution, which was, in that brief time, all I really cared about.

A similar lack of knowledge informed my audio digitisation work. Often the carefully planned, real-time transfers I did resulted in the highly compressed audio files that were part of my everyday technical lexicon: MP3s. As I now know after years of researching digital preservation practices, MP3s are of questionable quality because they are designed according to the logic of perceptual coding, 'forms of audio coding that use a mathematical model of human hearing to actively remove sound in the audible part of the spectrum under the assumption it will not be heard.'[63] MP3s are subject to destructive, lossy compression and are certainly *not* deemed by professionals to be of archival standard (currently 24 bit/96 kHz uncompressed B-WAV). In those early days I often digitised artifacts desperately. There was so much to do, and real-time transfers take up a lot of time. Digitisation was a means of extracting a feminist cultural heritage Holy Grail, whose afterlife I was facilitating and extending through those magnificent digital circuits (the number of visitors to the WLMA reached a total of 71,786 people as of 23 April 2013). I was propelled by the joy of access and immersive immediacy and, I confess, not thinking about the long term. What Chun calls 'superhuman digital programmability,'[64] the fantasy of digital permanence and indestructability, had clearly seduced me, but I was not alone in succumbing to the spectacular power and different competencies digital technologies appeared to offer.

In the first decade of the twenty-first century, many institutional projects, far better funded than the WLMA, also did not create robust digital *preservation* plans. The seductiveness of Van Heur's 'digital imperative,' a process whereby 'digital infrastructure was positioned as absolutely central to the development'[65] of a wide range of archival projects, could place pressure on institutions to adopt or integrate digital outputs within their projects, even if such an output was not appropriate. Furthermore, the funding available for such projects only covered the *creation* of digital collections (typically running for two to three years), and did not account for the long-term sustainability of the materials. This is all the more surprising because processes of active management and continual intervention define preservation practices for digital collections.[66] You cannot leave a hard drive on the shelf, forget about it and hope it will work in a hundred years' time. File integrity needs to be regularly monitored, while systems for receiving, managing, processing and ingesting digital information will inevitably change due to the innovation/obsolescence dynamic. The problem of sustaining digital collections becomes pressing within such a context. In an interview I conducted in 2013 with Paola Marchionni, head of digital resources for teaching, learning and research at Jisc, she described how the question of sustainability was managed within their organisation:

We've done quite a lot of work around sustainability but if you start unpacking what sustainability is, it is both about the technical aspects, the curation, and the kind of resources you need to put into post-digitisation—financial, staff resources. . . . It's about discoverability, so making sure that you don't just create a resource and preserve it, but that you keep on developing it, curating it, adapting to new technologies. Jisc has been doing work around the discoverability of digitised collections through the Spotlight on the Digital project,[67] and published a useful online guide of what managers of digital resources can do to ensure their collections are discoverable.[68] And it's also about what we refer to as 'embedding.' Making sure you do a project and it's not just you put it up there on the internet, 'build it and they will come.'

She then went on to reflect on a recent study[69] that

looked at the amount of money that people, institutions and funders put into creating the content is no way comparable to the little amount of money put toward maintaining, updating, refreshing, keeping the content sustainable, basically. On one level that's kind of obvious because you do have to put a big capital investment into digitisation, workforce, machines, but still they found that it was a tiny percentage of resources that went into sustaining the projects, so that's an issue, it's a big issue. Ideally, once new resources are created, their sustainability should become part of 'business as usual,' but this doesn't always happen.[70]

The focus on the creation, rather than the sustainable caring for digital archival material, implicitly privileges a culture of short-term access over long-term preservation. Digital culture, as it currently evolves from within the careless dynamic of the innovation-driven information economy, is then characterised by a '*systemic stupidity* that *structurally prevents the reconstitution of a long-term horizon.*'[71] The term digital *preservation* in this context is ironic, given how the creation, circulation and 'use' of digital data is deeply enmeshed within a volatile technical system that has '*systemically, and not accidentally*, been translated into the *decomposition of investment into speculation.*'[72] It is a system that cannot care for, and indeed destroys, the 'social faculty that *allows us* to take care of' the objects it produces.[73] Once the immediate euphoria about the access to archival information that digital technologies enable subsides, you don't have to dig too deep to see evidence of '*systemic stupidity*' in action. Consider the advice provided in the *Digital Preservation Handbook*, a resource last updated in 2008, which outlines the realities of managing such digital data within a techno-economic complex driven by accelerated, future-facing innovation.

While the media on which the information are stored may or may not fail, what is certain is that technology *will change rapidly so that even if the media is re-*

tained in pristine condition, it may still not be possible to access the information it contains. No matter how exemplary the care of the media is, it will not remove the requirement to deal with changes in technology, though responsible care should make it easier to manage technology changes.

The certainty that there will be frequent technological change poses a major challenge and it is therefore not surprising that collection managers . . . cited technological obsolescence as the greatest threat to successful digital preservation.[74]

This advice outlines an impossible situation. Even if the utmost care is taken of digital assets, it may all be fruitless because of rapid and inevitable technological change. When I started out on my archival adventure, I knew little of the information management *problem* the majority of the Western world had wholesale adopted. I just *did*. My concern was to flush the circuits with the lost information, to make the dead live again by refusing the prescription of hauntological feminist melancholia.[75] I was excited about the amount of people who could be reached and connected; I was excited about creating a long-circuit, about enabling others to enter the circuit. Yet length in the space-time compression of digital culture is not simply about extensiveness of space, which may well be 'uneven and patchy, with spots of concentration as well as areas with little or no connectivity,'[76] but it is also quite profoundly about time, a time however that *systematically* cannot be thought of as a '*long-term horizon*.' Considering the truncated horizon of innovation-driven market economies is crucial to devising a pragmatic, yet necessarily speculative approach to theorising—and responding to—the temporal extensiveness of lo-fi, low-resolution amateur archives.[77]

Standards

Sterne argues that 'a settled standard represents a crystallised moment in the negotiation process among different involved actors, whether companies, international standards-making bodies or governments. . . . [W]ithout standards, content could not travel as well as it does and could not be as well controlled as it is.'[78] It may come as a surprise that the question of establishing standards for professional digital archives has only been marked as a priority within the last two to three years. The US-based National Digital Stewardship Alliance (NDSA) argues that 'the need for integration, interoperability, portability, and related standards and protocols stands out as a theme across all of these areas of infrastructure development.'[79] The executive summary also stresses the negative impact rapid technological change can create, and the need to 'coordinate to develop comprehensive coverage on critical standards bodies, and promote systematic community monitoring of technology changes relevant to digital preservation.'[80] That such an agreement has not yet been reached among archive professionals indicates where priorities for managing digital information are. Significantly it is not within long-term preservation practices tabled by the cultural heritage sector, but rather in sustaining the innovation of technical systems that create, migrate, distribute and reuse—that is, monetise—archival data.[81]

Despite the slow evolution of technical standards, there is increasing evidence that the standardisation of digital information management processes is being placed at the forefront of information economy agendas. The recently established E-ARK project, for example, which aims 'to create a revolutionary method of archiving data, addressing the problems caused by the lack of coherence and interoperability between the many different systems in use across Europe,'[82] demonstrates this well. Yet the desire to cohere technical systems is done out of an overarching concern that information assets are currently not monetised effectively, rather than out of a benevolent desire to protect digitised cultural heritage per se. If an important aspect of the data-driven economy is the archival *market*, then that market needs to realise greater degrees of interoperability and standardisation if assets are to be traded effectively across borders.[83] File format collisions, complex systems, competing or poor resolution and the insular tyranny of propriety codecs are simply bad for business. Economising information has arguably moved beyond the creation stage discussed earlier in this chapter, into its *utilisation*. This may, of course, prove to be useful for the management of digital information in the long term. Creating standardised, interoperable data-sharing systems may help to lengthen the temporal extensiveness of ephemeral digitised information, the kind of 'good enough' archival data often produced by people on the margins of society, because its circuitry *potentially* has greater security.

This cannot detract from the fact that digitised collections like the WLMA are in a precarious position: the wily emergence of forgotten archival forms within connective consciousness remains at risk, despite their apparent—if low-resolution—potency. For such digital resources to remain operational within feminism's already-there in the long term, it is vital to exploit potential securitising openings if and when they arise. This also entails understanding the technical and systemic dynamics within which information is composed and transmitted. Such knowledge is, however, often inaccessible because of a persistent, immersive short-termism that structures expectations, perceptions and practices, a technical context that enables one to act, without, however, understanding the long-term implications of such actions. Such tempered sentiment is far away from the exuberant *archival play* described earlier in this chapter, which embraced both 'digital' and 'archive' as redemptive force. We have not yet considered, however, what the digital *does* to the archive of women's liberation music-making, which is the subject we turn to in the next chapter.

Notes

1. Jacques Derrida and Bernard Stiegler, *Echographies of Television*, Jennifer Bajorek, trans. (Cambridge: Polity, 2002), 72.
2. Cvetkovich, *An Archive of Feelings*, 268, italics mine.
3. Adi Kuntsman, 'Introduction: Affective Fabrics of Digital Cultures,' in Adi Kuntsman and Athina Karatzogianni, eds., *Digital Cultures and the Politics of Emotion* (Basingstoke: Palgrave, 2012), 1–21, 1.
4. Hesford, *Feeling Women's Liberation*, 151.
5. Bernard Stiegler, *For a New Critique of Political Economy*, Daniel Ross, trans. (Cambridge: Polity, 2010), 81–82, italics in original.
6. Deleuze, 'Postscript,' 5.
7. Stiegler, *Symbolic Misery*, 77, italics in original.
8. Mark Fisher, *Ghosts of My Life* (Winchester: Zer0, 2014).
9. Robinson, 'Touching the Void: Affective History and the Impossible'; Renée M. Sentilles, 'Toiling in the Archives of Cyberspace,' in Antoinette Burton, ed., *Archive Stories: Facts, Fictions and the Writing of History* (Durham, NC: Duke University Press, 2005), 136–157.
10. Bernard Stiegler, 'Distrust and the Pharmacology of Transformational Technologies,' Daniel Ross, trans., T. B. Zülsdorf et al., eds., *Quantum Engagements* (Heidelberg: AKA Verlag, 2011), 31–32.
11. Joanne Garde-Hansen et al., eds., *Save As . . . Digital Memories* (Basingstoke: Palgrave Macmillan, 2009).
12. Pierre Nora, 'Between Memory and History: *Les Lieux de Memoire*,' *Representations* 26 (1989): 11.
13. Grubbs, *Records Ruin the Landscape*, 144–146.
14. Jussi Parikka, 'Archival Media Theory: An Introduction to Wolfgang Ernst's Media Archaeology,' in Jussi Parikka, ed., *Digital Memory and the Archive: Wolfgang Ernst* (Minneapolis: University of Minnesota Press, 2012), 1–2.
15. Wolfgang Ernst, 'The Archive as Metaphor: From Archival Space to Archival Time,' archive public, 2005, accessed 27 March 2015, http://archivepublic.wordpress.com/texts/wolfgang-ernst/.
16. Daniel Ross, 'Pharmacology and Critique after Deconstruction,' in Christina Howells and Gerald Moore, eds., *Stiegler and Technics* (Edinburgh: Edinburgh University Press, 2013), 252.
17. David Carr, *Experience and History* (Oxford: Oxford University Press, 2014), 47.
18. Raphael Samuel, *Theatres of Memory* (London: Verso, 2012/1996), xxiii.
19. See Alexander Galloway, 'The Black Box of Philosophy: Compression and Obfuscation,' *Incredible Machines*, 2014, accessed 5 March 2015, http://incrediblemachines.info/keynote-speakers/galloway/. Galloway claims in this talk that alphabetic writing compresses experience into the combination of characters, and therefore operates a form of lossy—that is, reductive—compression acting on the transmission of knowledge. If this is so, then it becomes imperative to elaborate the different kinds of digital compression enacted by the digital, and the kinds of temporalities embedded within such compressive formations.

20. Katie King, *Networked Reenactments: Stories Transdisciplinary Knowledges Tell* (Durham, NC: Duke University Press, 2012), 12.

21. Vivian Sobchack, 'Afterword: Media Archaeology and Re-presencing the Past,' in Erik Huhtamo and Jussi Parikka, eds., *Media Archaeology: Approaches, Applications and Implications* (Berkeley and Los Angeles: University of California Press, 2011), 323.

22. Douglas Rushkoff, *Present Shock: When Everything Happens Now* (New York: Penguin, 2013).

23. See Mark Andrejevic, *Infoglut: How Too Much Information Is Changing the Way We Think and Know* (London: Routledge, 2013), and Mark Fisher's closing comments at the *Keeping Tracks: A One Day Symposium on Music and Archives in the Digital Age*, which echoed many of the points made by Reynolds's *Retromania*, which is discussed earlier in the book; accessed 6 May 2014, http://britishlibrary.typepad .co.uk/music/2014/04/keeping-tracks.html.

24. Benjamin, 'The Storyteller.'

25. Wendy Chun, 'The Enduring Ephemeral, or, The Future Is a Memory,' in Erik Huhtamo and Jussi Parikka, eds., *Media Archaeology: Approaches, Applications and Implications* (Berkeley and Los Angeles: University of California Press, 2011), 200.

26. Margaret Wertheim, *The Pearly Gates of Cyberspace: A History of Space from Dante to the Internet* (New York: W. W. Norton, 1999).

27. Bernard Stiegler, 'The Net Blues,' Sam Kinsley, trans., accessed 8 May 2014, http://www.samkinsley.com/2013/11/21/bernard-stiegler-the-net-blues/.

28. See also Trevor Owens, 'What Do You Mean by Archive? Genres of Usage for Digital Preservers,' *The Signal*, 27 February 2014, accessed May 2014, http://blogs .loc.gov/digitalpreservation/2014/02/what-do-you-mean-by-archive-genres-of-us age-for-digital-preservers/; Kate Eichorn, 'Archival Genres: Gathering Texts and Reading Spaces,' *Invisible Culture* 12 (2008), accessed 17 June 2014, http://www .rochester.edu/in_visible_culture/Issue_12/eichhorn/index.htm.

29. WLMA, 'Welcome to the Women's Liberation Music Archive!' accessed 17 June 2014, http://womensliberationmusicarchive.co.uk/.

30. See, for example, *Do You Remember Olive Morris?*

31. Sarha Moore, interview with author, 2010.

32. WLMA, 'About the Archive,' accessed 17 June 2014, http://womensliberation musicarchive.co.uk/about/.

33. WLMA, 'About the Archive.'

34. At the time of this writing, our MySpace page is still accessible; accessed 5 March 2015, http://www.myspace.com/drunkgranny.

35. Eichorn, *The Archival Turn*, 60.

36. Kenneth Goldsmith, 'If It Doesn't Exist on the Internet, It Doesn't Exist,' 2005, accessed 5 March 2015, http://epc.buffalo.edu/authors/goldsmith/if_it_doesnt_exist .html. The work of Goldsmith, founder of Ubuweb, is discussed at length in Grubbs, *Records Ruin the Landscape*, 135–167.

37. Eichorn, *The Archival Turn*, 203.

38. Stiegler, *Symbolic Misery*, 15. To explore this issue in depth, it is well worth reading the chapter from which this quote is selected because it delicately explores the central role that recorded music, as the epiphylogenetic *'sedimentary deposit'* (35),

performs in the fashioning of communities, and the fragilities of such a temporal bond. Yet while the *'already-there of our ill-being'* (29) is immediately accessible to Stiegler in recorded form, and serves as the basis for his observations, my example highlights the challenge of fashioning a 'we' via inoperable, or absent, iterations of feminism's already-there.

39. On the Gay Birmingham Remembered website, Hutton elaborates, 'I'd been to the Michigan Music festival, and met the women who were then running WRPM (Women's Revolutions Per Minute)—Nicolle Freny [*sic*] (an American, living here) and Teal Thompson [*sic*]—and then I got a phone call from my friend Mary McDonald who told me that it was my duty to take over WRPM as Nicolle had cancer and they were looking for someone to take it over and had decided that I was the person to do it'; http://gaybirminghamremembered.co.uk/memories/Women%92s%20Revolutions%20Per%20Minute%20(WRPM).

40. Eichorn, *The Archival Turn in Feminism*, 3.

41. This is not to paint a negative picture of Friend. Indeed, she was instrumental in moving the WRPM collection to the Women's Art Library, held at Special Collections at Goldsmiths, University of London, in 2012. The collection is now easy to access and, combined with the efforts of the WLMA, should ensure that the music-making of the WLM is an accessible part of feminism's already-there; http://www.gold.ac.uk/library/collections/wrpmcollection/.

42. Carly Guest, 'Young Women's Narratives and Memories of Becoming Feminist: A Multi-Method Study' (PhD diss., Birkbeck, University of London, 2014), 210.

43. Hesford, *Feeling Women's Liberation*, 17.

44. See http://www.kaffematthews.net.

45. Stiegler, *States of Shock*, 265.

46. See http://thefabulousdirtsisters.wordpress.com/.

47. Gail was interviewed for the *Sisterhood and After* project; accessed 17 June 2014, http://www.bl.uk/learning/histcitizen/sisterhood/bioview.html#id=144022&v=true&id=144022.

48. A sense of my excitement can be captured in this post on the Fabulous Dirt Sisters blog: 'Frankie Green and Jam Today,' accessed 27 March 2015, http://thefabulousdirtsisters.wordpress.com/2010/06/19/frankie-green-and-jam-today.

49. See, for example, the histories of the Chicago and New Haven Women's Liberation Rock Bands at http://www.uic.edu/orgs/cwluherstory/CWLUGallery/rock.html; the amazing J. D. Doyle is a one-man archiving machine at http://queermusicheritage.com/olivia.html; http://queermusicheritage.com/women.html.

50. See http://sistershowrevisited.wordpress.com.

51. See http://rememberolivemorris.wordpress.com/.

52. Deborah Withers and Ana Laura Lopez de la Torre, 'Blogging Olive,' *Do You Remember Olive Morris?* (London: ROC, 2010), 102–105.

53. Withers and Lopez de la Torre, 'Blogging Olive.'

54. See http://www.unfinishedhistories.com.

55. Andy Bennett, '"Heritage Rock": Rock Music, Representation and Heritage Discourse,' *Poetics* 37 (2009): 483. See also the research of Sarah Baker at http://diyarchives.blogspot.co.uk/.

56. Bennett, "'Heritage Rock": Rock Music, Representation and Heritage Discourse,' 483.

57. Bas Van Heur, 'From Analogue to Digital and Back Again: Institutional Dynamics of Heritage Innovation,' *International Journal of Heritage Studies* 16:6 (2010): 406.

58. 'British Library Preservation Strategy,' accessed 27 March 2015, http://www .bl.uk/aboutus/stratpolprog/collectioncare/discovermore/digitalpreservation/strat egy/BL_DigitalPreservationStrategy_2013-16-external.pdf.

59. Jisc, accessed 27 March 2015, http://www.jisc.ac.uk/about/history.

60. Eichorn, *The Archival Turn*, 71, italics mine.

61. Nora, 'Between Memory and History,' 13.

62. 'Good enough' is a phrase that recurs across discussions of digital preservation practice. See, for example, Meghan Banach Bergin, 'Digital Preservation Capabilities at Cultural Heritage Institutions: An Interview with Meghan Banach Bergin,' *The Signal*, 10 November 2014, accessed 13 November 2014, http://blogs.loc.gov/digi talpreservation/2014/11/digital-preservation-capabilities-at-cultural-heritage-institu tions-an-interview-with-meghan-banach-bergin/.

63. Jonathan Sterne, *MP3: The Meaning of a Format* (Durham, NC: Duke University Press, 2012), 21.

64. Chun, 'The Enduring Ephemeral,' 185.

65. Van Heur, 'From Analogue to Digital and Back Again,' 406.

66. In the British Library's 'Digital Preservation Strategy,' they write, 'The ever-changing nature of the technology and the fragility of digital content means *preservation actions can be needed from much earlier in the lifecycle than for traditional collections, and at a much greater frequency,'* 6.

67. See http://www.slideshare.net/PaolaMarchionni/dh-sheffield-pmarchionniap ril2014final?ref=http://digitisation.jiscinvolve.org/wp/2014/10/07/spotlight-on-the -digital-at-the-2014-digital-humanities-congress/.

68. See http://www.jisc.ac.uk/guides/make-your-digital-resources-easier-to-dis cover.

69. Ithaka S + R, *Appraising Our Digital Investment Sustainability of Digitized Special Collections in ARL Libraries*, 2013, accessed 12 January 2015, http://www .sr.ithaka.org/research-publications/appraising-our-digital-investment.

70. Paola Marchionni, interview with author, July 2013. See also 'The 4th Implementation Report of the *European Parliament and Council Recommendation on Film Heritage*' (2014), which states that 'resources devoted to film heritage . . . continue to represent a very small fraction of resources allocated to funding of new film productions by all Member States' (38). Accessed 8 January 2015, http://ec.europa.eu/ information_society/newsroom/image/4th_film%20heritage%20report%20final%20 for%20transmission_6962.pdf.

71. Stiegler, *For a New Critique of Political Economy*, 5, italics in original.

72. Stiegler, *For a New Critique of Political Economy*, 7.

73. Bernard Stiegler, *What Makes Life Worth Living: On Pharmacology*, Daniel Ross, trans. (Cambridge: Polity, 2013), 81–82.

74. Digital Preservation Coalition (2000/2008), 'Technological Issues,' *Digital Preservation Handbook*, accessed 17 June 2014, http://www.dpconline.org/advice/preservationhandbook/digital-preservation/preservation-issues.

75. McRobbie, *The Aftermath of Feminism*, 117. David M. Berry has also talked of a 'subjectivity that is embedded in the socio-technical networks of computational systems [which] points to a deathless existence.' David M. Berry, *The Philosophy of Software: Code and Mediation in the Digital Age* (Basingstoke: Palgrave, 2011), 154.

76. Anna Reading, 'Gender and the Right to Memory,' *Media Development* 2 (2010): 13.

77. Matthew G. Kirschenbaum observes that 'given sufficient resources—that is, elite technical and financial backing—data can be recovered from media even under the most extraordinary conditions.' However, it is clear that feminist archives have never been well endowed, or backed by powerful social and political elites. Matthew G. Kirschenbaum, *Mechanisms: New Media and the Forensic Imagination* (Cambridge, MA: MIT Press, 2012), xii. Digital forensic technology (some of which is open-source) does evolve alongside the creation of new digital archives, but it surely must be relied upon only as a very last resort.

78. Sterne, *MP3*, 23–24.

79. National Digital Stewardship Alliance, *2014 Agenda for National Digital Stewardship*, accessed 19 June 2014, http://www.digitalpreservation.gov/ndsa/documents/2014NationalAgenda.pdf, 2–3.

80. National Digital Stewardship Alliance, *2014 Agenda for National Digital Stewardship*, 2–3.

81. Default standards have, of course, emerged through common use over time, and these have come to inform large institutional policies. See, for example, Tim Gollins, 'Parsimonious Preservation: Preventing Pointless Processes! (The Small Simple Steps That Take Digital Preservation a Long Way Forward),' *Online Information Proceedings 2009*, accessed 8 January 2014, http://www.nationalarchives.gov.uk/documents/parsimonious-preservation.pdf.

82. Digital Preservation Coalition, 'DPC Joins Collaboration to Create an Electronic "Ark" for Digital and Paper-based Records,' 2014, accessed 19 June 2014, http://www.dpconline.org/newsroom/latest-news/1140-e-ark-announcement-feb-2014.

83. See numerous examples from the 'EU's Digital Agenda for Europe: A Europe 2020 Initiative' at http://ec.europa.eu/digital-agenda/en/our-goals, in general, and 'Towards a Thriving Data-Driven Economy' at http://ec.europa.eu/digital-agenda/en/towards-thriving-data-driven-economy, in particular.

6

Digital Archives of Process

B ELOW IS A LETTER, written in 1984, by Fabulous Dirt Sister Deb Mawby
to feminist record label Stroppy Cow:

> Dear Stroppy Cow,
>
> Enclosed is a tape which we thought might interest you. We made it in *ten hours
> on a very hot day so it could be lots better*. . . . We've had a lot of bad starts at
> getting the band going due *to women being too busy with other work, childcare
> or moving etc*. So the band has to continually reform—lose a trumpet, gain a
> bass, type thing![1]

This letter is an example of how artifacts in the WLMA communicate the
social, technical, economic and environmental conditions in which women's
liberation music-makers formed bands and recorded music. It transmits the
processes of women's liberation music-making. Mawby's letter clearly describes the pressured circumstances of feminist music-makers that, in turn,
have affected the quality of the recorded legacy we can access. The hurried
recording, further undermined by unpredictable environmental factors (note
the typically British appeal to the weather), fundamentally shaped the quality
of the 'finished' product. The caveat pronounced in the letter indicates that
the listener needs to know that 'it could be lots better,' that what they are
hearing is not a 'true' reflection of the band and what they sound like.

We might wonder, for a second, if it was not a good recording, why the
band did not record the material again and send off a better representation?
The absence of a different version, however, encourages us to remember

how difficult it could be to organise and finance recording sessions within an exclusively analogue context, even amid the rise of home-recording technologies and do-it-yourself practices. Such opportunities to record, like that fated *very hot day*, needed to be grasped, as it were, when they could, amid the grind of gendered caring responsibilities and everyday life that affected the evolution of the band. The difficult circumstances for women music-makers are clearly outlined by Mawby's hand, even within a speculative letter to what was, at that time, the UK's only feminist record label. The tone of the address demonstrates the expectations of care that Jolly suggests is characteristic of the epistolary cultures of women's liberation.[2] The letter is written assuming a shared context, with the hope that those listening to the tape will be sympathetic. Whether such sympathies were returned is not documented, although we may note that Stroppy Cow never released any of the Fabulous Dirt Sisters' work, but this may be reflective of 'organisational capacity' rather than critical rejection. The Nottingham band eventually set up their own label—Spinaround Records—on which they released two albums of their eclectic music, *Flapping Out* (1986) and *Five Strong Swimmers* (1989). We will learn more about these works later in this chapter.

What Kind of Archive Is This?

In the previous chapter, we began to reflect on how the category of the archive is being transformed by modes of access, to both content and practices, enabled by the digital. Some have argued that the term 'archive' has become so overused within twenty-first-century culture that it flirts with mediocrity simply by invoking it.[3] Yet if the WLMA is described as 'an archive,' particularly as a *digital archive*, in what ways does it contribute to the reconfiguration of archive-making in the twenty-first century? The WLMA consists of both physical artifacts and their digital doubles, with physical artifacts and digital files housed in the FAS, Bristol. As a low-financed, do-it-yourself archive, the WLMA is curated loosely. It is organised alphabetically, and each artifact—be it image, music, film, writing or ephemera—is posted one after the other within the band's entry. The material is displayed in a fairly random way: You may encounter a photo, followed by a video, another photo, some text, audio, another photo and so forth. Because each entry is a different length, and some acts have a lot of material and others only have very little, there appears to be limited standardisation. Moving through the site resembles rooting through the contents of a digitised shoe box, presenting contents tumbling out of a digital space. There is limited scope to jump between entries, aside from hyperlinked text embedded within entries; if the site visitor wants to scroll to the bottom of the entry, they have to move past all the other entries to go there. While the arrangement of the archive makes it more difficult to realise what Eichorn calls 'archival proximity'—that is, the ability to easily consult entities side by side, therefore opening up un-anticipated associations that enable different interpretations of feminism's already-there—it does have other values that are worth reflecting on.[4] For example, the WLMA forgoes the lightning speed that sparks the 'search-find-now' impulse that so often propels hungry information seekers. Due to this, it may encourage a kind of default lingering or dwelling within the pages, a situation that may also be lessened or heightened depending on browser capabilities, internet connection speeds and so forth.

As a community-led feminist archive, the *feel* of scrolling through the WLMA corresponds with Cait McKinney's description of her research at the Lesbian Herstory Archives, New York: 'The basement of the Lesbian Herstory Archives (LHA) in Brooklyn, NY seems a lot like the unfinished basement of a family home: stuff is everywhere, arranged into the kind of organized chaos befitting objects that don't belong upstairs, but are too important to discard, including a shelf crammed with books that haven't yet been cataloged and shelved in the mainfloor library.'[5] The WLMA site appears similarly 'home-made,'[6] improvised, skilled to a basic level, yet therefore potentially accessible to audiences who may not visit traditional archives.[7] None of these design and organisational choices was deliberate necessarily, at least at the level of conscious thought. They did, however, seem to be the best way to map the histories of the UK WLM's music-making communities in an accessible, coherent manner. Because of the lack of online information about many of the performers included in the WLMA, simple modes of presentation were deemed desirable. Decisions to present information in one way or another are not incidental to how they are accessed. As Shannon Mattern writes:

> Archives and libraries are intensely aesthetic environments. . . . These aesthetic variables have huge epistemological significance. Acknowledging archives and libraries as *aesthetic* entities not only helps patrons to better understand *how* they think and learn; but it also, ideally, helps practitioners recognize that the physical and digital environments they create aren't neutral containers of infor-mation: they give shape to data, information, knowledge, and history; condition how patrons access and process them—and, *in* the process, constitute what those intellectual constructs *are*.[8]

Had a different way to construct a digital archive been known, other organ-isational and aesthetic decisions might have been deployed. As the previous chapter made clear, the construction of the archive was very much a process of learning itself, using resources that were readily available, with very little

technical skill to adapt or modify how the material was presented. If the
WLMA has a particular archival aesthetic, then it is one of minimal order
and strategic randomness; it collects and transmits the *processual* histories of
women's liberation music-making.

Archives of Process

What do I mean when I say the WLMA can be understood as an *archive of
process*? This processuality is manifested in two principal ways. First, within
the quality of the artifacts themselves, many of which, like Mawby's letter,
wear their processes on their sleeve. Whether this is expressed descriptively
through words, in the quality or availability of recording (practices, live recordings and so forth) or through simply documenting a culture that was
keen to break down the processes of music-making as a political gesture,
all the artifacts share a resistance to the idea that they could be a final, or
finished, representation of women's liberation music culture. Indeed, all the
artifacts, in different ways, encourage a dragging[9] *within* the unfinished, ongoing quality of feminist cultural revolutions, transmitting a sensibility of and
techniques for culture *in the making*. This is not a contrived affair, because
such documentation can often be accidental, but it is what can be discerned
amid the remains of women's liberation music-making.

This sense of an active or 'present-focused,' processual temporality transmitted through the archival artifact may not, of course, be specific to women's
liberation cultures. Archival artifacts are often framed as historically contingent forms, marked by the singularity of the time they were created. They
therefore offer unique insight into circumstances and expectations of the
author(s) *at the time* they were recorded. Marina Warner has described such
evidential quality as 'that thing was there, that line of writing was there, was
made then, at that point in time' and from this 'we are then introduced *back
into the time* when the wound was open.'[10] The processual quality of WLMA
artifacts undoubtedly draws upon the potential-temporality of archival encounters *in general* to offer insight into the time of historical emergence.[11]
The historical context of women's liberation music-making, however, politi-
cises the temporality of process and therefore radicalises the transmission of
historical time as well. The processual temporalities emitted by these archive
fragments have particular value for our thinking of the politics of transmission because the political, cultural and economic processes they enact attempt to do things differently, and such urgency is embedded within their
artifactualities.[12] Furthermore, these artifacts help us to think of transmission
processes that further dislocate reliance on the $P \leftarrow P \rightarrow F$ constellation.

This leads on to the second manifestation of the WLMA as an archive of process: the conditioning mnemo-technical context of digital transmission from which, we recall, knowledge and perception arises, and within which the WLMA is embedded. Much has been made of the processual quality of the digital from computational, aesthetic and media archaeological perspectives. This processing is understood as so fast that it cannot be apprehended by human perception as such. Nonetheless, such processing is profoundly *there*, composing perceptive reality under the flat surface or screen. Discussing processual aspects of computational flows, David M. Berry has argued that

> a new industrial internet is emerging, a computational, real-time streaming ecology that is reconfigured in terms of digital flows, fluidities and movement. In the new industrial internet the paradigmatic metaphor I want to use is real-time streaming technologies and the data flows, processual stream-based engines and the computal interfaces that embody them. . . . Under the screen surface, however, there is *a constant stream of processing, a movement and trajectory, a series of lines that are being followed and computed.* . . . I am thinking about the difficulty we have in studying something unfolding in this manner, let alone archiving or researching, *without an eye on its processual nature.*[13]

Such a description is echoed by Timothy Scott Barker, who highlights the processes at play within the digital image, and indeed any kind of digital file:

> The digital image, whether static or in motion, is the result of continuous and ongoing computations. It does not exist as a thing made, but as a thing *that is continually in the making.* The digital image is linked to a stream of code; it would never attain existence, never come into being as an image upon the screen, without a constant flow of information.[14]

Finally, and perhaps of greatest relevance to this study, is Wolfgang Ernst's description of the digital archive:

> The traditional architecture of the archive has been based on classifying records by inventories; this is now being supplemented or even replaced by order in variation and fluctuation, that is, dynamic access. This 'archive' is no longer simply passive storage space *but becomes generative itself in algorithmically ruled processuality.*[15]

Ernst goes on to write, 'Since antiquity and the Renaissance, mnemotechnical storage has linked memory to space. But nowadays the static residential archive as permanent storage is being replaced by *dynamic temporal storage, the time-based archive as a topological place of permanent data transfer.*'[16] If we are to accept this conception of the digital archive as composed by time-based entities in continual movement—the 'dynarchive'[17]—how does this intersect with archival temporalities that are, in a sense, defined by their singular, open historical wounds? What happens to historical time in *general* when it is *processed* by the digital? The answer, it would seem from considering these writers, is that it comes *alive*. Alive, that is, if we consider descriptors such as 'dynamic,' 'continuously moving,' 'in the making,' 'flowing' and 'processual' to be convergent with a sense of 'liveness.'

Within digital culture, 'liveness' is often bracketed under the term 'real-time'; such conditions enable the transmission of real-time historicity—historical time processed by the digital. Yet 'real-time' has been sternly criticised. For Stiegler, real-time transmissions work by

> installing a permanent *present* at the core of the temporal flux where, hour after hour, minute by minute, a just-past world, disseminated through 'live,' 'real-time' devices of selection and retention are completely subservient to the calculations of the informatic machine. The development of industries of memory, imagination, and information engender the fact and feeling of a gigantic memory hole, a *loss* of connection with the past.[18]

Stielger's critique of real-time was initially developed as an interpretation of how television alters the transmission of historical events. In particular, it focuses on how the temporal compression between the production of the event and its reception annihilates the 'very essence of historical time . . . actualized in its *différance*.'[19] The interval between event and reportage, action and trace, supportive of the thinking act itself, is destroyed through real-time transmissions, Stielger contests,[20] whose operation, and pervasiveness, is extended and intensified by the internet.[21] Such a claim is surprising because it implies there can be *only one* conception of historicity and historical time accessible via *différance*: 'Writing, as a medium for recording history, identifies it (the historical event, what has happened).'[22] Yet does this suggest a singular technical essence of historicity rather than historicity as experientially composed through the conditioning context of the given mnemo-technical epoch? Is a '*différantial* situation, constantly forming and de-forming, that is, differentiating itself,' *ever* realisable via digital artifactual trace?[23] Arthur Bradley asks similar questions:

> Why—if all temporalisation is conducted through tertiary memory—should we see Real Time as any less 'real' than, say, the time afforded by analogue recording, alphabetic writing or even the first flint tool? . . . The critique of Real Time risks valorizing a simple, homogenous and ahistorical time of consciousness—a consciousness which is actually technically mediated all the way down. . . . Stiegler's critique of Real Time concerns its monopolization

over the processes of temporalisation: Real Time leaves us with no other ways
of (technically) temporalizing time.[24]

The idea of a totalising 'real-time' capture of temporal life has also been
criticised by a number of different scholars. Sarah Sharma has demonstrated,
for example, that the experience of the temporal within a digital milieu is
distributed unevenly, dependent on where one is occupationally positioned
within the transmissive circuits of global capital. She writes that 'the temporal operates as a form of social power and a type of social difference,' a point
often overlooked by the 'disorientated postmodern gaze . . . affected by the
acceleration of capital and time-space compression.'[25] Wajcman has made a
similar argument, suggesting that 'we should be looking at changing dynamics in the *distribution* of time' across different social groups.[26]

There is also an argument that real-time transmissions, although synchronic, are not necessarily homogenous. Weltevrede et al., for example, enable us to grapple with the specific ways real-time is produced as a mediatised
temporal structure, and the manner in which it creates specific forms of time-
consciousness. They suggest it is important not to

> think . . . about time online not as events happening in real-time, in the now, but
> as being entangled in the fabrication of *specific forms of real-timeness*. It is the
> continuous movement of new content, its request and display in devices, as well
> as the engagement by users through web activities and the filtering of content
> based on freshness and relevance, that constitute realtimeness. In this sense, *re-*
> *altimeness refers to an understanding of time that is embedded in and immanent*
> *to platforms, engines and their cultures.*[27]

Within this context, a 'stream is . . . not just the inflow of new content but also
its constant recombination or pacing based on algorithms, featured content
and user activities.'[28] Real-timeness then, as a temporal quality, does not exclusively relate to the 'the newest' or 'latest' 'news,' even if it may refer to the
most popular or highly ranked sites or stories generated by search engines.
The transmission of artifacts from 'internally different and multiple'[29] historical times can also be distributed through the vector of real-timeness, resulting
in the performative enactment of real-time historicities: 'Liveness cannot just
be proclaimed but has to be accomplished.'[30] Such a perspective challenges
the idea that real-time transmissions *always* produce a gigantic memory hole,
even if it does outline how transmissive practices are radically reconfigured
within a digital environment controlled, largely, by corporations invested in,
and profiting from, the rapid circulation of information. It is, however, possible to perceive the existence of an everyday milieu composed of historical
artifacts that are refreshed, released and rereleased, with each transmissive

act having the potential to operate at the temporal threshold of real-timeness. Such conditions engender access to a *différantial* situation via the transmitting digitised artifact, even if such potentials are not always realised or encouraged by the industrial operators of the internet.

Archives of Process in a Processual-Political Culture

To be clear, how I use the term 'process' in relation to the WLMA as an archive of process is different from the processual qualities ascribed to the digital by theorists such as Berry and Ernst. When using process in relation to the WLMA, I am referring to gestures of doing, acting and enacting, *as well as* the temporal dynamics bound into such practices: the temporalities unleashed when one is in the process of *doing something*, a sense of history occurring as it is happening. In this respect I understand process to be closely aligned with performativity, which, of course, we have discussed in relation to the intangible quality of women's liberation and wider social movement culture. This is arguably different from the streaming, real-time processuality of the computational, or the dynamic transfer of digital information, even if there is clear convergence in the continuousness of their temporal claims. Arguing that systemic transmissions are constantly turned on (always processing) is not the same as arguing that singular, historical times are performatively reenacted through transmission. The distinction to be made here is one of a movement of time composed by difference and differentiation (the *différantial* situation) and one that, although in continual movement, is often recognised as an expression of a homogenous real-time that congeals, rather than opens up, emergent modes of historicity. This chapter attempts to understand process in light of the former conception, even if it is necessary to acknowledge that processuality is a term used to describe the overall temporal condition of reality 'under the screen' in the digital milieu.

Another key point about the WLMA as an archive of process is that it is a multivalent document of how women's liberation music-makers dissected the *operations* of the cultural world in which they lived. A key aspect of women's liberation music-making was rendering transparent all aspects of the process, whether that was learning to play an instrument, releasing a record, plugging in an electric guitar, sitting behind a drum kit or carrying a massive amplifier up several flights of stairs.[31] All of these things—and many others—had been beyond the reach of women who were often handed very marginal, stereotyped roles in the music industry and in grassroots musical settings. Breaking down the processes in communiqués, workshops and performances was a key part of removing barriers to participation and fostering the conditions, women hoped, for substantial and sustainable cultural change. One example of this is when Jam Today 1 organised a benefit gig to support their musical activism. At their show they distributed invitations to discuss the role of music in the women's movement, as well as a list of the band's expenses. Such an action demonstrates the extent to which the band 'belonged' to the movement, and vice versa, but also that the raw economics of feminist culture making would be unpicked, step by step, as a means to explore alternative processes of social transformation. Jam Today 1's pamphlet revealed, 'Out of a total of 38 gigs done during this year, there were 14 benefits, 7 women's conference socials, 4 women's festivals, 5 women's fairs/events, 6 colleges/youth clubs, 1 children's party and 1 demonstration. Also we did five women only music workshops. . . . [A]part from Fran, our roadie, the other 7 of us pay £160.71 on average per year to be in the band. And none of us have another job.'[32]

Later generations of Jam Today were similarly concerned with the economics of women's liberation music-making and ensuring they were clear and accessible. 'We wanted to learn about making records from beginning to end. Small quantities of records are expensive to make and in the event of us getting more than the cost back for this EP, that money will go towards bringing out an LP by JAM TODAY if and when we can afford it,' we are told in a press release entitled 'About Stroppy Cow Records,' which accompanied the release of the 1981 *Stereotyping* EP.[33] Other women took a more irreverent approach, which poked fun at the patriarchal mystification of music-making with its 'technical knowledge and techno-jargon' that often put women 'in a position of relative powerlessness in a world where strange abbreviations abound.'[34] As part of their tape-only release, Newcastle-based Friggin Little Bits wrote that 'this tape was realised in dykeophonic sound using a totally new concept in reproductive technique called parthenogenesis which combines DH : 14 XL's with high frequency catatonic ZX4's to produce claustrophobic sound which comes of spending too much time in a Renault.'[35] While taking a less nuts-and-bolts approach than Jam Today, Friggin Little Bits disrupted the business as usual of music-making through humorous interventions that created more room for women's participation. Within the WLMA, process is transmitted through the content *and* form of digitised artifacts. How then might we grapple with the modes of transmission arranged by the digital, and how do they release emergent pathways to feminism's already-there?

Performativity

In chapter 4 we encountered the idea that the transmission of women's liberation music-making heritage is performative. As inheritors of cultures that 'left few records,' yet many 'smothered sounds,' this ephemeral legacy was reproduced in the cultural forms created by the women's liberation music-makers, im/materials that became lodged within feminism's already-there. Remains were embodied within the memories of participants or secreted in ephemeral documentation, such as the hastily scrawled letters above song lyrics denoting an appropriate chord to play as an accompaniment, or available documentary forms, such as the meticulously inscribed musical notation that operates as invitation to further interpretation. Such documentation cannot easily be replayed, as one would perhaps do with a vinyl record or cassette tape, complete with sleeve notes, marketing images and so forth. The record of women's liberation music-making does not appear to be fixed, but rather is encountered in forms that may be *played along with*, deciphered, interpreted and activated. These examples are a strong summation of how technics compose transmission practices—that is, both *what* can be transmitted and the *method* of its passage. Moreover, modes of transmission are also the means of preservation; through performative reinterpretations, cultural heritage is shared, interpreted, enlivened.

'Born-digital' cultural artifacts have similarly been noted for their performative quality—and the necessity of re-performance to their preservation. As Richard Rinehart and Jon Ippolito write in relation to the preservation of what they call 'new media art':

> New media art is as performative or behaviour-centric as it is artifactual or object-centric. . . . It exhibits variable form, much like music. . . . Computation may manifest physically in the flow of electricity and organization of magnetic bits, but it is not tied to any one specific physical instance. It is, definitively, a repeatable event. . . . This variability is not considered corruptive but rather as the inherent property of the medium and the work. Digital and related new media art will almost certainly use different hardware for presentation a hundred years from now, but can be still considered authentic.[36]

Rinehart and Ippolito challenge the ideal of authenticity within preservation practices. In its place, they propose a model of digital preservation—and therefore a model of transmission—that accounts for inevitable variability of technical context and can thereby embrace mutability of form. As discussed in relation to intangible cultural heritage, variability is key to understanding cultural traditions whose transmissive trajectories are located within performative practices and techniques. Within such contexts, the transmitted signal (*sign*-al) is modified as it moves across interpretive communities that embed material within the available technical, representational, economic and cultural lexicons. The temporality of such transmissions is the 'live event.' An artifact or tradition is transmitted when it is literally (re)performed or reenacted by a group or individual. The value of such activity is not derived from maintaining the *authenticity* of traditions. It is located in keeping cultural traditions *alive* through the *action* of transmission. Traditions are released, as it were, and what is already-there *activated*, within the scenes of these singular yet technic-configurative performativities. To court performativity as a key transmissive practice within the digital realm then, is to argue for the primal understanding of the active, live, inauthentic enaction of the already-there, rendered as a process of selection capable of *releasing* historical time. This is history understood as action, a doing of history, as it were. Such performativity occurs when the *digital processes historical time*, the results of which, in terms of the dissemination of historical time, could not be more different from the blanket containment of the $P{\leftarrow}P{\rightarrow}F$ we have discussed before. Peppered by all kinds of inauthentic temporal differences, the reenacted digital artifactual entity brought 'into play . . . artificially produced'[37] continually refreshes the content within the circuit, distributing real-time historicities.

What happens, then, when the digitised artifacts housed in the WLMA enter into such a circuit? How does such a conditioning context of mnemotechnical transmission amplify, distort or relay the WLMA's contents that are apparently as processual and ephemeral as their digital containers? How do such conditions enable the arrival of artifacts, practices and knowledges *whose time has come*, courting further evidence that what is already-there is never past as such, but always capable of operationalisation within amenable technical configurations? Victoria Browne describes such occurrences, following Nietzsche, as 'untimely events':

> The untimely event is not simply used up as it occurs. It does not fall back into the past: spent and wasted, but nor is it swept up and appropriated. . . . Nietzsche's untimely events and forgotten ideas are not subsumed within historical time. Nor do they disappear from it. They remain on the fringes of cultural memory and pop up again at unforeseen moments, to break apart and disrupt the sedimented time frames and syntheses that cannot entirely suppress or contain them.[38]

A significant number of recorded artifacts within the WLMA are of practices and live performances, the kind that could be easily made on a portable open-reel or cassette recorder—very few bands took advantage of the domestic multi-track recording technology that was becoming more widely available from the late 1970s onwards.[39] Sometimes these are the only recordings of the band, and clearly they have strong archival value for this reason. Such recordings indicate the kinds of access women's liberation music-makers had with recording technologies—the technics of transmission at their disposal.

In an article written in 1989 for the US journal of women's music and culture *Hot Wire*, Ova member Rosemary Schonfeld outlines very clearly the lack of resources for women, and how recording material was necessary to counter the radical ephemerality of women's culture in a profoundly sexist world: 'One of the main reasons for setting up our recording studio for women is that we have watched so many women's bands and individual women musicians virtually disappear because of a lack of financial support and decent venues, and we hoped to encourage more women to at least get their music down on tape. We have been quite successful in this respect, but very few women can afford to have albums pressed.'[40]

As I have emphasised throughout this book, the technical form of any recording conditions how it can be transmitted, and this process relates to the sender as well as the receiver. Within the digital, the digitised processual artifacts of women's liberation music-making find their ideal, if variable, container. Reemerging in the twenty-first century at a time when wide-ranging 'categories of archival sound'[41] are a staple part of media transmissions, and deciphering cryptic fragments is a normative, everyday communicative practice, it seems realistic to assume that noise-ridden recordings of unreleased, rare archival footage of women's liberation music-makers is widely recognisable *as a* cultural artifact. That is, its playback leverages a communicative signal *because* of its noise, rather than despite of it.[42] For writers such as Jaimie Baron, the proliferation of archival material within digital culture risks fetishising such rarities *as* authenticity, which lures audiences with the fantasy of historical truth and presence.[43] This perspective, however, overlooks the inauthentic, differential quality of digitised and born-digital artifacts, and how the mnemo-technical context is germane for the emergence of particular modes of historicity that are processual, such as the remains of women's liberation music-making.

Practices and live performances have different processual resonances that accrue particular meaning within the context of women's liberation music-making. Or, to put it another way, all recordings emit their processes, although some emit them differently from others. Recordings of live performances and rehearsals thrust those that discover the sound recordings into the active, raw and unpolished moments of music-making—the live performance, the practice and the demo—the times of rehearsing and performing. They jolt time into the moment of action, as we can listen to women practicing together, tarrying in time, going through the motions (in the motion) and trying (but often) failing to get the song right. We do not have access to the 'final' performance because there is no such recording in existence. We can hear the chatter of 'I missed that bit' in the corner of the recordings, followed by frustrated laughter as the women attempt again.[44] These archives are of practices; they indicate and reenact *learning*.

In contrast, a live recording of Abandon Your Tutu enacts undoing through performance. A trance-like rhythm beaten on the drum spirals out of control, overlaid with an outburst of hysterical laughter as the drummer declares that the kick drum is sliding away from her. The recording inserts the listener into this apparently hilarious moment when *performance as a process*, with a supposed beginning, middle and end, breaks down irrevocably. Breakdown, stutter and detour are all documented here as part of the process, and are released through the communicative, transmissive possibility of the digitised artifact—a different kind of processual learning to the rehearsal recording, but one still embodied in the action of trying, experimenting and doing. These vital aspects of any cultural practice are often marginalised within a cultural imaginary fixated on final products and finished representations. In the context where there are no final products as such, no commodities to fetishise, these evidentiary processes are valuable because they reflect the activity of women's liberation music-making—its messy, chaotic and unpredictable live manifestations, as well as the commitment and determination to *continue practising* in order to elaborate different rhythms and political worlds. The recordings thus release the temporality of practice as a process that never ends, but is bound up within the action of living. The documentation of such processes indicate the technical conditions in which women played and performed music, but are also suggestive, as Mawby's letter makes explicit, of the everyday conditions that shaped their practices as gendered music-makers. If, as Ernst suggests, to play back a media artifact is to also play back the singular temporalities recorded therein, what he calls the 'sensual and informational presence'[45] exuded by the operationalised media object, then the WLMA acts as a distributor for the different kinds of temporal knowledges embedded within each singular artifact. Such multivalent distribution creates an avenue into a time of action and doing, released by the performativity of digital objects, which render untimely temporalities operational. Each processual emission is defined by the singularity of temporal difference, a point that will be clarified in the next section.

Temporal Difference

So far I have been discussing how historical time processed by the digital releases temporal difference, real-time historicities occurring as live emergence. Such mnemo-technical conditions render conceptualisations of history and historical time that reside within the containing domain of P$\leftarrow$P$\rightarrow$F wholly inadequate for appreciating both the complexity and the actuality of artifactuality—temporality composed through technics—as it is arranged by the digital. Emergent concepts are then required to grapple with the conditions of historicity released by the digital. In the spirit of this book, these concepts are not new as such; they are modifications of what is already-there, with modification a necessary part of any exchange within and across a transmissive circuit. This is where I turn to the concept of temporal difference to orient action within the digital mnemo-technical conditions compositional of thought, expression and historical experience.

It is my contention that temporal difference has always existed as a condition of historical time; it is just that digital processing renders such conceptualisations salient and, moreover, pressing to decipher, recognise and *interpret*: 'Emancipation can only come from technics itself, from a technical intervention that can change the reception situation—from, for example, the possibilities for (a very different) decoding and encoding offered by the digital discretisation of the continuous, "real time" image.'[46] The condition of temporal difference arises most clearly in the process of digitisation itself: when non-digital singularities are processed digitally, when the paper file becomes its JPEG 2000 copy, the cassette tape meets its WAV counterpart, and so forth.[47] It is through this process, whereby what we understand to be the 'irreducible singularity'[48] of any archival artifact, its difference from other artifacts—*bifurcates* in structure, as difference emerges *within* itself. This difference is a *temporal* difference, because each incision within an artifact is a marking in and of time. Think of the painter who uses a brush to press paint against canvas a thousand or so times, with each stroke a unit composing the temporal order of the image. Often such an image is perceived as a flat whole, rather than a constellation of temporal incisions expressive of temporal differences. Recognising such temporal incisions is part of 'activating the materiality of making,' which foregrounds the 'politicised practice of opening up relationality.'[49] Arguably a similar interpretative process is required to activate the historico-temporal transmissions emitting from digital computations, commonly read as *flattening* historicity via the flat screen. As Berry writes, 'The interactional layer is extremely plastic and enables the computational presentation of appearance as such, usually through a visual register, but which can hold particular types of visual rhetoric that can be deployed *to support or produce preferred readings of the computational.*'[50] Yet it is precisely such *preferred readings* that must be challenged because they normatively operative at the 'commodity layer.' They therefore contain attempts to 'look . . . under the surface' at 'ontological layers of software' so that 'the structure and the construction'[51] *can be* examined. If preferred readings of the computational are not challenged, if the epistemic correspondences remain *stuck* within P←P→F historical time, the significance of temporal difference may not be perceived, and the necessity to develop a politics of transmission will not be elaborated with sufficient interpretive imagination.

When temporally multivalent artifacts are processed by the digital—whether they be scanned, photographed, 'shared' or placed within multiple and contingent orders of a digital archive—they are differentiated within themselves. This digital 'discretization radically affects the chain of memorial light, the Barthesian luminance, and by extension the *belief* we have in the image.'[52] Nevertheless, this 'chain of memorial light is not *absolutely* broken, it is rather *knotted in a different way.*'[53] Such artifactual splitting is the irrepressible contamination of historical time transmitting inauthentic difference. Deleuze described such an arrangement in *Difference and Repetition* as follows:

> Everything has become simulacrum, for by simulacrum we should not understand a simple imitation but rather the act by which the very idea of a model or privileged position is challenged and overturned. The simulacrum is the instance *which includes a difference within itself,* such as (at least) two divergent series on which it *plays,* all resemblance abolished *so that one can no longer point to the existence of an original and a copy.* It is in this *direction* that we must look for the conditions, not of possible experience, but of real experience (*selection, repetition,* etc). It is here that we find the *lived reality of sub-representative domain.* If it is true that representation has identity as its element and similarity as its unit of measure, then pure presence such as it appears in the simulacrum has the 'disparate' as its unit of measure—in other words, *always a difference of difference* as its immediate element.[54]

When historical time is processed by the digital, originals and copies are figured as expressions of *difference of difference,* released through the selection and performative transmission of the already-there. It is 'no longer about the real thing—the originary original. Instead, it is about its own real conditions of existence: about swarm circulation, digital dispersion, fractured and flexible temporalities.'[55] In such a context it is not sufficient to refer to processed digital historicity via the P←P→F schema, because both the descriptive and the conceptual value of these categories are attenuated by the mnemo-technical conditions that arrange vectors through which the already-there is accessed. One may well object here that the born-digital file, whose value derives from the capacity for exact replication, undermines these claims. Are born-digital files, then, composed through their sameness to one another? Born-digital files are also temporal singularities subject to the same digital processing and performativity as their digitised counterparts. Furthermore, born-digital files can exist in compressed and uncompressed formats, and although capable in theory of exact replication, are still prone to degradation, *particularly* when processed—that is, migrated and moved about.[56] The digitised and digital artifact, accrued with the textures of transmission, is a summation of what artist-theorist Hito Steyerl calls the 'poor image':

> *The poor image is a copy in motion.* Its quality is bad, its resolution substandard. As it accelerates, it deteriorates. It is a ghost of an image, a preview, a thumbnail, an errant idea, an itinerant image distributed for free, squeezed through slow digital connections, compressed, reproduced, ripped, remixed, as well as copied and pasted into other channels of distribution.
>
> The poor image is a rag or a rip; an AVI or a JPEG, a lumpen proletarian in the class society of appearances, ranked and valued according to its resolution. The poor image has been uploaded, downloaded, shared, reformatted, and reedited.[57]

Here Steyerl outlines how digital objects processually amass and shed materialised temporalities, due to being situated within the loops of destructive, lossy editing and wide circulation—that is, transmission. She points out how the sheer number and size of poor images in existence exceed transfer bandwidth and capacities as files clag through servers, operating at the threshold of the system's disseminative capabilities, caught in the lag between technological innovation and competent transmissive infrastructure.[58] These circulations of temporal differences must be appreciated for their singular qualities, deciphered for the times they release through performative transmission, as the already-there becomes arranged as a compositional mass of real-time historicities.

'Finished' Recorded Legacies

So far we have been discussing the contents of the WLMA with a focus on recordings whose processual qualities were manifest on playback: the live performance and the rehearsal. These are, however, not the only kind of recordings documented in the archive. There are a number of independently released albums, seven-inch singles and cassette albums—notably Jam Today (3)'s *Stereotyping* EP (seven-inch, 1981, Stroppy Cow); Ova's four albums (*Ova*, 1979; *Possibilities*, 1984; *Out of Bounds*, 1981; and *Who Gave Birth to the Universe*, 1988, all released on Stroppy Cow, tape and vinyl); Siren's *In Queer Street* (1985, self-released, tape only) and *Siren Plays* (Stroppy Cow, vinyl); the Fabulous Dirt Sisters (*Flapping Out*, 1986; *Five Strong Swimmers*, 1988, Spinaround Records, tape and vinyl); and the Mistakes (*Live at the Caribbean* album and a seven-inch single, 'Romance' b/w '16 Pins,' released on

Deviant Records). The recording and release of these works was largely due to the determination, organisational skills and willingness to take financial risks by some women's liberation music-makers. 'WE HAVE BORROWED THE MONEY TO MAKE THIS RECORDING SO PLEASE DO NOT COPY,' is a plea to the fans of the Fabulous Dirt Sisters written on the sleeve of their first album, *Flapping Out*.[59]

Compared with the relative ease of today's self-releasing musicians, doing it yourself in the late 1970s, prior to the mainstreaming of home-recording technologies in the early 1980s, was labour intensive and expensive.[60] Yet even professionally made recordings, which often become the final representation of a band's work, can emit their processes. Capturing the energy and 'essence' of a band in a recording is not always a simple or immediate task. For women with little experience of recording studios, working with in-house engineers who may never have heard them play live, the process of recording could be stressful, and the results disappointing. George Clarke, from Oxford-based pop-rock band the Mistakes, never listens to the seven-inch single and live album her band recorded because she doesn't like how it was mixed. In an interview she also revealed:

> The thing that went wrong for me when we were recording the LP and it was the first time I thought about leaving the band was I thought we were a good live band, I think people enjoyed watching us because we were lively and didn't take ourselves too seriously. When we got into the studio I felt some of the others in the group were a bit seduced by the recording techniques and being more into punk I wanted us to sound like we did live. There was this disgusting single that came out in the 80s by a band called the Corgis with zillions and zillions of over production noises on it and we'd been put in the same recording studio probably because somebody knew a bloke that ran it, and you know we were listening to 16 Annie's and 14 Mavis's, and I thought we're not the fucking Supremes we're The Mistakes. I can remember walking out in disgust.[61]

FIGURE 6.1
Fabulous Dirt Sisters in the recording studio (c. 1985/1986) (courtesy of the Fabulous Dirt Sisters).

The Fabulous Dirt Sisters had a particularly fraught relationship with their recorded work, a relationship that began with Mawby's letter used to open this chapter. In oral interviews conducted between 2010 and 2012, they often expressed disappointment with their albums, particularly *Flapping Out*, often citing their lack of expertise and confidence in the recording studio. Kaffe Matthews explains:

> Its only a few years ago when I was listening . . . and I was like Jesus Christ this is amazing, the song writing, Dorry's song writing was amazing but the production was really weak. The engineer was really weak, the studio we went to, he'd never done anything like this, he put down a click track, we should never have played to a click, we shouldn't have done that, so for us to record we needed to go into a studio and play live but we always did this bloody stupid overdub nonsense because we were totally naïve and didn't have a clue about this and we didn't have a producer. Basically the guy who engineered it suggested we did it like this and we just kinda go 'oh all right then.' We wanted it to sound as near to the live as possible.[62]

The contemporary reception of the album by critics and fans similarly reflected this sense of retrospective unease expressed by the Dirt Sisters. Consider these two reviews:

> Perhaps many people have told the Fabulous Dirt Sisters that they should go on record and spread the word. I wonder if they enjoyed recording it? It seems that success is determined by how many records you can spin off which is the wrong gauge of success in relation to the Fabulous Dirt Sisters. Their spirit is too valuable to be trapped and put on record. The feeling of celebration is better purveyed through live performance.[63]

> The Dirt Sisters' musical style defies definition, but their roots as a street band are clear. I don't think they've developed studio technique enough to appeal to those who haven't heard them live, though its worth listening to the tape just to hear Dorry's beautiful voice coming through clear and strong. . . . All Dirt Sisters fans should buy this album to keep them going between gigs, and I'd also recommend it, with condolences, to anyone who doesn't have the opportunity to see them live.[64]

For reviewers to pick up on the unease of a recorded piece of work seems fairly unusual, and both writers highlight the marked discrepancy of the recorded artifact in comparison to the vivacity of the band's live performances. The first review in particular suggests that there is something about the Dirt Sisters' music (its 'spirit') that cannot be 'trapped on record,' and that the very nature of the band is at odds with the culture of the popular music industry where 'success is determined by how many records you can spin off.' The questioning of whether the band enjoyed making the recording points to an awareness of the challenging processes surrounding feminist music-making, even among sympathetic reviews and fans. The sense communicated in the review that *Flapping Out*, as a *final representation* of the Dirt Sisters' work, is lacking reminds us to pay attention to the processes, to move under the surface of the screen (or in this case, the magnetic tape recording, or vinyl record) to interpret the material, historical and technical conditions that composed the action of feminist music-making and relay them within the scenes of transmission.

* * *

Walter Benjamin wrote that 'nothing that has ever happened should be regarded as lost for history.'[65] What emerges through the already-there never disappears entirely, even if its duration, depth or thickness can wane, become distilled or interrupted. Once an active transmission circuit has been dispersed, these exteriorised mnemonic resources exist as ongoing latencies. These compose within the already-there, remaining inoperable until appropriate technical systems are configured that enable embedded practices, knowledges, representations and ideas to become reinserted within the circuits that relay resources for collective and individual transformations. We have witnessed such occurrences with the cultural heritage of women's liberation music-making as the archive materials have been reintegrated within transmission circuits of digital mnemo-technicality. These archival forms may have arrived in a late or untimely fashion,[66] but such arrivals foreground the exigency of transmission as a conceptual-technical process through which (feminist) knowledge travels *across*: vertically, diagonally, horizontally and three-dimensionally, emergent from the dynamics of the *techniqual* system arranged by the digital. Transmissive systems are always intimately entangled with questions of spatial concentration (the length of the circuit) and duration (how long activated cultural entities can be sustained without thinning and disappearing within the already-there). Considering the role of transmission focuses on how the enlivening and utilising of traditions, techniques and knowledge—the circuits through which information is *kept alive*—occurs. This process is always different according to the actors involved, the resources available to them, cultural need, political context and so forth. Thus each occasion of transmission needs to be considered in its specificity, as I have done through my focus on the cultural heritage of the UK WLM as it was expressed through a particular cultural practice: music-making. The next and final chapter of this book outlines a number of pragmatic aspects that are necessary to elaborating a politics of transmission—a politics of the already-there—within the digital milieu: rethinking orientation and exploring how the informatic infrastructures that organise the already-there can be accessed and operationalised.

Notes

1. Deb Mawby, 'Letter to Stroppy Cow,' Feminist Archive South, DM2598/1.
2. Jolly, *In Love and Struggle*.
3. Jaimie Baron, *The Archive Effect: Found Footage and the Audiovisual Experience of History* (London: Routledge, 2014), 139–142; Eichorn, 'Archival Genres'; Owens, 'What Do You Mean by Archive? Genres of Usage for Digital Preservers.'
4. See Kate Eichorn, 'Beyond Digitisation: A Case Study of Three Contemporary Feminist Collections,' *Archives and Manuscripts* 42:3 (2014): 227–237.
5. Cait McKinney, 'Out of the Basement and on to Internet: Digitizing Oral History Tapes at the Lesbian Herstory Archives,' *No More Potlucks*, 'Failure' 34 (2014), accessed 24 July 2014, http://nomorepotlucks.org/site/out-of-the-basement-and -on-to-internet-digitizing-oral-history-tapes-at-the-lesbian-herstory-archives-cait -mckinney/.
6. A description Kaffe Matthews used to describe the Fabulous Dirt Sisters' music, interview with author, January 2010.
7. I would stop of short of describing this arrangement as 'democratic,' a word often used in relation to Web 2.0 participatory technologies, primarily because the internet, in its current corporate manifestation, is not democratic. Also see Eichorn, 'Beyond Digitization.'
8. Shannon Mattern, 'Preservation Aesthetics,' 18 July 2014, accessed 31 July 2014, http://www.wordsinspace.net/wordpress/2014/07/18/preservation-aesthetics -my-talk-for-the-locs-digital-preservation-conference/.
9. Freeman, *Time Binds*.
10. Marina Warner, 'Unhealing Time,' *Table of Contents: Memory and Presence* (London: Siobhan Davies Dance, 2014), 10–12.
11. To offer further conceptual grounding, we might also usefully turn to the work of Paolo Virno, *Dejà Vu and the End of History*, David Broder, trans. (London: Verso, 2015), when he talks about the temporality of the act/actual/actualities that 'always falls *in* time.' 'These acts are located within the progression of time along with so many other "nows," establishing reciprocal relations of anteriority and posteriority,' 66–67.
12. I am using this term in reference to Derrida's discussion of actuality and artifactuality: 'to think one's time . . . in order to bring it into play . . . the time of this speaking is artificially produced. It is an *artifact*.' Derrida, *Echographies*, 10. This point will be developed within the section of this chapter related to performativity.
13. Berry, *Critical Theory and the Digital*, 2–3, italics mine.
14. Timothy Scott Barker, *Time and the Digital: Connecting Technology, Aesthetics, and a Process Philosophy of Time* (Hanover, NH: Dartmouth College Press, 2012), 5, italics in original.
15. Wolfgang Ernst, *Digital Memory and the Archive*, Jussi Parikka, ed. (Minneapolis: University of Minnesota Press, 2012), 29, italics mine.
16. Ernst, 'The Archive as Metaphor: From Archival Space to Archival Time.'
17. Wolfgang Ernst, 'Between the Archive and the Anarchivable,' *Mnemoscape*, 1, 2014, accessed 23 April 2015, http://www.mnemoscape.org/#!Between-the-Ar

chive-and-the-Anarchivable-by-Wolfgang-Ernst/c1sp5/E1300B81-7A58-4F45-B8E3
-C89662ACC813.

18. Stiegler, *Technics and Time, 2: Disorientation*, 128.

19. Stiegler, 'Programs of the Improbable, Short-Circuits of the Unheard Of,' 82.

20. Stiegler, *Technics and Time, 2*, 115–136.

21. As Weltervrede et al. argue, there is a difference between the real-time internet of the 1990s, 'when the web was dominated by mainly static pages and very few
platforms and engines,' and the contemporary web 'dominated by platforms, engines
and their dynamically updating content.' By extension, there is a difference between
televisual real-time and these transmission systems, even if there is a similar concern
with immediacy and speed. Weltevrede et al., 'The Politics of Realtime,' 128.

22. Stiegler, 'Programs of the Improbable,' 82.

23. Stiegler, *States of Shock*, 53.

24. Arthur Bradley, *Originary Technicity: The Theory of Technology from Marx to
Derrida* (Basingstoke: Palgrave, 2011), 135.

25. Sarah Sharma, *In the Meantime: Temporality and Cultural Politics* (Durham,
NC: Duke University Press, 2014), 9.

26. Wajcman, *Pressed for Time*, 62, italics in original.

27. Weltevrede et al., 'The Politics of Realtime,' 143, italics mine.

28. Weltevrede et al., 'The Politics of Realtime,' 142.

29. Weltevrede et al., 'The Politics of Realtime,' 136.

30. Weltevrede et al., 'The Politics of Realtime,' 144.

31. Consider also the Sally Potter 'Sp-ark' archive (http://www.sp-ark.co.uk). It is
surely no coincidence that the former member of the Feminist Improvising Group
would create an educational archive deconstructing the process of making a film.
Even though the archive is astonishingly meticulous in breaking down the stages
through which a film is created, tracing genesis to delivery, covering script-writing,
attaining funding and designing costumes, it tellingly leaves out large amounts of
technical detail relating to the shooting of the film—which equipment was used
and so forth. That said, it is a compelling example of using digital technologies in a
processual manner—in a conceptually rigorous way—process by design, rather than
accident, like the WLMA. See also Sophie Mayer, 'Expanding the Frame: Sally Potter's
Digital Histories and Archival Futures,' *Screen* 49:2 (2008): 194–202.

32. 'Benefit for Jam Today,' Women's Liberation Music Archive, accessed 1
August 2014, http://womensliberationmusicarchive.files.wordpress.com/2010/10/
benefitforjt1backofflyer1.jpg/. To see the original copy, consult DM2598/1 at the
Feminist Archive South.

33. Stroppy Cow, 'About Stroppy Cow Records.' DM2598/1, Feminist Archive
South.

34. Mavis Bayton, *Frock Rock* (Oxford: Oxford University Press, 1998), 6.

35. Friggin Little Bits, 'Friggin Little Blitz-Come Together/Don't Die Wondering/
Bare (collective decision making),' Feminist Archive South, DM2598/1.

36. Richard Rinehart and Jon Ippolito, *Re-Collection: Art, New Media, and Social
Memory* (Cambridge, MA: MIT Press, 2014), 48.

37. Derrida, *Echographies*, 10.

38. Browne, 'Backlash, Repetition, Untimeliness,' 11.

39. An exception here being the Lupin Sisters' homemade album *Women Everywhere This Is For You* (1976) and Siren's *In Queer Street* (1985). Both were recorded on a two-track recorder.

40. Rosemary Schonfeld, 'Report from the Front Lines: Women's Music in Europe,' *Hot Wire: Journal of Women's Music and Culture* 5:2 (1989): 26–27. Note the tone of the title: the *front lines* of the cultural battlefield.

41. Grubbs, *Records Ruin the Landscape*, 136.

42. Furthermore, at an aesthetic level, grains, glitches and crackles might even be seen as edgy, cool and raw. See Julien Temple's claim regarding his footage of the Clash made on ½-inch open-reel videotape: 'Today monochrome footage would be perfectly graded with high-contrast effects. But the 1970s format has a dropout-ridden, glitchy feel which I enjoy now. *In fact, we cut in a couple of extra glitches we liked them so much.*' Vincent Dowd, 'Julien Temple on The Clash: "The Energy Of Punk Is Really Needed Now,"' BBC News, 1 January 2015, http://www.bbc.co.uk/news/entertainment-arts-30641500, italics mine.

43. Baron, *The Archive Effect.*

44. The recording of the Jam Today 2 practice 'Where Do We Go from Here?' is a good example of this. Available online: http://womensliberationmusicarchive.wordpress.com/j/.

45. Ernst, *Digital Memory and the Archive*, 58–59.

46. Mark Hansen, '"Realtime Synthesis" and the *Différance* of the Body: Techno-cultural Studies in the Wake of Deconstruction,' *Culture Machine* 6 (2004), accessed 4 March 2015, http://www.culturemachine.net/index.php/cm/article/view/9/8.

47. One now veering on anachronism if we are to accept what Berry has called the autonomy of the post-digital. See Stunlaw, 'The Post-Digital,' 1 January 2014, accessed 12 January 2014, http://stunlaw.blogspot.co.uk/2014/01/the-post-digital.html.

48. See the Emily Dickinson Radical Scatters, accessed 28 March 2015, http://archive.emilydickinson.org/radical_scatters.html.

49. Amelia Jones, *Seeing Differently: Visual Identification and the Visual Arts* (London: Routledge, 2012), 193. This process of identification and dis-identification Amelia Jones names 'queer feminist durationality' (193).

50. Berry, *Critical Theory and the Digital*, 70, italics mine.

51. Berry, *Critical Theory and the Digital*, 71–72.

52. Derrida and Stiegler, *Echographies*, 154, italics mine.

53. Derrida and Stiegler, *Echographies*, 154, italics mine.

54. Deleuze, *Difference and Repetition*, 69, italics mine.

55. Hito Steyerl, 'In Defence of the Poor Image,' *e-flux* 10:11 (2009) accessed 25 July 2014, http://www.e-flux.com/journal/in-defense-of-the-poor-image/.

56. See Barbara Sierman's website, *The Atlas of Digital Damages*. For example, read about the preservation migration of TIFF to JPEG 2000. 'During the migration action, the file was truncated, which resulted in losing vital information to create the correct JPEG2000 image. When an organization wants to preserve the JPEG2000 file for the long term, and is not aware of the damage that is done during the migration, then it

might be too late to repair it.' Accessed 11 January 2014, http://www.atlasofdigital
damages.info/v1/migration-issues/migration-tiff-to-jpeg2000/.

57. Steyerl, 'In Defence of the Poor Image,' italics.

58. This is particularly true of video files, which tend to be very large. Per Platou
from the Videokunstarkivet (Norwegian video art archive) told me in an interview
for the Great Bear Analogue & Digital Media tape blog that in establishing the
Videokunstarkivet they were 'pushing the limits of what is technically possible in
practice,' largely because internet servers are not built to handle large files, especially if those files are being transcoded back and forth across the file management
system. In this respect, the project is very much 'testing new ground,' creating an
infrastructure capable of effectively managing, and enabling people to remotely
access large amounts of high-quality video data. Accessed 27 July 2014, http://
www.thegreatbear.net/video-transfer/videokuntstarkivet-norways-digital-video
-art-archive/. See also the Presto Centre's *AV Digitisation and Digital Preservation
TechWatch Report #2, July 2014*: 'Transport of content was raised by one experienced archive workflow provider. They maintained that, especially with very high
bit-rate content (such as 4k) it still takes too long to transfer files into storage over
the network, and in reality there are some high-capacity content owners and pro-
ducers shipping stacks of disks around the country in Transit vans, on the grounds
that, in the right circumstances this can still be the highest bandwidth transfer
mechanism, even though the Digital Production Partnership (DPP) are pressing
for digital-only file transfer.' Accessed 29 July 2014, https://www.prestocentre.org/
system/files/library/resource/techwatch_report_final.pdf.

59. Fabulous Dirt Sisters, *Flapping Out*, Spinaround Records, 1986. Caps in original.

60. This raises an important question about the music-making communities of
queers and feminists in the twenty-first century. One would assume that given the
greater availability of recording and archival technologies that the availability and
preservation of twenty-first-century queer/feminist music, and those communities,
would be greater and more robust. Arguably similar problems of ephemerality and
'weak circuits' remain because technologies alone do not guarantee circulation, organisation and transmission. And there is also the question of file format, compressed
recordings and obsolescence.

61. George Clarke, interview with the author, 2009.

62. Matthews, interview with the author, 2010.

63. Amanda Tattamm, 'Review of Fabulous Dirt Sisters *Flapping Out*,' *Sanity*,
September 1986.

64. Linda Pierson, 'Review of Fabulous Dirt Sisters *Flapping Out*,' *Peace News*,
September 1986.

65. Benjamin, 'Theses on the Philosophy of History,' 256.

66. Browne, 'Backlash, Repetition, Untimeliness,' 11.

7

Orientation Within. *Already-There*

IN THE PREVIOUS CHAPTER I outlined what happens to historical time when
it is processed by the digital and how the digital alters conditions of access to the already-there. I explained this in terms of performatively enacted
real-time historicities that express inauthentic temporal differences through
a process of operationalisation. These digital mnemo-technical conditions
enact a profound dislocation from conceptions of historical time articulated
within the P$\leftarrow$P$\rightarrow$F constellation. Discussing the altered conditions of historicity within a digital milieu therefore necessitates qualification regarding
orientation. What does is it mean to be oriented within inauthentic temporal
differences, and how does this alter the conditions of access to the already-
there in general, and feminism's already-there in particular? Where, when
and how does the digital 'structure of *pros-thetic precedence*,' which acts as
'consciousness's "projective support", allowing us to inherit the past of all
preceding consciousnesses, and thus of *ourselves* at this moment,'[1] operate?
Stiegler, and many other theorists, have described the changing temporal
conditions wrought by digital mnemo-technics in terms of *disorientation*, a
disorientation often figured negatively in terms of disruption, loss and confusion, directed toward what one is, or we are, no longer orientated.[2] What is
being lost in these discussions, I want to suggest, is the P$\leftarrow$P$\rightarrow$F as organising
spatio-temporal principle ordering conditions of access to the already-there,
a 'law' that 'remains inaccessible, beyond everything,' according to Derrida.[3]

Orientation is embedded within the diagram I have used throughout the
second half of this book to gesture toward the categorisation of historical
time that must abandoned as we devise alternative access routes to the

already-there: P←P→F—the conception of 'the past' as always already oriented backwards, 'a present' turning point in the middle groundless site of articulation and a future always orientated forwards.[4] Such a program is no longer adequate to describe the transmission trajectories processed by the digital, and therefore other orientation schemas must be elaborated so that they may become tangible and *operative* techniques. This chapter thus responds to questions posed by Sara Ahmed: 'What does it mean to be orientated? . . . If we know where we are when we turn this or that way, then we are orientated. We have our bearings. We know what to do to get to this place or to that place. To be orientated is also to be turned toward certain objects, those that help us to find our way.'[5] I do so, however, within the arrangement of the already-there that refuses to be spatially limited by injunction to only look past-backwards or future-forwards. This is because to be oriented in the digital-processual already-there is to be reterritorialised; it is to be oriented in the everywhere. What follows, then, is an attempt to *adopt adequate techniques* to decipher, move within and operate within a recomposed already-there that, in turn, composes us, the conditioning *temporal* bond of a 'we.'[6] Let us then explore how Stiegler has understood disorientation before we offer alternative propositions to guide this movement.

Cardinality and Calendarity

In the previous chapter I outlined how a '*différantial* situation'[7] can be accessible via the digital artifact, challenging the idea that real-time transmissions inevitably install a 'permanent *present* at the core of the temporal flux' and therefore 'engender the fact and feeling of a gigantic memory hole, a *loss* of connection with the past.'[8] I argued that the digital is composed of multiple, internally different *real-time historicities* that enact the performative expression of inauthentic temporal differences. These artifacts, which may be a digitised item from 1851 or a born-digital twenty-first-century relic, have the potential to be continually refreshed, redistributed and repeated, more or less simultaneously, through the live vectors of real-time, or what Weltevrede et al. call *real-timeness*. These modes of digital transmission transform when, where and how artifacts are encountered, therefore altering normative conditions of historicity available to experience within the digital milieu.

Stiegler's main critique of real-time transmissions arises from how they are imbricated in the 'general seizure of control of inheritance, of retentions'[9] by the global, commercial programming industries. Such capture, which underscores the 'primordial nature of the current *disorientation*,'[10] assaults the very conditions of time and space whereby humans, composed within and by their technical environment, are oriented. Stiegler describes this as the undoing of 'calendarity and cardinality.'

> —*calendarity*, time, spanning the life of a society. . . . It is the calendar as such, but also the local events that make up the programmatics of *behavior* [*sic*], social synchronicities and the diachronic local manifestations, and
> —*cardinality*, space, tracing out actual territorial limits and boundaries, circumscribing social and cultural representations and forming *systems of orientation* and *navigational instruments* in space as well as time. . . .
> Calendarity and cardinality determine and manifest all collective movement, including history and geography.[11]

While the idea that digital technologies, and the internet in particular, have altered geographical boundaries and transformed conceptions of time has been an often-repeated claim, for Stiegler this kind of cardinal and calendarical disorientation has particularly disastrous effects because it undermines the possibility of 'the constitution of a *we* in general.'[12] Stiegler writes:

> For us to be able to say *we*, we must share the same calendar system and the same cardinal system. If we cannot refer to the same calendar, that is, if we do not share common time, and if we do not have a common representation of the spatial world in which we share systems of orientation—for example if we cannot read street names, maps or road signs—we amount to strangers.[13]

Part of what has become disoriented within the digital mnemo-technical epoch, I want to suggest, is the self-evident calendarity and cardinality that underpins the P←P→F constellation, the implicitly shared, yet unthought, conception of time and space that orders relationships to history and historical time. Within the digital mnemo-technical epoch, *the temporal force of historicity* has radically transformed orientation by becoming dislocated from P←P→F. Yet, as this effectively reroutes such 'a pivotal presupposition for a breath-taking array of Western concepts'[14] into a terrain that seems unimaginable or unthinkable, the impact *appears* to be one of devastation or disorientation. As Wajcman writes, 'Perhaps we are confused about what time we are living in. Part of the problem may be that the categories of speed and acceleration, and their association with progress, productivity and efficiency, *do not provide us with the appropriate language to formulate fresh ideas about how we might leverage the digital infrastructure.*'[15] It is vital, therefore, that appropriate categories, language and techniques are developed that can respond to, but also care for and operationalise, what is already-there—the exteriorised forms of inheritance that form the conditions for thinking and acting.[16] While the question of the industrial control of tertiary retentions cannot be ignored, 'the generally hidden and forgotten fact that society is already a process of

adoption'[17] similarly cannot be overlooked, particularly when this amounts
to the adoption of different modes of calendarity and cardinality emergent
within the digital mnemo-technical epoch.

This is, then, primarily, a question of orientation. Quite literally how we
turn toward, touch, encounter, enter and locate, in terms of both space and
time, the already-there within the digital milieu. These acts of turning toward,
which are also acts of turning within, through, under, against, touching the
surface of and so forth, can be imagined abstractly as the refusal to only perceive inheritance, of accessing the already-there, in terms of a backwards and
forwards movement, no matter how dynamic that movement may be.[18] It
demands the development of pragmatic techniques—navigational tools—that
enable access to the emergent digital mnemo-technical already-there, using
equipment that is appropriate, as well as conceptually and categorically fit
for purpose, to elaborate what exists, and endures through perpetual modification within the transmission process.[19] These modes of orientation are
situated within performative expressions of inauthentic temporal differences,
operationalised by specific transmission processes arranged by the digital.
This temporal ordering of the digital already-there challenges Stiegler's own
conception of calendarity and cardinality located, primarily, within a logic of
temporal-spatial sameness. That is, an 'adoption . . . presupposed by the constitution of a *we*'[20] resident within a shared time that is only possible because
it occurs *at the same time*. The temporal-spatial conditions for individual
and collective transformation within the digital, however, are composed by
temporal *differences* operating at the same time. There are different histories
and different geographies (there always have been), multiple and internally
diverse through bifurcation, simultaneously existing and operable via the
digitised trace.[21] Such temporal conditions necessitate pragmatic theorisation
of how to apprehend the arrangement and expression of these different historicities. Writing about how communities share time, Bastian argues:

> [T]he call to share time [should] recognize more clearly the way that a commu-
> nity's co-temporality is always multiple and never absolutely synchronous. To
> recognize coevalness would then entail breaking the conceptual bond that links
> 'harmonious community' with a 'synchronized time' in order to instead develop
> notions of community that would admit the possibility of being in different
> times, *at the same time*.[22]

Bastian outlines a way of thinking community and sharing time that is
not coordinated by the *same* map or the *same* calendar system. Instead, she
suggests, communities are composed by simultaneous experience of temporal differences. The challenge is to explore social models that can apprehend
and express those differences, rather than attempt to contain them through
exclusive appeals to synchronisation. A comparable operation is neces-

sary for reorientation within the already-there that can be attuned to the movement of temporal differences composing the digital mnemo-technical milieu—in short, the possibility of admitting that different historical times coexist at the same time: the digital '*différantial* situation.' Furthermore, because our digital times are normatively archival, *we* are conditioned by the temporal recursiveness that Eichorn describes as 'archival time,' *reparative* historiographic technologies capable of realigning historical actors and events that interrupt established historical designs, including standardised temporalisations of what happened across history and when.[23] Stiegler made a similar point when he wrote:

> *A combination of new texts/data and instruments make an entirely new mobilization of the already-there conceivable.* Citation and arrangement of the various elements furnished by available patrimonic and informational sources open the possibility of a qualitative leap from a new reading and writing at 'light-time' laminated onto an other, deferred time. Calculation as light-time, as information processing, then appears as a *new condition* for the irreducible textuality of texts—meaning of *traces* in general—in the *incalculability of their effects.*[24]

Yet this *entirely new mobilisation of the already-there* has not been thought by Stiegler in terms of the performative expression of inauthentic temporal differences. The 'meaning of traces *in general*' remains framed for him within the containing categorisations of P←P→F and their attendant spatial-temporal orientations. As I have argued in the second half of this book, if what is already-there is thought only within the categorical organisation of the P←P→F—indeed, if the P←P→F is not apprehended as a technique of thought produced by technics that arrange access and operationalisation of the already-there—there is the risk of mis-recognising the condition of transmission itself, which *is to move everywhere* as/through difference. Transmission within the digital mnemo-technical already-there is tessellating, obverse, tall and deep; its time-space orient(o)ntologies are coeval, crowded, perspectival, differentiated, performative and inauthentic—simultaneously supportive and potentially corrosive. For other kinds of 'we' to emerge, for other kinds of knowledge to emerge as part of this 'new relation to technics,'[25] it is crucial to outline interpretative techniques and practices that can elaborate the conditions of operation within the digital. One such technique that I will reflect on to end this book relates to a key archival technology: metadata.

Processes of Adoption, Metadata and Informatic Infrastructures

Tagging, categorisation and the production of metadata are key elements of accessing the already-there within the digital. These archival techniques aid the long-term discovery of digital information, creating vital information-infrastructures through which ephemeral feminist histories may achieve greater stability, concentration and access. As Stiegler writes,

> [W]ith digitalisation, for the first time in human history, metadata is produced through a bottom up and not a top down process, resulting in metadata that makes it possible not only to navigate through data, but also to link them and thus to trace within information the circuits that transform this information into knowledge. This . . . affects and will affect more and more both the elaboration of knowledge as well as the conditions for its socialization and transmission.[26]

Within the digital context, where metadata accrues added significance because of its capacity to link information entities, it is important that we consider carefully how artifacts are categorised and described. As discussed in previous chapters, my search and desire for WLM feminist musical histories was born from a *lack* of access to these legacies at a particular moment in historical time: 2007. Yet if we were to assign a descriptive category to the archive material I searched for, it may well be 'second wave' rather than 'music-making,' 'feminist activism' or 'cultural activism.' While wave-based distinctions may be useful to a degree, such categories are themselves not neutral. They are what van der Tuin calls 'classi*fix*ations,' which can often contain, overdetermine and motivate knowledge claims about feminism in particular times and places.[27] Yet in the archive, in a very pragmatic sense, employing categorisation and classification cannot be avoided. 'Organising the archive necessitates confronting the most pressing issues in feminist thought—even if it's just a matter of deciding where to shelve a book.'[28] While it sometimes appears as if there is *too much* categorisation preventing expansive, dynamic movements into feminism's already-there, I want to suggest there is *not enough* categorisation, both within feminism as an epistemic field and beyond—that is, the ability of feminist ideas to infect and change other fields of practice and knowing. Within the UK, and no doubt elsewhere, significant amounts of archive holdings pertaining to feminist and women's history remain either undercatalogued or uncatalogued. This means that parts of feminism's already-there do not have the *luxury* of categorisation and, as such, are, if not entirely invisible, then certainly barely accessible—merely existing as inoperable points within the circuitry of feminism's already-there. As archivist Hannah Little explains, 'For feminist archives, most energy has been put into saving/creating/collecting the archives, mainly by those who created the records themselves, so little has been done to arrange, appraise, describe and catalogue them.'[29] *The question of categorisation* occupies a central place, especially the problem of how feminism's already-there can be *discovered* and *operationalised* across generations. Categorisation performs a key role *enabling* modes of transmission; it need not render 'calculable what, being incomparable (the singular is in essence that which cannot be compared with anything else), is irreducibly incalculable.'[30] Classification is a means of description and association that links knowledge categories in the formation of robust circuits, a key process through which these 'objects of desire [which] are intrinsically singular' can 'intensify the singularity of [they] who desire.'[31]

How, then, are such practices to be done? Traditionally, archivists ascribe to a professional practice of neutrality. This 'major axiom that lies at the heart of archival practice' has been challenged by 'several [theorists who] have argued that given the power and instrumentality that are associated with the archive and its practices, as well as those of the record, neutrality is fundamentally a professional illusion and should be exposed as such.'[32] Yet, given the importance of metadata within the digital as a means to not only categorise but also link information entities so that they may become discoverable, I want to advocate for *strategic neutrality* in the description of feminism's digital already-there, in order to take account of the intimate relation between information, transmission and categorisation, and how this enables access to feminism's already-there. Conscientious metadata practices can place feminist artifacts within networks of reference and association that may help to assuage the ephemeral conditions of feminist histories that are often subject to dramatic cycles of recovery and loss. This will only be possible, however, if the metadata that describe entities within feminism's already-there facilitates the widest possible associations *across* the field of feminist inheritance, rather than be contained within a particular category that, due to its conceptual-descriptive power, risks undermining further connections and associations. Of course, such a suggestion may be 'much more desirable for those of us who theorize feminism than for our colleagues charged with the task of making feminist knowledges retrievable in the increasingly complex information networks where knowledges circulate.'[33] Yet I want to stress that attending to description is both pragmatic and necessary, particularly if we follow Stiegler's suggestion that 'the epistemic, political and economic stakes of the "digitalisation to come" rest on the conception, development and mass socialisation of such production models of the épistémè founded on polemical *annotation systems*.'[34] It is vital, therefore, to think through and reassess the normative processes of categorisation at play within fields such as feminism, where they often remain un-thought, yet, in fact, define the points of access to information *in the process of becoming* knowledge.

Taking Care of Categorisation

Within feminism, as we have heard, there can be less of a distinction between those who take care of and collect archives (professional archivists) and those who interpret their contents (researchers, curators and so forth). The process of collating a feminist archive and ensuring its long-term survival is often an activist endeavour, even if professional archivists and librarians help secure stable homes for materials and are usually central to any research process involving archive collections. Given the central role metadata and categorisation perform and will perform within the digital domain, greater exchange between information managers, researchers and others belonging to communities of interest whose knowledge is in/directly affected by the terms of categorisation will become a pressing concern. *We all need to become information managers in this information management society*, in other words, in a manner that challenges the mere instrumentality enforced by profit-hungry corporations that require vast swathes of data-producing (and managing) subjects.[35] Despite being surrounded by archival metaphors, as Parikka attests, there is the risk of eliding the lived responsibility and attaining none of the skills essential to the practice of (digital) information management—as evidenced by my early forays with the construction of the WLMA described in chapter 5. Collecting material is not enough to furnish a long-circuit; information needs to be embedded within further information so that it can be both preserved (a resilient already-there) and discoverable (an emergent already-there).

Creating metadata and, through this, *taking care of categorisation*, is an archival practice that helps spread categories of knowledge.[36] It is to become *skilled* at not only interpreting and learning from knowledge but also adopting techniques to implement the necessary informatic architectures that enable the sustainable transmission of feminism's already-there. As Little explains, 'Metadata is vital for digital material's preservation, so—as with most digital material—we can only hope that those creating the stuff care enough about it, or aren't too modest, and *are educated enough* to create the metadata.'[37] Creating appropriate metadata ensures that information has a 'context [that] gives us orientations, and reconstitutes our memories, something not afforded merely by storage. Dropbox, Google Drive, and so on are repositories . . . but they do not give us any *orientation*.'[38] Metadata acquires added importance given that the duration of digital circuits are as ephemeral as the artifacts they distribute. As the head of the UK's National Archives wrote in 2009, the next digital generation may be only five years away because of rapid cycles of innovation and obsolescence.[39] This means that it is vital that digital artifacts are appropriately annotated, including (but not limited to) description of file formats, transfer and storage history.

Creating metadata is a direct-action practice that tinkers with and reorganises the terms of association, categorisation and annotation that can maneuver orientations facilitating access to feminism's already-there. It is not foolproof: creating metadata offers no firm guarantee that the integrity of any digital object will be preserved in its entirety. There is always the risk of data loss as information is ingested by data management systems; *modification* is inherent to the transmission process. Yet this digital environment enables the dynamic movements across categorisation that van der Tuin so desires for her cartographical modes of association that 'advance links between existing schools of thought and breathe life in many categories at once.'[40] Devising nubile tagging and categorisation systems may also enable emergent forms of archival proximity to arise, something Eichorn struggles to envisage as possible within the digital context.[41] As Little, who worked as an archivist at the Glasgow Women's Library, elaborates:

> Electronic cataloging enables more ways in which to describe and arrange material, enabling multiple routes of discovery (taking cataloguing as a form of metadata) and also tagging (not only by archivists but by communities), subject indexing and multiple descriptions, so material can be arranged more easily in many different conceptual ways. I aimed to be as flexible and sensitive as possible, opting for open source cataloguing software that was interoperable with other systems. *Most terms are best worked out in a community.* In all the archives I've worked in, there is never enough time for cataloguing and most archives are still struggling to put their catalogues online.[42]

Education, skills and technique are the necessary armory required to ensure feminism's already-there is tagged, described and associated through descriptive metadata. Such systems do not just emerge, as if by magic. They are the result of very deliberate technical processes, the building of informatic architectures that enable access to feminism's already-there. These informatic architectures need instead to be designed, updated and widely contributed to so that *selected categories* can enable feminism's already-there to *spread*, but also connect in ways that cannot be anticipated because descriptions are premised within *strategic neutrality*. This is the means to implement categories that help the multiple knowledges of the already-there to spread with expansive differentiation.

Metadata, whose exigency is intensified within the digital, is thus key to the processual emergence of different temporal artifactualities. With such a context there is a pressing need *to adopt* a variety of skilled roles that cares not just for artifacts as finished work but also for its ongoing place within information architectures that are never static, always a site of struggle *and* an important arena for social transformation. Adoption here is synonymous with technical integration, the acquisition of almost-automatic habits that furnish one with appropriate skills to intervene, shape and transform one's environment. It requires an investment in economic and temporal terms, an investment that is so often scarce, as Little reminds us, but also an investment of will to dislocate the individual scholar *as individual*, who can then adopt a different role within 'intrinsically contributive'[43] mnemo-technical conditions. These are the processual circumstances whereby the animate sites of power and knowledge are the annotated circuits of transmission operating the digital. What accrues critical importance is not exclusively what is said but also where it travels, when and for how long. This has always been, or has potentially always been, the case. It is simply that contemporary mnemo-technical conditions render it salient and knowable as *everyday technique*.

Mobilising Tradition without $P \leftarrow P \rightarrow F$

Mobilising a politics of tradition is key to my articulation of the emergent already-there within the digital. Often tradition, as a concept, gets misrecognised as innately conservative, static, embarrassing, something to be distanced from. Yet the question of inheritance, in terms of both how knowledge is transmitted—the technical processes through which information is organised, preserved and disseminated—and how such information can be interpreted, is intensely political. As I have made clear throughout this book, how different communities are positioned in relation to the traditions that are meaningful to or meant for them can be, and usually are, sites of profound political and cultural struggle. Furthermore, the question of tradition—that is, placing the knowledges and techniques that are already-there within transmissive circuits in order to operationalise or enliven them—is particularly salient within a cultural context profoundly fixated upon the new, the innovative and the future, a context always oriented in moving or looking forward: $\rightarrow F$. To argue for the radical potentials of traditions, particularly those that keep alive cultural memories of social movements and world-making activities resistant to global capitalism, may seem innocuous or even quirky, an attachment to anachronism or even an expression of nostalgia. Yet, with processes of transmission, where the signal is modified and bifurcated by difference as it moves across temporal, spatial and generational entities, other worlds are not merely remembered—they are kept *alive*.

The mnemo-technical conditions presented by digitisation are then an invitation to *reorient* calendarities and cardinalities as an alternative elaboration of politicised tradition, an elaboration that always remains attributable to material, lived acts of transmission. I want to underscore that this political invocation of tradition never moves backwards, but always *within* and *everywhere*. If traditions are preserved, it is not for the obscure ideal of 'the future,' which Franco Berardi decries as a 'mythological temporalization . . . of an ever progressing development' that is 'rooted in modern capitalism.'[44] Traditions are instead preserved and reactivated for the benefit of communities of people and things, animating both the living and the dead. When what is already-there is transmitted and *panned* within animate circuits of transformative exchange, exteriorised mnemonic traces continue to speak and emit *infinite*[45] temporal knowledges. Or, as Stiegler explains,

> Technics opens the possibility of transmitting individual experience beyond the individual's life. . . . Inheriting and adopting a tool means inheriting part of the experience of the one(s) who bequeathed it: It is to adopt an experience, to make it part of one's own past even if one did not live it oneself.[46]

Inheriting tools and adopting pragmatic techniques from radical traditions such as feminism—the political movement *whose time has come*—can make other cardinalities and calandarities apparent, other ways of being oriented in the time-spaces of worlds. This is why generational exchange within the already-there is undergirded by multispatial, multitemporal dynamics; it is not uni- or bi-lateral (from old to the young, the young to old, backward to forward, forward to backward); transmission, and the potential relationships it can engender, is throughout, pan, everywhere. *'I am of this world; there is no other'*—the world that is already-there.[47]

These calendrical and cardinal orientations within the already-there are not always liberating; indeed, they may be deeply painful. For refusing the passed-ness of 'the past,' and resisting the habit of projection toward the future that thinks tradition for us without having to examine the messiness of inheritance, the lives lived but not lived, also means confronting ongoing-ness of devastating traditions wrought by colonialism, slavery, sexual violence, ecocide and war. These deeply regrettable instances of our history continue to shape all lives and orientations in the world, as well as perpetuating entrenched forms of deep social inequality. Investigating such issues with the care and attention that is necessary is, however, beyond the scope of this book, even if the possibility of other politics must be gestured to. As practices of historical redress, repatriation and political apologies suggest, reorienting cultural conceptions of historical time may have profound implications for collective identities and the distribution of cultural, economic and political power, even if such processes are unevenly or insufficiently delivered and practiced, and have varying degrees of success.[48] Yet what is already-there cannot ultimately be escaped, but it can be worked through—confronted. It has to be *lived with* because it infuses everything, and that *living with* should, ideally, not be debilitating of the body and soul of anyone or thing, organic or inorganic. It should, at the very least, be lived to enable the widest sense of persistence and flourishing[49] for living and non-living things, and the many traditions that can compose them. To do so, adjustments have to be made, orientations named, practiced and honed to the level of technique. If we accept that 'there is quite simply no history before the possibility of considering history *through* its technological medium,'[50] then the different tenor of historical time processed by the digital must be processed, and other means of orientation within the already-there expressed. Here the green shoots of unfinished worlds—their thoughts, sentences, feelings, images, noises, revolutions and traumatic constituencies—are emerging, already-there. Such conditions are an opportunity to learn how to *operate* within such rhythms.

For feminism, the conditions of the digital present a unique chance to learn from and take care of the traditions that have been toiled for, denigrated, misunderstood, ridiculed, hated, abjected, romanticised, mourned, desired, searched for and rejected so that they may be all these things and more. The vocabularies and techniques for accessing the already-there that I have laid out are to be picked up and used, and 'in case of success, the page is turned, the habits of thought are modified; others will be able to take up the baton.'[51] *My desire* is to have impressed upon the reader a sense that transmission is an active and activating practice that is an integral part of the encounter with knowledge. The transmission of traditions arranges the world; it arranges the possibility of the world. It is enormously powerful, yet often unthought or overlooked, because it composes it without our knowledge. Yet *we are* responsible for what is already-there, what gets transmitted, what becomes tradition—it is crucial that critical communities become skilled at processes of selection and learn the criteria through which nefarious social norms and traditions are fashioned, while seeking to affirm nurturing and loving ones. 'The question . . . "Who selects, and by what criteria?"'[52] must be taken seriously and responded to. My aim in this work is to orient the curious searcher for feminist traditions *within* the already-there. Go further, rest and stay awhile within. Linger in its midst. The flat dimensions of time and space, as correspondent with facing forward/back, exist as echoes. A band starts playing. There is singing, anguish and laughter.

I am spending the weekend visiting Maggie Nicols at her home in Drefach Felindre, Carmarthenshire. Maggie had been an original member of the now iconic Feminist Improvising Group (FIG) in late 1970s. In 2012 I helped migrate a number of live audiocassette recordings of FIG, and her other collective project, Contradictions, *to digital files as part of the Heritage Lottery Funded* Music & Liberation *exhibition.*

I browse her bookshelf as I often do with friends—I am a nosy visitor. Lodged between books about tarot and yoga is another cassette of FIG that clearly didn't make it to the digitising pile. I pull the tape off the shelf, dust curls under the inside of the cassette box corner and a wispy dead spider draped across the black shell. When was the last time it was played? *I wonder.*

In the kitchen is a tape machine, which I connect to my ad-hoc, digitisation device—a Zoom 4hN set to capture at 24bit/96kHz. I press Play, the tape warps and woozes, eventually the signal is stabilised and continuous sound is emitted. The side ends, I repeat the process for side 2. Listening back the migrated file could definitely be better in quality, since there is interference at the beginning and end of the tape, but given the equipment it was the best I could do. The opportunity had to be grasped at that moment—there might not be another chance. After everything is packed away, I push the tape back into its place on the shelf. That copy is good enough, I thought, and I get on with my day.

Notes

1. Stiegler, *Technics and Time, 3*, 49.
2. Wajcman, *Pressed for Time.*
3. Derrida and Stiegler, *Echographies of Television*, 8–9.
4. Indeed the self-evident assumption that historical thinking is synonymous with acts of looking backwards or forwards permeates the discipline, but also acts as a metaphysics of orientation within wider Western thinking (Bastian, 'Political Apologies and the Question of a "Shared Time"').
5. Sara Ahmed, *Queer Phenomenology: Orientations, Objects, Others* (Durham, NC: Duke University Press, 2006), 1.
6. Stielger, *Symbolic Misery.*
7. Stiegler, *States of Shock*, 53.
8. Stiegler, *Technics and Time, 2*, 128.
9. Stiegler, *Technics and Time, 3*, 223.
10. Stiegler, *Technics and Time, 3*, 223.
11. Stiegler, *Technics and Time, 3*, 121.
12. Stiegler, *Acting Out*, 45.
13. Stiegler, *Acting Out*, 45–46.
14. Bastian, 'Political Apologies and the Question of a "Shared Time,"' 116.
15. Wajcman, *Pressed for Time*, 183–184.
16. I am referring here Stiegler's claim that the I and we are composed together in the individuation process, as discussed in chapter 1.
17. Stiegler, *Acting Out*, 44.
18. See Browne, *Feminism, Time and Non-Linear History.*
19. Steyerl, 'Politics of the Archive.'
20. Stiegler, *Acting Out*, 45.
21. Tantalisingly, Browne quotes Paul Ricouer's contention that 'the trace' is 'an actual operator of historical time' in Browne, *Feminism, Time and Non-Linear History*, 72.

22. Bastian, 'Political Apologies and the Question of a "Shared Time,"' 112, italics in original.

23. Eichorn, *The Archival Turn in Feminism*, 90.

24. Stiegler, *Technics and Time, 2*, 148.

25. Stiegler, *States of Shock*, 137.

26. Stiegler, 'Distrust and the Pharmacology of Transformational Technologies,' 33.

27. See Withers and Chidgey, 'Complicated Inheritance: Sistershow and the Queering of Feminism,' and Hemmings, *Why Stories Matter*.

28. Stephanie Boland, '"She Blinded Me with Library Science": Why the Feminist Library Is More Vital Than Ever,' *New Statesman*, 26 February 2015, accessed 26 April 2015, http://www.newstatesman.com/culture/2015/02/she-blinded-me-library-science-why-feminist-library-more-vital-ever.

29. Hannah Little, interview with author, 5 November 2014.

30. Stiegler, *The Re-Enchantment of the World*, 12.

31. Stiegler, *The Re-Enchantment of the World*, 12.

32. Anne Gilliland, 'Neutrality, Social Justice and the Obligations of Archival Education and Educators in the Twenty-First Century,' *Arch Sci* 11 (2011): 196–197.

33. Eichorn, *The Archival Turn*, 149.

34. Stiegler, 'Distrust and the Pharmacology of Transformational Technologies,' 33.

35. Yuk Hui, 'A Contribution to the Political Economy of Personal Archives,' in Greg Elmer et al., eds., *Compromised Data: From Social Media to Big Data* (London: Bloomsbury, 2015). See also Christian Fuchs, *Digital Labour and Karl Marx* (London: Routledge, 2014), 243–283.

36. Bernard Stiegler, 'Chapter 1 Categorisation and Transindividuation,' 2013, accessed 23 August 2014, http://digital-studies.org/wp/categorisation-transindividuation/.

37. Hannah Little, personal correspondence with author, 5 November 2014.

38. Hui, 'A Contribution to the Political Economy of Personal Archives.'

39. Gollins, 'Parsimonious Preservation,' 76.

40. Van der Tuin, *Generational Feminism*.

41. Eichorn, 'Beyond Digitisation.'

42. Hannah Little, personal correspondence with author, 5 November 2014.

43. Stiegler, 'Distrust and the Pharmacology of Transformational Technologies,' 32.

44. Franco 'Bifo' Berardi, *After the Future*, Arianna Bove et al., trans. (Edinburgh: AK Press, 2011).

45. Stiegler, *States of Shock*, 161.

46. Stiegler, *Technics and Time, 3*, 206.

47. Rosi Braidotti and Timotheus Vermeulen, 'Borrowed Energy,' *Frieze* 165 (2014), accessed 15 October 2014, http://www.frieze.com/issue/article/borrowed-energy/, italics mine.

48. Elizabeth Crooke, 'Dealing with the Past: Museums and Heritage in Northern Ireland and Cape Town, South Africa,' *International Journal of Heritage Studies* 11:2 (2005): 131–142; Bastian, 'Political Apologies and the Question of a "Shared Time."'

49. Judith Butler, *Frames of War* (London: Verso, 2008).

50. Stiegler, 'Programs of the Improbable, Short-Circuits of the Unheard Of,' 83, italics mine.

51. Stengers and Despret, *Women Who Make a Fuss*, 68.

52. Stiegler, *Technics and Time, 3*, 223.

Bibliography

Adorno, Theodor. *The Culture Industry: Selected Essays on Mass Culture.* London: Routledge, 2001.

Ahmed, Sara. *The Cultural Politics of Emotion.* Edinburgh: Edinburgh University Press, 2004.

———. *Queer Phenomenology: Orientations, Objects, Others.* Durham, NC: Duke University Press, 2006.

Alexander, M. Jacqui. *Pedagogies of Crossing: Meditations on Feminism, Sexual Politics, Memory and the Sacred.* Durham, NC: Duke University Press, 2005.

'Alexis Pauline Gumbs.' Accessed 25 March 2015. http://alexispauline.com/.

Andrejevic, Mark. *Infoglut: How Too Much Information Is Changing the Way We Think and Know.* London: Routledge, 2013.

Anon. 'Here Is Julie Burchill's Censored *Observer* Article.' *The Telegraph.* 14 January 2013. Accessed 5 November 2013. http://blogs.telegraph.co.uk/news/toby young/100198116/.

———. Interview with Elizabeth Bird. 14 January 1999. Feminist Archive South. DM2123.

Anzaldúa, Gloria. 'Bridge, Drawbridge, Sandbar, or Island: Lesbians-of-Color *Hacienda Alianzas.*' Gloria Anzaldúa and AnaLouise Keating, eds. *The Gloria Anzaldúa Reader,* 140–56. Durham, NC: Duke University Press, 2009a.

———. 'Metaphors in the Tradition of the Shaman.' Gloria Anzaldúa and AnaLouise Keating, eds. *The Gloria Anzaldúa Reader,* 121–23. Durham, NC: Duke University Press, 2009b.

———. 'Preface: (Un)natural Bridges, (Un)safe Spaces.' Gloria Anzaldúa and AnaLouise Keating, eds. *This Bridge We Call Home: Radical Visions for Transformation,* 1–5. London: Routledge, 2002.

Arizpe, Lourdes. 'The Cultural Politics of Intangible Cultural Heritage.' *Art, Antiquity and Law* 12 (2007): 355–370.

Armstrong, Frankie. Interview with author. April 2012.

'The Atlas of Digital Damages.' Accessed 11 January 2014. http://www.atlasofdigital damages.info/v1/migration-issues/migration-tiff-to-jpeg2000/.

Aune, Kristin, and Catherine Redfearn. *Reclaiming the F-Word: The New Feminist Movement.* London: Zed Books, 2013.

Banach Bergin, Meghan. 'Digital Preservation Capabilities at Cultural Heritage Institutions: An Interview with Meghan Banach Bergin.' *The Signal.* 10 November 2014. Accessed 13 November 2014. http://blogs.loc.gov/digitalpreservation/2014/11/digital-preservation-capabilities-at-cultural-heritage-institutions-an-interview-with-meghan-banach-bergin/.

Banyard, Kat. *The Equality Illusion: The Truth About Men and Women Today.* London: Faber, 2011.

Barad, Karen. 'Quantum Entanglements and Hauntological Relations of Inheritance: Dis/continuities, SpaceTime Enfoldings, and Justice-to-Come.' *Derrida Today* 3:2 (2010): 240–268.

Barker, Timothy Scott. *Time and the Digital: Connecting Technology, Aesthetics, and a Process Philosophy of Time.* Hanover, NH: Dartmouth College Press, 2012.

Baron, Jaimie. *The Archive Effect: Found Footage and the Audiovisual Experience of History.* London: Routledge, 2014.

Bastian, Michelle. 'Political Apologies and the Question of a "Shared Time" in the Australian Context.' *Theory, Culture & Society* 30:5 (2013): 94–121.

Batra, Kanika. 'The Home, the Veil and the World: Reading Ismat Chughtai towards a "Progressive" History of the Indian Women's Movement.' *Feminist Review* 95 (2010): 27–44.

Bauer, Petra, and Dan Kidner, eds. *Working Together: Notes on British Film Collectives in the 1970s.* Southend: Focal Point Gallery, 2013.

Bayton, Mavis. 'Feminist Music Practice: Problems and Contradictions.' Tony Bennett et al., eds. *Rock and Popular Music: Politics, Policies, Institutions*, 177–193. London: Routledge, 1993.

——. *Frock Rock.* Oxford: Oxford University Press, 1998.

Beins, Agatha. 'Sisterly Solidarity: Politics and Rhetoric of the Direct Address in US Feminism in the 1970s.' *Women: A Cultural Review* 21:3 (2010): 292–309.

'Benefit for Jam Today.' Women's Liberation Music Archive. Accessed 1 August 2014. http://womensliberationmusicarchive.files.wordpress.com/2010/10/benefit forjt1backofflyer1.jpg/.

Benjamin, Walter. 'The Storyteller.' *Illuminations*, 83–108. Glasgow: Fortuna, 1977.

——. 'Theses on the Philosophy of History.' *Illuminations*, 255–267. Glasgow: Fortuna, 1977.

Bennett, Andy. '"Heritage Rock": Rock Music, Representation and Heritage Discourse.' *Poetics* 37 (2009): 474–489.

Berardi, Franco 'Bifo.' *After the Future.* Arianna Bove et al., trans. Edinburgh: AK Press, 2011.

Berliner, David. 'New Directions in the Study of Cultural Transmission.' L. Arizpe and C. Amescua, eds. *Anthropological Perspectives on Intangible Cultural Heritage.* Springer Briefs in *Environment, Security, Development and Peace* 6 (2013): 71–77.

Berry, David M. *Critical Theory and the Digital.* London: Bloomsbury, 2014.

———. *The Philosophy of Software: Code and Mediation in the Digital Age.* Basingstoke: Palgrave, 2011.

Bird, Elizabeth. 'Women's Studies and the Women's Movement in Britain.' *Women's History Review* 12:2 (2003): 263–288.

Boland, Stephanie. '"She Blinded Me with Library Science": Why the Feminist Library Is More Vital Than Ever.' *New Statesman.* 26 February 2015. Accessed 26 April 2015. http://www.newstatesman.com/culture/2015/02/she-blinded-me-library-sci ence-why-feminist-library-more-vital-ever.

Bolmer, Grant David. 'Virtuality in Systems of Memory: Toward an Ontology of Collective Memory, Ritual, and the Technological.' *Memory Studies* 4:4 (2011): 450–464.

'Bolton Women's Liberation Oral History' Project. Accessed 24 January 2015. http://www.bolton-womens-liberation.org/.

Boylan, P. J. 'The Intangible Heritage: A Challenge and an Opportunity for Museums and Museum Professional Training.' *International Journal of Intangible Heritage* 1 (2006): 54–65.

Bradley, Arthur. *Originary Technicity: The Theory of Technology from Marx to Derrida.* Basingstoke: Palgrave, 2011.

Brah, Avtar. 'Journey to Nairobi.' Gail Lewis, Shabnam Grewal, Jackie Kay, Liliane Landor and Pratibha Parmar, eds. *Charting the Journey,* 74–89. London: Sheba Press, 1988.

Braidotti, Rosi, and Timotheus Vermeulen. 'Borrowed Energy.' *Frieze* 165 (2014). Accessed 15 October 2014. http://www.frieze.com/issue/article/borrowed-energy/.

'British Library Preservation Strategy.' Accessed 27 March 2015. http://www.bl.uk/aboutus/stratpolprog/collectioncare/discovermore/digitalpreservation/strategy/BL_DigitalPreservationStrategy_2013-16-external.pdf.

Brocken, Michael. *The British Folk Revival: 1944–2002.* Aldershot: Aldgate, 2003.

Browne, Victoria. 'Backlash, Repetition, Untimeliness: The Temporal Dynamics of Feminist Politics.' *Hypatia* 2012. Accessed 27 October 2013. DOI: 10.1111/hypa.12006.

———. *Feminism, Time and Non-Linear History.* Basingstoke: Palgrave, 2014.

———. 'Feminist Historiography and the Reconceptualisation of Historical Time.' PhD diss., University of Liverpool, 2013.

'Butetown History & Arts Centre.' Accessed 13 February 2015. http://bhac.org.c31.sitepreviewer.com/.

Butler, Judith. *Frames of War.* London: Verso, 2008.

———. *Gender Trouble.* London: Routledge, 2006.

Burin, Yula, and Ego Ahaiwe Sowinski. 'Sister to Sister: Developing a Black Feminist Archival Consciousness.' *Feminist Review* 108 (2014): 112–119.

Byrne, Denis. 'A Critique of Unfeeling Heritage.' Laurajane Smith and Natsuko Akagawa, eds. *Intangible Heritage,* 229–253. London: Routledge, 2009.

Campbell, Gary, and Laurajane Smith. 'Association of Critical Heritage Studies Manifesto.' 2012. Accessed 1 April 2014. http://criticalheritagestudies.org.preview .binero.se/site-admin/site-content/about-achs.

Carr, David. *Experience and History.* Oxford: Oxford University Press, 2014.

Caruth, Cathy, ed. *Trauma: Explorations in Memory.* Baltimore: Johns Hopkins University Press, 1995.

Caughie, Pat. 'Theorizing the "First Wave" Globally.' *Feminist Review* 95 (2010): 5–9.

Chidgey, Red, '"A Modest Reminder": Performing Suffragette Memory in a British Feminist Webzine.' Anna Reading and Tamar Katriel, eds. *Powerful Times: Cultural Memories of Nonviolent Struggles.* Basingstoke: Palgrave Macmillan, 2015.

Chun, Wendy. 'The Enduring Ephemeral, or, The Future Is a Memory.' Erik Huhtamo and Jussi Parikka, eds. *Media Archaeology: Approaches, Applications and Implications,* 184–207. Berkeley and Los Angeles: University of California Press, 2011.

Clarke, George. Interview with the author. 2009.

Cochrane, Kira. 'The Fourth Wave of Feminism: Meet the Rebel Women.' *The Guardian.* 10 December 2013. Accessed 13 December 2013. http://www.theguardian .com/world/2013/dec/10/fourth-wave-feminism-rebel-women.

Cohen, Sara, and Les Roberts. 'Unauthorising Popular Music Heritage: Outline of a Critical Framework.' *The International Journal of Heritage Studies* 20:3 (2014): 241–261.

Coley, Rob, and Dean Lockwood. *Cloud Time: The Inception of the Future.* Winchester: Zer0 Books, 2012.

Combahee River Collective. 'The Combahee River Collective Statement.' 1977. Accessed 25 March 2015. http://www.sfu.ca/iirp/documents/Combahee%201979.pdf.

Cooke, Rachel. 'Taking Women Off the Shelf.' *The Guardian.* 2 April 2008. Accessed 28 October 2014. http://www.theguardian.com/books/2008/apr/06/fiction .features1.

Cooper, Lindsay/Sally Potter. 'Seeing Red.' *The Gold Diggers.* 1983. Sync Pulse 0617.

Coote, Anna, and Beatrix Campbell. *Sweet Freedom: The Struggle for Women's Liberation.* London: Pan, 1982.

Cowman, Krista. '"Carrying a Long Tradition": Second-Wave Presentations of First-Wave Feminism in Spare Rib c. 1972–80.' *European Journal of Women's Studies* 17:3 (2010): 193–210.

Crary, Jonathan. *24/7.* London: Verso, 2013.

Crogan, Patrick. 'Experience of the Industrial Temporal Object.' Christina Howells and Gerald Moore, eds. *Stiegler and Technics,* 102–118. Edinburgh: Edinburgh University Press, 2013.

Crooke, Elizabeth. 'Dealing with the Past: Museums and Heritage in Northern Ireland and Cape Town, South Africa.' *International Journal of Heritage Studies* 11:2 (2005): 131–142.

——. 'The Politics of Community Heritage: Motivations, Authority and Control.' *International Journal of Heritage Studies* 16:1–2 (2010): 16–29.

Cubitt, Geoffrey. *History and Memory.* Manchester: Manchester University Press, 2007.

Cvetkovich, Ann. *Archives of Feelings: Trauma, Sexuality, and Lesbian Public Cultures*. Durham, NC: Duke University Press, 2003.

deLanda, Manuel. *A Thousand Years of Non-Linear History*. New York: Swerve Editions, 2000.

Deleuze, Gilles. 'Desert Islands.' Michael Taormina, trans. *Desert Islands and Other Texts 1953–1974*, 9–15. Los Angeles: Semiotexte, 2004.

———. *Difference and Repetition*. Paul Patton, trans. London: Athlone Press, 1994.

———. 'Postscript on Societies of Control.' *October* 59 (1992): 3–7.

Deleuze, Gilles, and Félix Guattari. *Kafka: Towards a Minor Literature*. Dana Polan, trans. Minneapolis: University of Minnesota Press, 1986.

Derrida, Jacques. *Dissemination*. Barbara Johnson, trans. London: Continuum, 2004.

———. *Spectres of Marx*. Peggy Kamuf, trans. London: Routledge, 2006.

Derrida, Jacques, and Bernard Stiegler. *Echographies of Television*. Jennifer Bajorek, trans. Cambridge: Polity, 2002.

Digital Preservation Coalition. 'DPC Joins Collaboration to Create an Electronic "Ark" for Digital and Paper-based Records.' 2014. Accessed 19 June 2014. http://www.dpconline.org/newsroom/latest-news/1140-e-ark-announcement-feb-2014.

———. 'Technological Issues.' *Digital Preservation Handbook*. 2000/2008. Accessed 17 June 2014. http://www.dpconline.org/advice/preservationhandbook/digital-preservation/preservation-issues.

do Mar Pereira, Maria. 'Feminist Theory Is Proper Knowledge, But . . . : The Status of Feminist Scholarship in the Academy.' *Feminist Theory* 13:3 (2012): 283–303.

Downes, Julia. 'DIY Subcultural Resistance in the UK.' PhD diss. University of Leeds, 2010.

'East London Suffragette Festival.' Accessed 24 January 2015. http://eastlondonsuffragettes.tumblr.com/.

Edelman, Lee. *No Future: Queer Theory and the Drive*. Durham, NC: Duke University Press, 2004.

Eichhorn, Kate. 'Archival Genres: Gathering Texts and Reading Spaces.' *Invisible Culture* 12 (2008). Accessed 17 June 2014. http://www.rochester.edu/in_visible_culture/Issue_12/eichhorn/index.htm.

———. *The Archival Turn in Feminism: Outrage in Order*. Philadelphia: Temple University Press, 2013.

———. 'Archiving the Movement: The Riot Grrrl Collection at the Fales Library and Special Collections.' Liz Bly and Kelly Wooton, eds. *Make Your Own History: Documenting Feminist and Queer Activism in the 21st Century*, 23–39. Los Angeles: Litwin Books, 2013.

———. 'Beyond Digitisation: A Case Study of Three Contemporary Feminist Collections.' *Archives and Manuscripts* 42:3 (2014): 227–237.

'Emily Dickinson Radical Scatters.' Accessed 28 March 2015. http://archive.emilydickinson.org/radical_scatters.html.

Ernst, Wolfgang. 'The Archive as Metaphor: From Archival Space to Archival Time.' *Archive public*. 2005. Accessed 27 March 2015. http://archivepublic.wordpress.com/texts/wolfgang-ernst/.

———. 'Between the Archive and the Anarchivable.' *Mnemoscape*, 1. 2014. Accessed 23 April 2015. http://www.mnemoscape.org/#!Between-the-Archive-and-the-Anar chivable-by-Wolfgang-Ernst/c1sp5/E1300B81-7A58-4F45-B8E3-C89662ACC813.

———. *Digital Memory and the Archive.* Jussi Parikka, ed. Minneapolis: University of Minnesota Press, 2012.

European Union. *European Parliament and Council Recommendation on Film Heritage.* 2014. Accessed 8 January 2015. http://ec.europa.eu/information_society/newsroom/ image/4th_film%20heritage%20report%20final%20for%20transmission_6962.pdf.

Eyerman, Ron, and Andrew Jamison. *Music and Social Movements: Mobilizing Traditions in the Twentieth Century.* Cambridge: Cambridge University Press, 1998.

Fabulous Dirt Sisters. *Flapping Out.* Spinaround Records. 1986.

———. Interview with author. 20 May 2010.

Farthing, Anna. 'Authenticity and Metaphor: Displaying Intangible Human Remains in Museum Theatre.' Anthony Jackson and Jenny Kidd, eds. *Performing Heritage: Research, Practice and Innovation Museum Theatre and Live Interpretation*, 94–106. Manchester: Manchester University Press, 2011.

Feigenbaum, Anna. '"Now I'm a Happy Dyke!" Creating Collective Identity and Queer Community in Greenham Women's Songs.' *Journal of Popular Music Studies* 22:4 (2010): 367–388.

———. 'Tactics and Technology: Cultural Resistance at the Greenham Common Women's Peace Camp.' PhD diss., McGill University, 2008.

'Feminist Archives and Libraries Network.' Accessed 24 January 2015. http://femi nistlibrariesandarchives.wordpress.com/.

'Feminist Archive South.' Accessed 27 October 2013. http://feministarchive.org.uk.

Feminist Archive South. 'Personal Histories of Second Wave Feminism.' Accessed 12 November 2014. http://feministarchivesouth.org.uk/collections/personal-histo ries-of-second-wave-feminism-oral-history-project-2000-2001/.

'The Feminist Seventies.' Accessed 13 February 2015. http://www.feministseventies .net/.

Fisher, Mark. *Ghosts of My Life.* Winchester: Zer0, 2014.

Foucault, Michel. *The Archaeology of Knowledge.* London: Routledge, 2002.

'Frankie Green and Jam Today.' Accessed 27 March 2015. http://thefabulousdirtsis ters.wordpress.com/2010/06/19/frankie-green-and-jam-today.

Freeman, Elizabeth. *Time Binds: Queer Temporalities, Queer Histories.* Durham, NC: Duke University Press, 2010.

Friedan, Betty. *The Feminine Mystique.* London: Penguin, 2010.

Friggin Little Bits. 'Friggin Little Blitz-Come Together/Don't Die Wondering/Bare (collective decision making).' Feminist Archive South. DM2598/1.

Fuchs, Chrisitan. *Digital Labour and Karl Marx.* London: Routledge, 2014.

Fuggle, Sophie. 'Stiegler and Foucault: The Politics of Care and Self-Writing.' Christina Howells and Gerald Moore, eds. *Stiegler and Technics*, 192–207. Edinburgh: Edinburgh University Press, 2013.

Fuss, Diana. *Essentially Speaking: Feminism, Nature and Difference.* London: Routledge, 1989.

'The F-Word.' Accessed 15 November 2014. http://www.thefword.org.uk/.

Galloway, Alexander. 'The Black Box of Philosophy: Compression and Obfuscation.' *Incredible Machines*. 2014. Accessed 5 March 2015. http://incrediblemachines.info/ keynote-speakers/galloway/.

Garde-Hansen, Joanne, Andrew Hoskins and Anna Reading, eds. *Save As . . . Digital Memories*. Basingstoke: Palgrave Macmillan, 2009.

Gibson-Graham, J. K. 'Querying Globalisation.' John C. Hawley, ed. *Post-Colonial, Queer*, 239–277. New York: SUNY Press, 2001.

Gilfillan, Caroline. Interview with author. March 2012.

Gill, Rosalind. 'Postfeminist Media Culture: Elements of a Sensibility.' *European Journal of Cultural Studies* 10 (2008): 147–66.

Gill, Rosalind, and Christina Scharff. 'Introduction.' Rosalind Gill and Christina Scharff, *Postfeminism, Neoliberalism and Subjectivity*, 1–21. Basingstoke: Palgrave, 2011.

Gilliland, Anne. 'Neutrality, Social Justice and the Obligations of Archival Education and Educators in the Twenty-First Century.' *Arch Sci.* 11 (2011): 193–209.

Gillis, Stacy, Gillian Howie and Rebecca Munford, eds. *Third Wave Feminism: A Critical Introduction*. Basingstoke: Palgrave Macmillan, 2007.

Goldsmith, Kenneth. 'If It Doesn't Exist on the Internet, It Doesn't Exist.' 2005. Accessed 5 March 2015. http://epc.buffalo.edu/authors/goldsmith/if_it_doesnt_exist .html.

Gollins, Tim. 'Parsimonious Preservation: Preventing Pointless Processes! The Small Simple Steps That Take Digital Preservation a Long Way Forward.' *Online Information Proceedings*. 2009. Accessed 8 January 2014. http://www.nationalarchives. gov.uk/documents/parsimonious-preservation.pdf.

Gould, Deborah M. *Moving Politics: Emotion and Act Up's Fight Against AIDS*. Chicago: Chicago University Press, 2010.

Graff, Agnieszka. 'A Different Chronology: Reflections on Feminism in Contemporary Poland.' Stacey Gillis, Gillian Howie and Rebecca Munford, eds. *Third Wave Feminism: A Critical Exploration*, 142–155. Basingstoke: Palgrave, 2007.

'Grassroots Feminism.' Accessed 24 January 2015. www.grassrootsfeminism.net.

Gratton, Peter, 'Review of *Taking Care of Youth and the Generations*.' *Notre Dame Philisophical Reviews*. 2010. Accessed 11 December 2013. http://ndpr.nd.edu/ news/24441-taking-care-of-youth-and-the-generations/.

'Great Bear Tape Blog.' Accessed 27 July 2014. http://www.thegreatbear.net/video -transfer/videokuntstarkivet-norways-digital-video-art-archive/.

Green, Frankie. 'London Women's Liberation Rock Band.' Women's Liberation Music Archive. 2010. Accessed 19 December 2012. http://womensliberationmusi- carchive.wordpress.com/l/.

Grosz, Elizabeth. 'The Practice of Feminist Theory.' *differences: A Journal of Feminist Cultural Studies* 21:1 (2010): 94–108.

Grubbs, David. *Records Ruin the Landscape: John Cage, the Sixties, and Sound Recording*. Durham, NC: Duke University Press, 2014.

Guest, Carly. 'Young Women's Narratives and Memories of Becoming Feminist: A Multi-Method Study.' PhD diss., Birkbeck, University of London, 2014.

Gumbs, Alexis Pauline. 'Eternal Summer of the Black Feminist Mind.' Lyz Bly and Kelly Wooten, eds. *Make Your Own History: Documenting Feminist & Queer Activism in the 21st Century*, 59–69. Los Angeles: Litwin Books, 2013.

Gunnarsson, Lena. 'A Defence of the Category "Women."' *Feminist Theory* 12:1 (2011): 23–37.

Hall, Stuart, and Alan O'Shea. 'Common Sense Neo-liberalism.' *Soundings* 55 (2013): 1–18. Accessed 24 March 2015. https://www.lwbooks.co.uk/journals/soundings/pdfs/Manifesto_commonsense_neoliberalism.pdf.

Hanmer, Jalna. Email message to the author. 20 October 2013.

Hansen, Mark B. N. *Feed-Forward: On the Future of Twenty-First-Century Media*. Chicago: University of Chicago Press, 2015.

———. 'Memory.' W. J. T. Mitchell and Mark B. N. Hansen, eds. *Critical Terms for Media Studies*, 64–88. Chicago: University of Chicago Press, 2010.

———. '"Realtime Synthesis" and the Différance of the Body: Technocultural Studies in the Wake of Deconstruction.' *Culture Machine* 6 (2004). Accessed 4 March 2015. http://www.culturemachine.net/index.php/cm/article/view/9/8.

Harrison, Brian. 'Oral Evidence of the Suffrage Movement.' 'Women's Library.' Accessed 27 October 2013. http://twl-calm.library.lse.ac.uk/CalmView/Record.aspx?src=CalmView.Catalog&id=8SUF.

Harrison, Rodney. 'Forgetting to Remember, Remembering to Forget: Late Modern Heritage Practices, Sustainability and the "Crisis" of Accumulation of the Past.' *International Journal of Heritage Studies* 19:6 (2013): 579–595.

———. *Heritage: Critical Approaches*. London: Routledge, 2013.

Harrison, Rodney, and Deborah Rose. 'Intangible Heritage.' Tim Benton, ed. *Understanding Heritage and Memory*, 238–277. Manchester: Manchester University Press, 2010.

Hartman, Saidya. *Lose Your Mother: A Journey Along the Atlantic Slave Route*. New York: Farrar, Straus and Giroux, 2007.

Harvey, David C. 'Heritage Pasts and Heritage Presents: Temporality, Meaning and the Scope of Heritage Studies.' *International Journal of Heritage Studies* 7:4 (2001): 319–338.

Hemmings, Clare. 'Generational Dilemmas: A Response to Iris van der Tuin's "Jumping Generations": On Second- and Third-wave Feminist Epistemology.' *Australian Feminist Studies* 24:59 (2009): 33–37.

———. *Why Stories Matter: The Political Grammar of Feminist Storytelling*. Durham, NC: Duke University Press, 2011.

Henry, Astrid. *Not My Mother's Sister: Generational Conflict and Third Wave Feminism*. Bloomington: Indiana University Press, 2004.

Hesford, Victoria. *Feeling Women's Liberation*. Durham, NC: Duke University Press, 2013.

Hesford, Victoria, and Lisa Diedrich. 'Experience, Echo, Event: Theorising Feminist Histories, Historicising Feminist Theory.' *Feminist Theory* 15 (2014): 103–117.

Hirsch, Marian. 'The Generation of Postmemory.' *Poetics Today* 29:1 (2008). Accessed 26 March 2015. DOI: 10.1215/03335372-2007-019.

Hoel, Aud Sissel, and Iris van der Tuin. 'The Ontological Force of Technicity: Reading Cassirer and Simondon Diffractively.' *Philosophy & Technology* (2012). Accessed 25 March 2015. Philos. Technol. DOI: 10.1007/s13347-012-0092-5.

Hoskins, Andrew. 'Media, Memory, Metaphor: Remembering and the Connective Turn.' *Parallax* 17:4 (2011): 19–31.

'How the Vote Was Won.' Accessed 24 March 2015. http://www.thesuffragettes.org/.

Hui, Yuk. 'A Contribution to the Political Economy of Personal Archives.' Greg Elmer, Ganaele Langlois and Joanna Redden, eds. *Compromised Data: From Social Media to Big Data*. London: Bloomsbury, 2015.

Humm, Maggie, ed. *Feminisms: A Reader*. Hemel Hempstead: Harvester Wheatsheaf, 1992.

Hunt, Teresa. Interview with author. 2012.

Hutton, Caroline. Interview with author. 2009.

Ippolita. *The Dark Side of Google*. Amsterdam: Institute of Network Cultures, 2013.

Ithaka S + R. *Appraising our Digital Investment Sustainability of Digitized Special Collections in ARL Libraries*. 2013. Accessed 12 January 2015. http://www.sr.ithaka .org/research-publications/appraising-our-digital-investment.

Jameson, Fredric. *Postmodernism, or the Cultural Logic of Late Capitalism*. London: Verso, 1992.

Jisc. Accessed 27 March 2015. http://www.jisc.ac.uk/about/history.

John, Angela V. 'To Make That Future Now: The Women's Library and the TUC Library.' *History Workshop Journal Online*. 20 April 2012. Accessed 24 October 2013. http://www.historyworkshop.org.uk/to-make-that-future-now-the-womens -library-the-tuc-library/.

Jolly, Margaretta. 'Assessing the Impact of Women's Movements: Sisterhood and After.' *Women's Studies International Forum* 35 (2012): 150–152.

———. *In Love and Struggle*. New York: Columbia University Press, 2008.

Jones, Amelia. *Seeing Differently: Visual Identification and the Visual Arts*. London: Routledge, 2012.

Jonsson, Terese. 'White Feminist Stories: Locating Race in Representations of Feminism in *The Guardian*.' *Feminist Media Studies* 14:6 (2014): 1012–1027.

Kaloski, Ann, ed. *The Feminist Seventies*. York: Raw Nerve, 2003.

Kearney, Mary Celeste. 'Riot Grrrl—Feminism—Lesbian Culture.' Sheila Whiteley, ed. *Sexing the Groove: Popular Music and Gender*, 207–225. London: Routledge, 1997.

Kidd, Jenny, Sam Cairns, Alex Drago, Amy Rayall and Miranda Stearn, eds. *Challenging History in the Museum*. Aldershot: Ashgate, 2014.

Kidd, Jenny, and Anthony Jackson. 'Introduction.' Anthony Jackson and Jenny Kidd, eds. *Performing Heritage: Research, Practice and Innovation Museum Theatre and Live Interpretation*, 1–11. Manchester: Manchester University Press, 2011.

Kimball, Gayle, ed. *Women's Culture in a New Era: A Feminist Revolution*. Lanham, MD: Scarecrow Press, 2005.

Kimball, Gayle. *Women's Culture: The Women's Renaissance of the Seventies*. Lanham, MD: Scarecrow Press, 1981.

King, Katie. *Networked Reenactments: Stories Transdisciplinary Knowledges Tell.* Durham, NC: Duke University Press, 2012.

Kirschenbaum, Matthew G. *Mechanisms: New Media and the Forensic Imagination.* Cambridge, MA: MIT Press, 2012.

Kuntsman, Adi. 'Introduction: Affective Fabrics of Digital Cultures.' Adi Kuntsman and Athina Karatzogianni, eds. *Digital Cultures and the Politics of Emotion*, 1–21. Basingstoke: Palgrave, 2012.

Lebedeva, Kristina. 'Review Article: Bernard Stiegler: *Technics and Time, 2.*' *Parrhesia* 7 (2009): 81–85. Accessed 11 December 2013. http://www.parrhesiajournal.org/parrhesia07/parrhesia07_lebedeva.pdf.

Lehrer, Erica, Cynthia E. Milton and Monica Eileen Patterson. *Curating Difficult Knowledge: Violent Pasts in Public Places.* Basingstoke: Palgrave, 2011.

Lewis, Gail. 'Against the Odds: Feminist Knowledge Production and Its Vicissitudes.' *European Journal of Women's Studies* 17:2 (2010): 99–103.

——. 'Black Feminist Texts.' *Sisterhood and After.* 2013. Accessed 25 March 2015. http://www.bl.uk/learning/histcitizen/sisterhood/viewhtml#id=143433&id2=143140.

——. Interviewed by Rachel Cohen. *Sisterhood and After.* 2011. Transcribed by the author from the audio file. Accessed 24 March 2015. http://cadensa.bl.uk/uhtbin/cgisirsi/?ps=dftkoGSvHL/WORKS-FILE/97220073/9.

——. 'Oral Histories of the Black Women's Movement: The Heart of the Race Project.' ORAL/1. Black Cultural Archives (2009/2010).

Lewis, Gail, Shabnam Grewal, Jackie Kay, Liliane Landor and Pratibha Parmar. 'Preface.' Gail Lewis, Shabnam Grewal, Jackie Kay, Liliane Landor and Pratibha Parmar, eds. *Charting the Journey*, 1–6. London: Sheba Press, 1988.

Liddington, Jill. 'Fawcett Saga: Remembering the Fawcett Library Across Four Decades.' *History Workshop Journal* (2013): 266–280. Accessed 27 October 2013. DOI: 10.1093/hwj/dbt026.

Little, Hannah. Interview with author. 5 November 2014.

Logan, William, and Keir Reeves. *Places of Pain and Shame: Dealing with 'Difficult Heritage.'* London: Routledge, 2008.

Lorde, Audre. 'Litany for Survival.' *Collected Poems of Audre Lorde*, 255–256. New York: W. W. Norton, 1997.

——. 'An Open Letter to Mary Daly.' *Sister Outsider: Essays and Speeches*, 66–72. New York: The Crossing Press, 1984.

——. *Zami: A New Spelling of My Name.* Watertown, MA: Persephone Press, 1982.

Loxley, Diana. *Problematic Shores: The Literature of Islands.* New York: St. Martin's, 1990.

'Make Your Own Herstory.' Accessed 24 January 2015. http://nicgreen.wix.com/makeyourownherstory.

Malabou, Catherine. *The Ontology of the Accident: An Essay on Destructive Plasticity.* Carolyn Shread, trans. Cambridge: Polity Press, 2012.

Mann, Regis. 'Theorizing "What Could Have Been": Black Feminism, Historical Memory, and the Politics of Reclamation.' *Women's Studies* 40:5 (2011): 575–599.

Marchionni, Paola. Interview with author. July 2013.

Massumi, Brian. 'Painting: The Voice of the Grain.' Bracha Ettinger, ed. *The Matrixial Borderspace*, 201–215. Minneapolis: University of Minnesota Press, 2006.

Mattern, Shannon. 'Preservation Aesthetics.' 18 July 2014. Accessed 31 July 2014. http://www.wordsinspace.net/wordpress/2014/07/18/preservation-aesthetics-my -talk-for-the-locs-digital-preservation-conference/.

Matthews, Kaffe. Interview with author. January 2010.

Mawby, Deb. 'Letter to Stroppy Cow.' Feminist Archive South. DM2598/1.

May, Chris. 'Step Forward, Daughters.' Unknown publication. Feminist Archive South. DM2123.

Mayer, Sophie. 'Expanding the Frame: Sally Potter's Digital Histories and Archival Futures.' *Screen* 49:2 (2008): 194–202.

Mayhall, Laura. 'Creating the "Suffragette Spirit": British Feminism and the Historical Imagination.' Antoinette Fraser, ed. *Archive Stories: Facts, Fictions and the Writing of History*, 232–251. Durham, NC: Duke University Press, 2005.

McBean, Sam. *Feminism's Queer Temporalities*. London: Routledge, 2015.

McKinney, Cait. 'Out of the Basement and on to Internet: Digitizing Oral History Tapes at the Lesbian Herstory Archives.' *No More Potlucks*. 'Failure' 34 (2014). Accessed 24 July 2014. http://nomorepotlucks.org/site/out-of-the-basement-and -on-to-internet-digitizing-oral-history-tapes-at-the-lesbian-herstory-archives -cait-mckinney/.

McRobbie, Angela. *The Aftermath of Feminism: Gender, Culture and Social Change*. London: Sage, 2009.

'Mechanical Curator.' Accessed 28 March 2015. http://mechanicalcurator.tumblr .com/.

Merla-Watson, Cathryn Josefina. 'Metaphor, Multitude, and Chicana Third Space Feminism.' *ACME: An International E-Journal for Critical Geographies* 11:3 (2012): 492–511.

Meskell, Lynn. *Archaeology Under Fire: Nationalism, Politics and Heritage in the Eastern Mediterranean and Middle East*. London: Routledge, 1998.

Minh-Ha, Trinh T. *The Digital Film Event*. London: Routledge, 2004.

Mohanty, Chandra Talpade. 'Under Western Eyes: Feminist Scholarship and Colonial Discourses.' *Boundary 2* 12:3 (1986): 333–358.

Moi, Toril. *Sexual/Textual Politics*. London: Methuen, 1985.

Moore, Niamh. *The Changing Nature of ECO/Feminism: Telling Stories from Clayoquot Sound*. Vancouver: University of British Columbia Press, 2013.

——. 'Eco/Feminism and Rewriting the Ending of Feminism: From the Chipko Movement to Clayoquot Sound.' *Feminist Theory* 12:1 (2011): 3–21.

Moore, Sarha. Interview with author. 2010.

Moraga, Cherríe. 'Foreword.' Cherríe Moraga and Gloria Anzaldúa, eds. *This Bridge Called My Back: Writings by Radical Women of Color*. New York: Kitchen Table: Women of Color Press, 1983.

Munford, Rebecca, and Melanie Waters. *The Post-Feminist Mystique: Feminism and Popular Culture*. London: IB Tauris, 2013.

Muñoz, José Esteban. *Cruising Utopia: The Then and There of Queer Futurity*. New York: New York University Press, 2009.

'Music & Liberation.' Accessed 27 October 2013. http://music-and-liberation.tumblr
.com.

Neiger, Motti, Oren Meyers and Eyal Zandberg. 'Localizing Collective Memory:
Radio Broadcasts and the Construction of Regional Memory.' Motti Neiger, Oren
Meyers and Eyal Zandberg, eds. *On Media Memory: Collective Memory in a New
Media Age*, 156–174. Basingstoke: Palgrave, 2011.

Nietzsche, Friedrich. 'On the Use and Disadvantages of History for Life.' Daniel
Breazeale, trans. *Untimely Meditations*, 57–125. Cambridge: Cambridge University
Press, 1997.

Nora, Pierre. 'Between Memory and History: *Les Lieux de Memoire*.' *Representations*
26 (1989): 7–24.

Northern Women's Liberation Rock Band. *Manifesto: Why Are There Hardly Any
Women Rock Bands?* 1974. Accessed 27 November 2013. http://womensliberation
musicarchive.files.wordpress.com/2010/10/northern-womens-liberation-rock
-band-manifesto-and-lyrics-booklet.pdf.

——. 'Women Together: Edinburgh Sixth National Women's Liberation Conference.' *Spare Rib* 27 (1974). Accessed 26 March 2015. http://womensliberationmu
sicarchive.files.wordpress.com/2010/10/nwlrb-article-spare-rib-27-1974.jpg.

Novaczek, Ruth. Interview with author. 2012.

O'Keefe, Theresa. 'My Body Is My Manifesto! SlutWalk, FEMEN and Femmenist
Protest.' *Feminist Review* 107 (2014): 1–19.

Owens, Trevor. 'What Do You Mean by Archive? Genres of Usage for Digital Preservers.' *The Signal*. 27 February 2014. Accessed 7 May 2014. http://blogs.loc.gov/
digitalpreservation/2014/02/what-do-you-mean-by-archive-genres-of-usage-for
-digital-preservers/.

'Oxford Dictionaries.' Accessed 26 March 2015. http://www.oxforddictionaries.com/.

Papadopoulos, Dimitris. 'Generation M: Matter, Makers, Microbiomes: Compost for
Gaia.' *European Institute for Progressive Cultural Politics*. 2014. Accessed 26 March
2014. http://eipcp.net/n/1392050604.

Parikka, Jussi. 'Archival Media Theory: An Introduction to Wolfgang Ernst's Media
Archaeology.' Jussi Parikka, ed. *Digital Memory and the Archive: Wolfgang Ernst*,
1–23. Minneapolis: University of Minnesota Press, 2012.

——. *The Anthrobscene*. Minneapolis: University of Minnesota Press, 2014.

Parmar, Pratibha, and Trinh T. Minh-ha. 'Women, Native, Other.' *Feminist Review*
36 (1990): 65–74.

Perrier, Maud. 'The Fear of Depoliticization in Feminist Critiques of the Affective
Turn: The Necessity of the Unstable Psyche for Reframing Affect Debates.' Paper
presented at the 8th European Feminist Research Conference, Budapest, Hungary,
17–20 May 2012.

Phelan, Peggy. *Unmarked: The Politics of Performance*. London: Routledge, 1993.

Pierson, Linda. 'Review of Fabulous Dirt Sisters *Flapping Out*.' *Peace News*, September 1986.

Pietrobruno, Sheenah. 'Between Narrative and Lists: Performing Digital Intangible
Heritage Through Global Media.' *International Journal of Heritage Studies* 20:7–8
(2014): 742–760.

Power, Nina. 'Why Diet When You Could Riot.' *Riots Not Diets Compilation.* Tuff Enuff Records, LP. *Music & Liberation: A Compilation of Music from the Women's Liberation Movement.* CD. 2012. Accessed 23 December 2014. http://music-and -liberation.tumblr.com/post/35555849335/nina-power-reviews-music-liberation -compilation.

Presto Centre. *AV Digitisation and Digital Preservation TechWatch Report #2, July 2014.* Accessed 29 July 2014. https://www.prestocentre.org/system/files/library/ resource/techwatch_report_final.pdf.

Reading, Anna. 'Gender and the Right to Memory.' *Media Development* 2 (2010): 11–15.

——. 'Restitution Is Impossible.' Keynote presented at Memory and Restitution conference, 5–6 July 2013. http://www.memoryandrestitution.co.uk/.

——. 'Seeing Red: A Political Economy of Digital Memory.' *Media, Culture & Society* 36:6 (2014): 748–760.

——. 'Singing for My Life: Memory, Nonviolence and the Songs of Greenham Common Women's Peace Camp.' Anna Reading and Tamar Katriel, eds. *Powerful Times: Cultural Memories of Nonviolent Struggle.* Basingstoke: Palgrave, forthcoming.

'Reclaim the Night.' Accessed 27 October 2013. http://www.reclaimthenight.co.uk.

'Remember Olive Morris.' Accessed 24 January 2015. https://rememberolivemorris .wordpress.com/.

Reynolds, Simon. *Retromania: Pop Culture's Addiction to Its Own Past.* London: Faber, 2011.

Rinehart, Richard, and Jon Ippolito. *Re-Collection: Art, New Media, and Social Memory.* Cambridge, MA: MIT Press, 2014.

Robinson, Emily. 'Touching the Void: Affective History and the Impossible.' *Rethinking History* 14:4 (2010): 503–520.

Roseneil, Sasha. *Common Women, Uncommon Practices: The Queer Feminisms of Greenham.* London: Continuum, 2000.

Ross, Daniel. 'Pharmacology and Critique after Deconstruction.' Christina Howells and Gerald Moore, eds. *Stiegler and Technics*, 243–259. Edinburgh: Edinburgh University Press, 2013.

Rowbotham, Sheila. *Hidden from History.* London: Pluto, 1975.

Rowlands, Mike, and Beverly Butler. 'Conflict and Heritage Care.' *Anthropology Today* 23:1 (2007): 1–2.

Runnalls, Jana. Interview with author. 2012.

Rushkoff, Douglas. *Present Shock: When Everything Happens Now.* New York: Penguin, 2013.

Samuel, Raphael. *Theatres of Memory.* London: Verso, 2012/1996.

Schneider, Rebecca. *Performing Remains: Art and War in Times of Theatrical Reenactment.* London: Routledge, 2011.

Schonfeld, Rosemary. Interview with author. 18 December 2010.

——. 'Report from the Front Lines: Women's Music in Europe.' *Hot Wire: Journal of Women's Music and Culture* 5:2 (1989): 26–27.

Schor, Naomi, and Elizabeth Weed, eds. *The Essential Difference.* Bloomington: Indiana University Press, 1994.

Scott, Joan W. *The Fantasy of Feminist History.* Durham, NC: Duke University Press, 2011.

Sebesteyen, Amanda. 'Tendencies in the Women's Movement.' The Women's Library, *Ms Understood: The Development of the Movement.* 2012. London Metropolitan University.

'See Red Women's Workshop.' Accessed 24 January 2015. https://seeredwomens workshop.wordpress.com/.

Segal, Lynne. 'Generations of Feminism.' *Radical Philosophy* 83 (1997): 6–16.

Sentilles, Renée M. 'Toiling in the Archives of Cyberspace.' Antoinette Burton, ed. *Archive Stories: Facts, Fictions and the Writing of History*, 136–157. Durham, NC: Duke University Press, 2005.

'Shape and Situate: Posters of Inspirational European Women.' Accessed 24 January 2015. http://www.spacestationsixtyfive.com/exhibitions_and_projects .php?project_id=140.

Sharma, Sarah. *In the Meantime: Temporality and Cultural Politics.* Durham, NC: Duke University Press, 2014.

Shocking Pink. n.d. Feminist Archive South. DM2123/5.

'Sisterhood and After.' Accessed 24 January 2015. http://www.bl.uk/learning/histciti zen/sisterhood/.

'Sistershow Revisited.' Accessed 27 October 2013. http://sistershowrevisited.word press.com.

Smith, Laurajane. 'The "Doing" of Heritage: Heritage as Performance.' Anthony Jackson and Jenny Kidd, eds. *Performing Heritage: Research, Practice and Innovation in Museum Theatre and Live Interpretation*, 69–81. Manchester: Manchester University Press, 2011.

———. *The Uses of Heritage.* London: Routledge, 2006.

Smith, Laurajane, and Emma Waterton. '"The Envy of the World?" Intangible Heritage in England.' Laurajane Smith and Natsuko Akagawa, eds. *Intangible Heritage*, 289–303. London: Routledge, 2009.

Sobchack, Vivian. 'Afterword: Media Archaeology and Re-Presencing the Past.' Erik Huhtamo and Jussi Parikka, eds. *Media Archaeology: Approaches, Applications and Implications*, 323–335. Berkeley and Los Angeles: University of California Press, 2011.

Spivak, Gayatri Chakravorty. 'Feminism, Criticism and the Institution.' *Thesis Eleven* 10–11 (1984/1985): 175–187.

Starosielski, Nicole. *The Undersea Network.* Durham, NC: Duke University Press, 2015.

Stengers, Isabelle. 'Experimenting with Refrains: Subjectivity and the Challenge of Escaping Modern Dualism.' *Subjectivity* 22 (2008): 38–59.

Stengers, Isabelle, and Vinciane Despret. *Women Who Make a Fuss: The Unfaithful Daughters of Virginia Woolf.* Minneapolis, MN: Univocal, 2014.

Sterne, Jonathan. *MP3: The Meaning of a Format.* Durham, NC: Duke University Press, 2012.

Steyerl, Hito. 'In Defence of the Poor Image.' *e-flux* 10:11 (2009). Accessed 25 July 2014. http://www.e-flux.com/journal/in-defense-of-the-poor-image/.

——. 'Politics of the Archive, Translations in Film.' *Transversal*. 2008. Accessed 25 March 2015. http://eipcp.net/transversal/0608/steyerl/en.

Stiegler, Bernard. *Acting Out*. David Barison, Patrick Crogan and Daniel Ross, trans. Stanford: Stanford University Press, 2009.

——. 'Chapter 1: Categorisation and Transindividuation.' 2013. Accessed 23 August 2014. http://digital-studies.org/wp/categorisation-transindividuation/.

——. *The Decadence of Industrial Democracies*. Daniel Ross, trans. Cambridge: Polity, 2011.

——. 'Distrust and the Pharmacology of Transformational Technologies.' Daniel Ross, trans. T. B. Zülsdorf et al., eds. *Quantum Engagements*, 27–39. Heidelberg: AKA Verlag, 2011.

——. *For a New Critique of Political Economy*. Daniel Ross, trans. Cambridge: Polity, 2010.

——. *The Lost Spirit of Capitalism: Disbelief and Discredit, vol. 3*. Daniel Ross, trans. Cambridge: Polity, 2014.

——. 'The Net Blues.' Sam Kinsley, trans. Accessed 8 May 2014. http://www.sam kinsley.com/2013/11/21/bernard-stiegler-the-net-blues/.

——. 'Programs of the Improbable, Short-circuits of the Unheard Of.' Robert Hughes, trans. *DIACRITICS* 42:1 (2014): 70–109.

——. *The Re-Enchantment of the World: The Value of Spirit Against Industrial Populism*. Trevor Arthur, trans. London: Bloomsbury, 2014.

——. *States of Shock: Stupidity and Knowledge in the 21st Century*. Daniel Ross, trans. Cambridge: Polity, 2015.

——. *Symbolic Misery: Vol. 1, The Hyperindustrial Epoch*. Barnaby Norman, trans. Cambridge: Polity, 2014.

——. *Taking Care of Youth and the Generations*. Stephen Barker, trans. Stanford: Stanford University Press, 2010.

——. *Technics and Time, 1: The Fault of Epimetheus*. Richard Beardsworth and George Collins, trans. Stanford: Stanford University Press, 1998.

——. *Technics and Time, 2: Disorientation*. Stephen Barker, trans. Stanford: Stanford University Press, 2009.

——. *Technics and Time, 3: Cinematic Time and the Question of Malaise*. Stephen Barker, trans. Stanford: Stanford University Press, 2011.

——. *What Makes Life Worth Living: On Pharmacology*. Daniel Ross, trans. Cambridge: Polity, 2013.

Stiegler, Bernard, and Irit Rogoff. 'Transindividuation.' *e-flux* (2010). Accessed 26 March 2014. http://www.e-flux.com/journal/transindividuation/.

Stoler, Ann Laura. *Along the Archival Grain: Epistemic Anxieties and Colonial Common Sense*. Princeton, NJ: Princeton University Press, 2010.

'Striking Women.' Accessed 24 January 2015. http://www.striking-women.org/main -module-page/striking-out.

Stroppy Cow. 'About Stroppy Cow Records.' DM2598/1. Feminist Archive South.

Stunlaw. 'The Post-Digital.' 1 January 2014. Accessed 12 January 2014. http://stunlaw .blogspot.co.uk/2014/01/the-post-digital.html.

Tasker, Yvonne, and Diane Negra, eds. *Gendering the Recession: Media and Culture in an Age of Austerity.* Durham, NC: Duke University Press, 2014.

Tattamm, Amanda. 'Review of Fabulous Dirt Sisters *Flapping Out.*' *Sanity.* September 1986.

Taylor, Diana. *The Archive and the Repertoire: Performing Cultural Memory in the Americas.* Durham, NC: Duke University Press, 2003.

Thompson, Tierl, Andrea Webb and Janie Fairchild. 'Introduction.' *Sisters in Song: Collection of New Songs from the Women's Liberation Movement,* 4–7. Only Women Press, 1978.

'Translation/Transmission Women's Film Season.' Accessed 24 January 2015. http://translationtransmission.wordpress.com.

Tripp, Aili Mari. 'The Evolution of Transnational Feminisms: Consensus, Conflict and New Dynamics.' Myra Marx Ferree and Aili Mari Tripp, eds. *Global Feminism: Transnational Women's Activism, Organising and Human Rights,* 51–79. New York: New York University Press, 2006.

UNESCO. 'Recommendation on the Safeguarding of Traditional Culture and Folklore.' 1989. Accessed 26 March 2015. http://portal.unesco.org/en/ev.php-URL_ID=13141&URL_DO=DO_TOPIC&URL_SECTION=201.html.

———. 'Text for the Safeguarding of Intangible Cultural Heritage.' 2003. Accessed 24 March 2014. http://www.unesco.org/culture/ich/index.php?lg=en&pg=00006.

'Unfinished Histories: Histories of Alternative Theatre, 1968–1988.' Accessed 24 January 2015. http://www.unfinishedhistories.com.

Van der Tuin, Iris. *Generational Feminism: New Materialist Introduction to a Generative Approach.* New York: Lexington, 2014.

———. 'Jumping Generations: On Second- and Third-wave Epistemology.' *Australian Feminist Studies* 24:59 (2009): 17–31.

Van Heur, Bas. 'From Analogue to Digital and Back Again: Institutional Dynamics of Heritage Innovation.' *International Journal of Heritage Studies* 16:6 (2010): 405–416.

Virno, Paolo. *Dejà Vu and the End of History.* David Broder, trans. London: Verso, 2015.

VT West, Pat. Oral History with Viv Honeybourne. 2000. Transcribed by the author. Feminist Archive South. DM2123/1/Archive Boxes 79.

Wajcman, Judy. *Pressed for Time: The Acceleration of Life in Digital Capitalism.* Chicago: University of Chicago Press, 2015.

Walker, Alice. *In Search of Our Mothers' Gardens: Womanist Prose.* London: Women's Press, 1983.

Wardrop, Alex. 'A Procrastination.' Alex Wardrop and Deborah Withers, eds. *The Para-Academic Handbook: A Toolkit for Making-Learning-Creating-Acting,* 6–14. Bristol: HammerOn Press, 2015.

Warner, Marina. 'Unhealing Time.' *Table of Contents: Memory and Presence,* 6–15. London: Siobhan Davies Dance, 2014.

Weltevrede, Esther, Anne Helmond and Carolin Gerlitz. 'The Politics of Realtime: A Device Perspective on Social Media Platforms and Search Engines.' *Theory, Culture & Society* 31:6 (2014): 125–150.

Wertheim, Margaret. *The Pearly Gates of Cyberspace: A History of Space from Dante to the Internet.* New York: W. W. Norton, 1999.

Whiteley, Gillian. "'New Age" Radicalism and the Social Imagination: Welfare State International in the Seventies.' Laurel Foster and Sue Harper, eds. *British Culture and Society in the 1970s: The Lost Decade,* 35–51. Newcastle Upon Tyne: Cambridge Scholars, 2010.

Winch, Alison. *Girlfriends and Postfeminist Sisterhood.* Basingstoke: Palgrave, 2013.

Winter, Tim. 'Heritage Studies and the Privileging of Theory.' *International Journal of Heritage Studies.* Accessed 27 October 2013. DOI: 10.1080/13527258.2013.798671.

Withers, Deborah. *Sistershow Revisited: Feminism in Bristol, 1973–1975.* Bristol: HammerOn Press, 2011.

——. 'What Is Your Essentialism Is My Immanent Flesh! The Ontological Politics of Feminist Epistemology.' *European Journal of Women's Studies* 17:3 (2010): 231–247.

Withers, Deborah, and Red Chidgey. 'Complicated Inheritance: Sistershow and the Queering of Feminism.' *Women: A Cultural Review* 12:3 (2010): 309–323.

Withers, Deborah, and Ana Laura Lopez de la Torre. 'Blogging Olive.' *Do You Remember Olive Morris?,* 102–105. London: ROC, 2010.

Women in Moving Pictures. *In Our Own Time.* 1981. Feminist Archive South. DM2123/1/Archive Boxes 35.

'Women's Liberation Music Archive.' Accessed 13 February 2015. http://womensliberationmusicarchive.co.uk.

Women's Liberation Workshop Group. *Shrew* 4:1 (1972).

Woodward, Sophie, and Kath Woodward. *Why Feminism Matters: Feminism Lost and Found.* Basingstoke: Palgrave Macmillan, 2011.

Young, Rob. *Electric Eden: Unearthing Britain's Visionary Music.* London: Faber, 2010.

Zelizer, Barbie. 'Cannibalizing Memory in the Global Flow of News.' Motti Neiger, Oren Meyers and Eyal Zandberg, eds. *On Media Memory: Collective Memory in a New Media Age,* 27–37. Basingstoke: Palgrave Macmillan, 2011.

Zobl, Elke, and Ricarda Drüeke, eds. *Feminist Media: Participatory Spaces, Networks and Cultural Citizenship.* Bielefield: Verlag, 2012.

Index